community LIVABILITY

What is a livable community? How do you design and develop one? What does government at all levels need to do to support and nurture the cause of livable communities?

Using a blend of theory and practice, the second edition of *Community Livability* addresses evidence from international, state and local perspectives to explore what is meant by the term "livable communities." The second edition contains new chapters from leading academics and practitioners that examine the various factors that constitute a livable community (e.g., the influence and importance of transportation options/alternatives to the elderly, the importance of walkability as a factor in developing a livable and healthy community, the importance of good open space providing for human activity and health, restorative benefits, etc., the importance of coordinated land use and transportation planning), and the relationship between livability and quality of life. A number of chapters focus on livable communities with case studies from an international perspective in the USA, Canada, Australia, Peru, Sweden, South Korea, Japan, and Austria.

Fritz Wagner has a doctorate in urban and regional planning from the University of Washington. On completion of his degree he moved to New Orleans, where he joined the University of New Orleans. During his 28-year tenure at the University of New Orleans, he served for 20 years as Dean/Director of the College of Urban and Public Affairs. In 2002, he joined the Department of Urban Design and Planning at the University of Washington.

Roger W. Caves is Professor Emeritus of City Planning, School of Public Affairs, San Diego State University. He received his doctorate in urban affairs and public policy from the University of Delaware in 1982. He has authored and edited many planning volumes, including *Exploring Urban America: An Introductory Reader* (1995) and *Livable Cities from a Global Perspective* (2018) with Fritz Wagner. His research areas include urban planning, direct democracy, smart cities, housing and information technology, and community development.

community LIVABILITY

ISSUES AND APPROACHES TO SUSTAINING THE WELL-BEING OF PEOPLE AND COMMUNITIES

Second Edition

Edited by
Fritz Wagner and Roger W. Caves

Routledge
Taylor & Francis Group

LONDON AND NEW YORK

Second edition published 2020
by Routledge
2 Park Square, Milton Park, Abingdon, Oxon OX14 4RN

and by Routledge
52 Vanderbilt Avenue, New York, NY 10017

Routledge is an imprint of the Taylor & Francis Group, an informa business

First edition published by Routledge 2012

British Library Cataloguing-in-Publication Data
A catalogue record for this book is available from the British Library

Library of Congress Cataloging-in-Publication Data
Names: Wagner, Fritz W., editor. | Caves, Roger W., editor.
Title: Community livability : issues and approaches to sustaining the well-being of people and communities / edited by Fritz Wagner and Roger W. Caves.
Description: Second Edition. | New York : Routledge, 2020. | "First edition published by Routledge 2012"–T.p. verso. | Includes bibliographical references and index.
Identifiers: LCCN 2019016948 (print) | LCCN 2019017695 (ebook) | ISBN 9781315111636 (ebook) | ISBN 9781138084858 | ISBN 9781138084858(hardback) | ISBN 9781138084865(paperback) | ISBN 9781315111636(ebook)
Subjects: LCSH: Sustainable living–Case studies. | Community life–Case studies.
Classification: LCC GE196 (ebook) | LCC GE196 .C65 2020 (print) | DDC 307–dc23
LC record available at https://lccn.loc.gov/2019016948

ISBN: 978-1-138-08485-8 (hbk)
ISBN: 978-1-138-08486-5 (pbk)
ISBN: 978-1-315-11163-6 (ebk)

Typeset in Garamond
by Wearset Ltd, Boldon, Tyne and Wear

Without the support of community members of Chelsea, Michigan, my hometown, this book would not have been possible. Special thanks to the following people: Pat and Sandra Merkel, Doug Elser, David McLaughlin, Jack Merkel, Tim Merkel, Earl Heller, Loren Heller, Gail Thomas, Fred Klink, Bill Coltre, Kandie Waggoner, Larry Schramm, Peter Flintoft, Eugene Seitz, and Erin Owens.

To my sister, Carolyn Labanowski, for her love and support over the years.

CONTENTS

CONTENTS

LIST OF FIGURES AND TABLES

Figures

Tables

NOTES ON CONTRIBUTORS

David Amborski is a professional urban planner, professor at Ryerson University's School of Urban and Regional Planning, and the founding director of the Centre for Urban Research and Land Development (CUR). His research and consulting work explores topics where urban planning interfaces with economics, including land and housing markets. His specific interests include the area of municipal finance, land development, and land value capture tools. He has served as president of the Association of Canadian Urban Planning Programs, is an academic advisor to the National Executive Forum on Public Property, and is a member of Lambda Alpha (Honourary Land Economics Society). He has undertaken studies for the federal, provincial, and a range of municipal governments. At the international level, he has undertaken work for both the Canadian International Development Agency (CIDA), World Bank, the InterAmerican Development Bank, and several other organizations in Eastern Europe, Latin America, and Asia. He also serves on the editorial boards of a number of international academic journals.

Ana Sabogal Dunin Borkowski is an engineer agronomist, academic, and Peruvian scholar/environmentalist. Her current research includes human impact of the agriculture and ecology of tropical forest, plant distribution, and influence of human impact of the plant distribution and society and study of vegetation, grazing in the fog-forests ecosystems in south Peru. Her previous research and publications included ecology of moorland ecosystems, study of vegetation, grazing in the forests of northern Peru (with emphasis on the distribution of *Ipomoea carnea* Jacq), and management of dry forests on the northern coast of Peru. Sabogal is the Director of Master Studies in Environment Development at the Pontificia Universidad Catolica del Peru and was the Director of Research and Information to the Peruvian Ministry of Environment (2012–2013). Her academic interests include the impact of environment changes in vegetation and the study of human impact in the ecosystem.

Anne-Marie Broudehoux is associate professor at the School of Design of the University of Quebec at Montreal. She received her doctorate in architecture from the University of California at Berkeley and her Master of Architecture from McGill University in Montreal. She is the author of *Mega-Events and Urban Image Construction: Beijing and Rio de Janeiro*, published by Routledge in 2017. She has edited a few collective volumes and published multiple articles and book chapters on the socio-spatial impacts of large-scale urban transformations. Her 2004 book, *The Making and Selling of Post-Mao Beijing*, published by Routledge, was awarded the International Planning History Society book prize in 2006.

Roger W. Caves is Professor Emeritus of City Planning, School of Public Affairs, San Diego State University. He received his doctorate in Urban Affairs and Public Policy from the University of Delaware in 1982. He is the author of *Land Use Planning: The Ballot Box Revolution* (1992), editor of *Exploring Urban America: An Introductory Reader* (1995), co-author of *Planning in the USA: Policies, Issues, and Processes* (2003, 2008, and 2014) with Barry Cullingworth, editor of *Encyclopedia of the City* (2005), co-editor of *Community Livability: Issues and Approaches to Sustaining the Well-Being of People and Communities* (2012) with Fritz Wagner, and co-editor of *Livable Cities from a Global Perspective* (2018) with Fritz Wagner. His research areas include urban planning, direct democracy, smart cities, housing and information technology, and community development.

Sabina Deitrick is associate professor at the Graduate School of Public and International Affairs and co-director of the urban and regional analysis research program at the University Center for Social and Urban Research (UCSUR) at the University of Pittsburgh. Professor Deitrick teaches courses and conducts research in the areas of economic and community development, urban planning, and regional policy, with an emphasis on regional restructuring, revitalization, and brownfields redevelopment. She is co-editor of *Boom or Bust? Governance, Planning, and the Economic Impacts of Fracking* (Cornell Press, forthcoming). She received her B.A. and M.A. from the University of Pennsylvania and Ph.D. from the University of California at Berkeley. She also serves on the City of Pittsburgh Planning Commission.

Billy Fields, Ph.D., Urban Studies, University of New Orleans, is an associate professor of political science at Texas State University. His research focuses on understanding the key elements of resilient communities. He has examined resiliency from transportation, urban planning, public health, and hazard mitigation perspectives with publications in the *Journal of Planning, Education, and Research* (JPER), *Journal of Public Health Policy*, the *Journal of Urbanism*, the *Journal of Urban Design*, and *Cityscape*. He is also co-editor of the spring 2013 release by Island Press, *Transport Beyond Oil*. He leads the International Sustainable Transportation Engagement Program with an annual study abroad program to the Netherlands to explore best practices in active transportation. Prior to joining Texas State University, Dr. Fields was director of the Center for Urban and Public Affairs at the University of New Orleans and Research Director for the Rails to Trails Conservancy, where he developed and explored the concept of trail-oriented development.

Cecilia Giusti, Ph.D., is associate dean in the College of Architecture at Texas A&M University, where she is also associate professor in the Department of Landscape Architecture and Urban Planning. Her doctorate is from the University of Texas at Austin; M.A. from the Institute of Social Studies, The Hague; and bachelor's and professional degrees from the Catholic University, Lima, Peru. In 2002 she was selected as a HUD Urban Scholar, getting funding to research microbusiness in Colonias in Texas. Her research on economic development and planning has a multidisciplinary approach focusing on informality, microlending among marginalized populations, land values, public spaces, and equity. Dr. Giusti has published at multiple venues, from peer-reviewed academic journals to non-academic settings and has presented her research in the U.S. and abroad. She is a Fulbright expert on urban issues 2017–2020.

Edward G. Goetz is professor of urban planning at the Humphrey School of Public Affairs and director of the Center for Urban and Regional Affairs, University of Minnesota. He specializes in housing and local community development and how issues of race and poverty affect housing policy, planning, and development. His most recent books are *The One Way Street of Integration: Fair Housing and the Pursuit of Racial Justice in American Cities* (2018, Cornell University Press), *New Deal Ruins: Race, Economic Justice and Public Housing Policy* (2013, Cornell University Press), and *Clearing the Way: Deconcentrating the Poor in Urban America* (2003, Urban Institute Press), which won the Paul Davidoff Award from the Association of Collegiate Schools of Planning in 2005. Goetz is a member of the Planning Accreditation Board and serves on the editorial board of the *Journal of the American Planning Association*. He has held visiting positions at Université Paris Ouest-Nanterre, Tsinghua University—Beijing, and DeMontfort University—Leicester, England.

Tigran Haas, Ph.D., is associate professor of urban planning and urban design as well as the director of the Centre for the Future of Places (CFP) at the School of Architecture and the Built Environment at KTH. Tigran Haas' expertise, current research, and teaching focus on contemporary trends and paradigms in urban planning and design, new urbanism, sustainable urbanism, social housing and urban transformations, and city development and design. His latest publication is *In The Post-Urban World: Emergent Transformation of Cities and Regions in the Innovative Global Economy*, with Hans Westlund (Routledge, New York, and London, 2017).

Mark Hinshaw FAIA FAICP is an architect, urban planner, and writer with more than 45 years of experience in cities and towns throughout the country. He has worked in public agencies, directing urban design policies, programs, and projects. He has headed a design review function for a city. As a consultant, he has advised communities about downtown development, urban design framework plans, streetscape projects, public spaces, and design-oriented codes. He has developed design guidelines for numerous jurisdictions that focus on the public realm and how adjacent development can support walkability and social life. Mark has both headed planning and design teams and contributed to other teams as an urban designer or planner. Mark has also had a 30-year career as a journalist, writing hundreds of articles on urban development. He has written for *Landscape Architecture, Architecture, Planning Magazine, Places, 'scape*, and other journals. For 12 years he had a regular column in the *Seattle Times*. Most recently, he has been a frequent contributor to crosscut.com, an online daily magazine of civic affairs in the Pacific Northwest. He also has published two books, *Citistate Seattle: The Making of a Metropolis* and *True Urbanism: Living In and Near the Center*, as well as a recent Planning Advisory Service Report entitled *Design Review: Guiding Better Development*. He has also taught urban design at the University of California, Davis. Finally, he has served on a number of organizational boards, including, most recently, Feet First, an advocacy group in Washington State that promotes streets and routes for walking.

Robert Kerstein is an emeritus professor at the University of Tampa. He taught courses on urban politics and policy, public policy analysis, and American government. Kerstein is the author of *Politics and Growth in Twentieth-Century Tampa* and *Key West on the Edge*, both published by the University Press of Florida.

Ji Hei Lee is a lecturer in real estate and planning at Henley Business School, University of Reading, Malaysia. She holds a Master's in Urban Planning (Seoul National University) and Ph.D. (Texas A&M University). Her research focuses on built environment and human behavior in aging societies. Her previous research deals with older adults' socializing behavior, wellbeing and mental health, and place-making. She is currently working on research on older adults' use of technologies in socializing and shopping experiences in cross-cultural contexts. She teaches international perspectives on planning practices and policies in her modules.

Ray Lister is a graduate of the Urban Development Master's degree program at Ryerson University. She currently works as a policy analyst for the Friends of the Greenbelt Foundation in Toronto.

Stefan Lundberg graduated from the Royal Institute of Technology (KTH) as a civil engineer in 1977 in the area of urban planning. In 2007 he took his doctorate at KTH and is now an associated professor at KTH. He has been working in the industry both at Ericsson and different housing companies as well as at the government. His area of interest is how to plan for the inclusion of old people in the city and how to support aging-in-place.

Mats J. Lundström, MSc in Urban Planning and Design, is a Ph.D. candidate at the School of Architecture and the Built Environment at KTH, as well as a practicing urban planning and design consultant at Tyréns. Mats' expertise, current research, and teaching focus is on sustainable urban development, energy efficiency and climate mitigating urban planning, age-friendly urban planning and design, cross-disciplinary planning processes, and public space and socially sustainable cities. He will finish his doctorate in October 2018.

Pauline McGuirk is senior professor of human geography at UOW and director of ACCESS. Her research focuses on the geographies and politics of urban governance. Her current projects focus on urban regeneration, urban energy transition, and the governance practices involved in making cities smart in Australia. Pauline is an editor of *Progress in Human Geography*.

Kathleen Mee, associate professor, is a cultural geographer from the discipline of geography and environmental studies at the University of Newcastle and co-director of the Centre for Urban and Regional Studies. She is an award-winning teacher, having won the University of Newcastle Excellence in Teaching Award in 1998, the Faculty of Science and IT Excellence in Teaching Award in 2008 and 2017, and the Vice Chancellor's Award for Teaching Excellence and Contribution to Student Learning (Science) in 2017. Kathy's research explores three major themes: the changing nature of social vulnerability in urban and regional areas; housing for socially vulnerable groups; and the diverse workings and practices of urban regeneration.

Kristian Ruming, associate professor, is an urban geographer in the Department of Geography and Planning at Macquarie University. His current research explores urban regeneration and governance, social and affordable housing provision, and planning system reform. Kristian is editor of *Urban Regeneration in Australia* (Routledge, 2018).

Fumihiko Seta is currently an associate professor of the Department of Urban Engineering (DUE), Faculty of Engineering, the University of Tokyo. He was born in 1972 in Tokyo, graduated from the University of Tokyo in 1995, and worked at the University of Tokyo from 1998 to 2005 and Osaka City University from 2005 to 2012. His major is national, regional, and urban planning in Japan and foreign countries, especially for both growing and depopulating cities and towns.

Katharina Soepper-Quendler, Ph.D., works for the Urban Planning Department (MA 18) of the City of Vienna, Austria, with a focus on strategic urban planning. She is an urban planner and graduated in 2008 at HafenCity University of Hamburg, Germany. Her master's as well as doctoral thesis focused on neighborhood management and the role of private partners in public funding programs. She did her research in Germany and the US (affiliated with San Diego State University, California) and received her doctorate from the Vienna University of Technology. Her practical work in the planning field took place in Germany as well as in Austria in the private sector and municipalities. She did land use planning as well as strategic development concepts. In her current appointment at the City of Vienna, Austria, she has worked on the urban development plan; her current focus lies on urban center development.

Elizabeth Strom is associate professor in the School of Public Affairs at the University of South Florida, where she teaches in the Urban and Regional Planning program. Her research interests include downtown development, housing policy, tourism, and the role of the arts. Her work has been published in numerous urban affairs journals.

Jill Sweeney, Ph.D., is a lecturer in human geography at the University of Newcastle, Australia. Her research interests include placemaking, urban regeneration, and geographies of ocean spaces.

Fritz Wagner has a doctorate in urban and regional planning from the University of Washington (1974). On completion of his degree he moved to New Orleans, where he joined the University of New Orleans as an assistant professor. During his 28-year tenure at the University of New Orleans, he served for 20 years as dean/director of the College of Urban and Public Affairs and its prior academic unit names. In 2002, he joined the Department of Urban Design and Planning at the University of Washington (Seattle) and subsequently co-founded the Northwest Center for Livable Communities. He has chaired the Department of Landscape Architecture and served as associate dean and interim dean of the College of Architecture and Urban Planning. Presently, he serves as a research professor and director of the Northwest Center for Livable Communities in the Department of Urban Design and Planning at the University of Washington (Seattle).

Robert Whelan is retired as clinical professor of public affairs at the University of Texas-Dallas. He is co-author of *Urban Policy and Politics in a Bureaucratic Age* and author of numerous articles and papers. His current major research interest is urban redevelopment in a comparative perspective.

FOREWORD
Robert Whelan

Since the publication of the first edition of this book in 2012, *livability* has become a concern for cities all around the globe. Some of this stems from professional predilections for buzzwords and trendiness. Much of the livability discussion, however, centers on very real and important problems for cities, as the chapters in this collection demonstrate.

In the introduction to the first edition, I dated the recent concern with livability to the latter decades of the 20th century. In particular, I was thinking of the Brundtland Commission Report, which created awareness of the need for sustainable development on a worldwide basis. In the United States, 13 states passed (and, sometimes, updated) statewide plans beginning in the 1960s. These plans were variously called *smart growth*, *growth management*, etc. Livability was a common thread in these plans.

Certainly, livability is not a new idea for urban planners. The early 20th-century planners wanted to improve public health, sanitation, and housing conditions. The City Beautiful movement wanted to make our cities more livable. Olmsted, Vaux, and the other founders of Central Park wanted to create a democratic space for all city dwellers to enjoy public recreation (Rogers, 2018).

The chapters included herein have been divided into three parts, for organizational purposes. One group of chapters enlightens our understanding of livability. A second group emphasizes urban and regional planning issues. The third focuses on issues of poverty, equity, and environmental problems. All of the chapters address all three categories, to some extent.

Understanding of Livability

We need not discuss the concept of livability at length here. Suffice it to say that livability centers on quality of life, and livability includes objective and subjective dimensions. Each of the chapters in the first part illuminate aspects of livability.

Despite a harsh winter climate, Montreal ranks high on indices of livability. In her chapter, Anne-Marie Broudehoux attributes this to *Montrealite*, a unique urban culture. This includes a deeply rooted social democratic culture. The arts and culture are extremely important to Montrealers, with a steady array of outdoor summer festivals and symphony, theater and museums in the winter. The quality of life is well above average, with subsidized health care, inexpensive higher education, and affordable housing by North American standards. Transportation mobility is good. Public use of the metro and bus systems is high, and car-sharing and bicycle use have risen significantly. Broudehoux's academic study is supported by at least one Anglo-Canadian journalist. In a recent *Globe and Mail* column, Denise Balkissoon (2018) wrote of falling in love with Montreal. Born in Toronto, Balkissoon is attracted by the same things that Broudehoux and her students admire: housing affordability, transportation, and fun. Montreal is a special place, and livability is a big reason for that distinction.

Pittsburgh is another city that we might not associate with livability. As Sabina Dietrick points out in her chapter, the city improved its urban environment and restructured its economy throughout the middle decades of the 20th century. Pittsburgh has ranked high on the livability index for the last 30 years and continues to do so. Using a 2011 Quality of Life survey, Dietrick notes substantial differences between the responses of African-American and white residents. Thus, livability may not be the same for all residents.

Stockholm, as we might expect, ranks very high in world indices of livability. Stefan Lundberg and his co-authors explain why this is the case. Stockholm has an extraordinary array of urban plans, and they have been implemented, in large part. Sustainability and a walkable city have been the focus of recent urban plans. The city's latest planning effort envisions a *Stockholm for Everyone* by 2040. The only discordant notes are housing affordability and spatial segregation, shared by most other Western metropolises.

Seoul, a city of 10 million plus, with a high urban density, might not be the first place we think of in terms of livability. Like the other cities in this section, Seoul ranks high on livability indices. Ji Hei Lee's chapter indicates that one reason might be the city's policy of village community building. In essence, the city is creating *third places*—community gathering centers other than home and work. Seoul does this through public–private partnerships. In creating these small community support centers, the city is also encouraging community planning. We have seen how important third places are for Korean-Americans, and we can understand this contribution to livability.

Fumihiko Seta's chapter on Iga City in Japan's Osaka Region is extremely provocative, and it is very different from the others in this part. Iga City once had more than 100,000 people and now has a population of around 50,000. Moreover, this population is aging. How do local governments maintain livability? Seta hints at a strategy of planned shrinkage, recalling similar debates in the United States in the 1970s.

Urban and Regional Planning Issues

Intuitively, we understand that sound urban and regional planning is a pre-requisite for livable communities. It's possible, but not likely, that livability can arise from fortuitous circumstances. The four chapters in this part demonstrate the relationship of good planning to livability.

Asheville, North Carolina, with a population of about 90,000, is probably the smallest city in this collection. Its beautiful mountain surroundings and agreeable climate have attracted retirees and tourists. In some respects, Asheville confronted the Yogi Berra dilemma: "Nobody goes there anymore, it's too crowded." Elizabeth Strom and Robert Kerstein show us how the city's recent plans deal with growth and equity issues. A comprehensive downtown plan in the early 2000s aimed at preserving downtown livability. This has included the encouragement of traditional crafts and microbreweries. In their account of "successful" American towns, Fallows and Fallows (2018) note the presence of microbreweries almost universally. More recently Asheville is working on a new 2035 comprehensive plan and a city council strategic plan. Both stress livability concerns.

Seattle is a city that always ranks high in livability, and, thus, we'd expect good regional planning. Mark Hinshaw's lively account of Seattle's planning history shows that gaining livability is not a linear process. Hinshaw sees two major turning points in Seattle's planning efforts. The first was the preservation of the Pike Place market and keeping the interstate highway away from the waterfront. The second was the passage of a series of bond issues under the name *Forward Thrust*, which provided funds for parks and recreation and regional waste management, among other things. These turning points occurred in the late 1960s and early 1970s. Some of the city's livability can be attributed to enlightened state legislation. The Washington legislature passed an environmental protection act and a seashore protection act early on. Later, the state enacted a substantial growth management plan. Finally, Seattle is a city that follows the idea of urban villages and has neighborhood design review. Hinshaw is frank about Seattle's mistakes. He discusses failed plans for a downtown park and monorail development. As Seattle moves forward, the biggest challenges are affordable housing and extension of the light rail system.

David Amborski and Ray Lister begin their chapter on Toronto by stating three prerequisites for livability: good governance, good planning, and good financial capability. Toronto has enjoyed all three. The region's metropolitan governance has been a model for urbanists since the 1950s, and it underwent major revisions in the 1990s. The province of Ontario, often the key actor in government and planning, passed planning legislation in 1946. In 1970, a growth plan was passed. In recent years, Toronto's environment has benefitted from growth management legislation and planning for the Toronto waterfront. The city evidences almost all the elements of good livability. Toronto has a very good public transit system. Its health care is excellent. As one of the most diverse cities on the planet, Toronto is a center for multiculturalism. The city is great for culture, with many fine museums and a large number of theaters. Toronto has significant green space, and the city is a leader in environmental efforts. Despite a recent influx of gang-related violence, the crime rate is low when compared with U.S. cities. Amborski and Lister cite two future concerns. First, the public transportation infrastructure hasn't kept up with increased demand and usage. Second, there is the problem of housing affordability, shared by many of these cities.

Vienna is a city that had to rebuild completely after the Second World War. It not only succeeded in doing that, but in the last decade, Vienna has ranked consistently among the highest cities in terms of livability. Katharina Soepper-Quendler's chapter focuses on how the city maintains its high livability ranking. With a high urban density, Vienna has a large amount of green space (50%), and it provides excellent public transportation. The city constantly monitors public opinion on livability questions. Like the other cities in this part, it has thorough, updated plans dealing with livability issues.

Issues of Poverty, Equity, and the Environment

It is a bit surprising to have Minneapolis-St. Paul included in a section on poverty and equity issues. The metropolitan area always ranks high in livability. The region is known for its policy initiatives, such as regional tax base sharing and affordable housing development. Yet, as Edward Goetz points out in his chapter, none of this has made a dent in persistent racial inequities.

Goetz gives us a rich case study involving recent transit initiatives. A new light rail system was supposed to pass directly through a majority African-American neighborhood. In response, a collaborative foundation effort focused on affordable housing, small business preservation, and the placement of stations in the corridor. This resulted in a large funding initiative in the threatened corridor. Minneapolis-St. Paul's ameliorative efforts are more substantial than those of most metropolitan regions.

Unlike the Twin Cities, New Orleans, historically, has had serious problems caused by poverty and inequity, as well as substantial environmental issues. And that was before Hurricane Katrina hit in 2005. Billy Fields is a native and student of New Orleans. His chapter on post-disaster amenity planning in New Orleans examines the multitude of neighborhood plans related to the creation of the Lafitte Greenway, post-Katrina. The Lafitte Greenway is a 2.8-mile linear park and trail, extending through several neighborhoods. It is clear that the greenway increased livability and abetted increasing gentrification of these neighborhoods. The plans usually did not address the housing affordability issue.

Cecilia Giusti discusses a very different kind of community in her chapter on the Las Lomas community located near the Texas–Mexico border. By traditional definition, a colonia lacks many of the elements of livability. Giusti makes the case that empowerment and attachment to a home can be considered elements of livability. She details several community efforts. Colonia Unidas helped people to get title to their property. Nuestra Casa makes micro-loans for home improvements. Entrepreneurial efforts have been encouraged. Giusti's chapter makes us think about non-traditional elements of livability.

Lima, Peru, is a different entity from most metropolitan areas in this collection. As a large, Latin-American megacity, Lima has been overwhelmed by population growth in recent decades. Ana Sabogal Dunin Borkowski outlines the challenges for Lima in her chapter. Livability is threatened by air pollution, resulting from great increases in automobile traffic. The city also faces problems in providing green space. Generally, there is a lack of public green space. Existing green space is distributed inequitably. Poorer areas have little or no green space. She concludes the chapter with suggestions for improvement.

Kathleen Mee and her co-authors present a study of livability of two suburbs of Newcastle, New South Wales, Australia. They find that housing affordability is a key component of livability. Residents also thought that access to facilities (such as shopping) and to the natural environment were important for livability. Like Giusti's chapter, the contributions of residents were a key component of livability. Their research demonstrates the multilevel scales of livability.

Considered as a whole, this collection adds greatly to our understanding of livability and how community livability has advanced since the first edition of this book. On the negative side, almost every chapter raises problems of poverty and inequity. Individually, the authors offer many positive suggestions for planners and policymakers.

References

Balkissoon, D. (2018, June 29). Cities are for the people. *Globe and Mail.*

Fallows, J., & Fallows, D. (2018). *Our Towns: A 100,000-Mile Journey into the Heart of America.* New York: Pantheon.

Rogers, E. B. (2018). *Saving Central Park: A History and a Memoir.* New York: Knopf.

PART I

UNDERSTANDING OF LIVABILITY

Chapter 1

MONTREALISM OR MONTRÉALITÉ? UNDERSTANDING MONTREAL'S UNIQUE BRAND OF LIVABILITY

Anne-Marie Broudehoux

As one of the oldest cities in North America, which celebrated its 375th anniversary in 2017, Montreal emerged in the 1960s as a modern, dynamic metropolis that now ranks among the world's most livable. In spite of having lost the status of Canada's economic center to Toronto in the late 1970s, Montreal remains the nation's cultural capital and Quebec's principal city, home to half of the province's 7 million residents. In recent years, Montreal has invariably figured within the top 25 of Most Convivial Cities rankings published by magazines such as the *Economist*, *Forbes*, and *Monocle* (Bloom, 2017; EIU, 2017; Monocle, 2016).

What is the recipe for this high livability index? This chapter attempts to identify some of the key ingredients that make Montreal such a convivial place to live. It argues that livability in the Montreal sense is not so much the work of planners, managers, and decision-makers, or an urban model (like Vancouverism) that can be branded and exported, but it is much more the product of a unique urban culture, sometimes referred to as Montrealness (or Montréalité) that is deeply rooted in local reality and history (Olazabal, 2006; Charney, 1980).

This chapter is the fruit of a collective effort. Nine graduate students at the University of Quebec at Montreal's School of Design[1] have helped document various aspects of what we have called the *convivial city*. From quality of life issues such as social climate, crime, mobility, economic development, to access to culture, housing, health education, public spaces, and employment, they have sought to define Montreal's unique recipe for a convivial city. Since the term livability has no equivalent in French, Quebec's official idiom and the language used at our university, we have chosen the term *convivial* to best translate Montreal's reality. Etymologically, convivial comes from the Latin *con* and *vivo*, which means to live together. The term does not carry the same festive connotations in French as it does in English, but rather suggests amiability, tolerance, and openness. It also carries easy-going, user-friendly, and welcoming undertones, which are all equally suited to characterize Montreal. We thus adopted the term for our study, using it widely when approaching informants, commentators, and participants. The main sources used in this investigation were newspaper and periodical articles, official websites, and blogs, as well as interviews with local elected officials, NGO activists, specialists such as planners, architects, environmentalists, creative industry workers, and members of the general public. The several debates that occurred throughout our semester-long seminar also inform the chapter.

A Deeply Rooted Social Democratic Culture

Our investigations revealed that many contributing factors to Montreal's great livability stem from a deep-seated social democratic culture and innovative response to harsh living conditions. With a long tradition of unionism and cooperatism, this political culture has given rise to a strong sharing economy, modes of collaborative consumption, and well-developed solidarity networks (Dumont, 1993). It is also behind the social, political, and economic innovation for which both the city of Montreal and the province of Quebec are known. This particular culture can be traced to the city's historical and multicultural heritage and difficult beginnings as a pioneer colony faced with harsh climatic conditions, which made solidarity an essential survival strategy. The domination of a rich and powerful minority ruling class after the 1759 British conquest may also explain the importance of unionism, cooperation, and the social-democrat leaning of the majority population, as well as its highly protectionist stance towards French language and culture (Dumont, 1993).

Montreal's cultural makeup is central to the city's uniquely convivial character. Because of its particular history, Montreal is one of the rare North American metropoles with a largely bilingual population, who can live and work in both English and French. Often described as the most European of North American cities, Montreal is the fourth largest francophone city in the world, after Kinshasa, Paris, and Abidjan (Demographia, 2017). As a major port city, Montreal has always been a city of immigrants, welcoming newcomers from all parts of the world. This openness and multiculturalism may be behind the culture of tolerance that has contributed to the city's very low crime rate,[2] relative social peace, and welcoming attitude.

Arts and Culture as Factors of Livability

The arts are known to contribute to the quality of life of communities and to their social and economic vitality, and creative people are said to prefer living where "diversity, tolerance and openness to new ideas" prevail (Stolarick, Florida, & Musante, 2005). One of Montreal's greatest assets in terms of livability is undoubtedly its rich cultural landscape, made up of a well-developed cultural industry, a vibrant artist community, plentiful cultural institutions, and an affordable access to culture, thanks to generous government subsidies (Stolarick et al., 2005).

Quebec's recognition of the importance of culture as a social, political, and economic asset goes back to the 1950s, as part of the province's nation-building endeavors and self-definition as a distinct society within the Canadian confederacy. Cultural vitality and artistic production have always played both a social and political role in Quebec society. Quebec set up its Ministry of Cultural Affairs in 1961, long before many nations, including Canada, created such an institution (Handler, 1985). This ministry not only sought to assert the province's cultural identity, it also aimed to boost economic activity by fostering the production of cultural goods and services. The ministry was also responsible for setting up diverse institutions to support artistic production and democratize access to culture (Handler, 1985).

The city of Montreal has long made culture accessible to its citizens, notably through initiatives such as the Maisons de la culture (Houses of Culture), a neighborhood-based, freely accessible facility for the diffusion of culture. Since 1981, 12 such community centers were created throughout the city, hosting art shows, theater, and music performances. Throughout the year, the city holds over 120 various cultural festivals, including the Journées de la culture (Days of Culture), a weekend-long event that gives free access to all cultural institutions.

Since the 1990s, Montreal's economy has gradually shifted towards creativity and knowledge. In 1996, the city's tourism bureau, Tourisme Montréal, acknowledged the central role of culture in the city's economic development by proposing to rebrand Montreal as a City of Festivals. More recently, Montreal has embraced cultural production as an engine of development and economic activity and a strategy of prosperity and influence. Montreal was among the first world cities to recognize culture as one of the pillars of sustainable development, as part of its Agenda 21 action plan in 2011.

In recent years, Montreal implemented a host of actions to secure its global position among a growing network of creative cities, investing massively in cultural production, cultural tourism, and the knowledge-based economy. Apart from granting generous tax breaks, Montreal also supports various funding and scholarship programs in the arts and culture. The city's artists population is one and a half times the average for Canadian cities, and up to 44% of Quebec's listed artists live in Montreal. A great majority of those are concentrated in the Plateau borough, recognized as Canada's most creative neighborhood, with a concentration ten times the Canadian average (VdM, 2017a). Between 1998 and 2008, the cultural industry sector grew three times faster in terms of employment compared with all other industries, and is still dominant today. Half of creative industry employment are concentrated in four areas: film and video (14%), specialized design services (12%), advertising (12%), and independent artists, writers, and performers (12%). In 2016, the total economic windfalls in the cultural sector were estimated at C$12 billion, about 6% of Montreal's GDP (VdM, 2017a).

Montreal is also thriving in the design arena. In 2005, the world headquarters of the International Design Alliance was established in Montreal, to promote the role of design on the international scene. The following year, UNESCO granted Montreal a City of Design designation, and the city remains the only Canadian urban entity to have integrated the organization's network of 116 creative cities around the world. This designation recognizes "the potential for designers to contribute to the future of Montréal, and the commitment and determination of the city, governments and civil society to build on this strength to improving the quality of life of Montrealers" (Design Montréal, 2015).

Quality of Life and Living Standards

Montrealers in general are not wealthy, but they enjoy a relatively high standard of living. In 2015, the average Montrealer had an annual disposable income of about C$27,000 (VdM, 2015a). However, thanks in part to the province's universal health care, and high-quality, free public education system, with a large network of subsidized daycare centers and universities, Montreal's cost of living remains comparatively low. A 2014 Mercer study of 211 cities worldwide ranked Montreal 128th in terms of cost of living (Mercer, 2014), while a Union of Swiss Banks 2012 analysis of 72 urban centers found Montrealers to enjoy the 28th highest purchasing power. Another factor explaining this inverse relationship between disposable income and high purchasing power is the city's relatively stable inflation rate. Rents, goods, and services, as well as food, are much more affordable in Montreal compared in relative terms with other cities. While the average net hourly wage is 22% lower in Montreal than in New York City, residents of both cities enjoy a similar purchasing power. Goods and services are 24% cheaper in Montreal, rents are a sixth of New York's and food costs 16% less than in New York (VdM, 2015b). These conditions all contribute to the attractiveness of the city and to its perceived quality of life, especially for students. A 2017 Best Student City ranking placed Montreal as the number one city to study in the world (Quacquarelli Symonds, 2017)

The Role of Climate and Its Influence on Livability

The way the city has adapted to its unique climatic conditions over the centuries also contributes to Montreal's livability. Over its four distinct seasons, the city experiences vast temperature variations, from hot muggy summers to cold, snowy winters. This seasonality has greatly shaped the city's infrastructure, architecture, modes of transportation, and lifestyles. Flexibility is deeply ingrained within the city's urban culture, as both city administrators and residents have learned to adapt to fast-changing conditions to allow urban life to go on unimpeded.

This means that urban spaces, mobility solutions, and public services are planned with seasonality in mind. For example, the city has developed various forms of indoor public spaces, including its so-called underground city, built along with the subway system in the 1960s. This network of underground pedestrian passages runs over 33 kilometers and connects office buildings, hotels, restaurants, shopping malls, colleges, theaters, and apartment buildings. With more than 120 access points, it is linked to 12 major metro stations and is used by an average of 500,000 people a day (MUC, 2017).

Public infrastructure is also seasonally transformed to respond to climatic conditions. Parklets built over street parking are dismantled every fall and put away for winter. The city's bike-sharing stations were designed to be entirely removable and stored during the cold season. Montreal's public spaces also undergo seasonal transformations, as ice rinks and snowshoe trails replace sports fields and picnic areas. By giving all-year-round access to the city's public spaces, this adaptation contributes to residents' quality of life and minimizes the negative impacts of forced hibernation.

Montreal's Economic Environment

As Canada's second most populous province, Quebec stands out in the North American economic landscape thanks to plentiful natural resources, innovative industries, and low operating costs. Another economic asset is the province's low hydro-electric energy costs, one of the most reliable, cleanest, and cheapest energy sources in North America (Warin, Sinclair-Desgagné, & Van Assche, 2015). Quebec's economic and social environments are also highly conducive to research and innovation, with one of the most intensive industrial research and development economies in the world, aided by a generous tax regime (Warin et al., 2015).

The province's favorable position in the global economy could not be sustained without Montreal's input as an important hub for trade. Strategically located on the shore of the St. Lawrence River, with access to both the sea and the interior of the continent via the Great Lakes, Montreal has long been well connected to major North American economic centers. Montreal's port is the largest inland port in the world, the largest port on the Canadian east coast, and the second largest container port in the country, where two-thirds Canada's annual trade transits (Port of Montreal, 2015).

Montreal generates half of the province's economic activity and is the 16th largest financial center in the world, with more than 3,000 companies employing more than 100,000 people in business, finance, and administration (Warin et al., 2015). A 2013 study found Montreal, with its low labor, rent, and energy costs, to have the lowest operating expenditures for running a business among the 20 largest urban centers in North America (Montréal International, 2013).

In recent decades, Montreal's economy has specialized in research, development, and innovation. Its industrial and entrepreneurial landscapes have been transformed by the emergence of organized industrial clusters in the fields of aerospace, aluminum, film and television, transport and logistics, fashion, life sciences, financial services, information technologies, and clean technologies. By pooling human resources and developing collaborative projects, these clusters rely upon the collaboration of businesses, institutions, and universities. They facilitate interaction and complementarity, thereby fostering productivity, creativity, and cooperation[3] (Grappes Montreal, 2016).

Montreal's tourism industry is also booming, thanks to the city's diversified cultural products and conferences facilities. In 2014, Montreal was the number one North American host for international conferences, with 347 events bringing 194,000 business visitors to the city (Port of Montreal, 2015). The year 2017, which marked the 375th anniversary of the city, was a record year for tourism, with over 10.7 million visitors, spending C$3.6 billon, surpassing, for the first time, the mark set by the 1976 Olympic Games (Tourisme Montréal, 2017).

However, in spite of a favorable economic context, a host of factors have deterred investors from flocking to the province, and prevent the city from reaching its full economic potential. A complex, multilevel taxation system with high income and capital taxes, a strong union movement, stringent language laws, and perceived political instability with the threat of separation from Canada make foreign investors uneasy. Other deterrents include high transportation costs and decaying public infrastructure.

The Social Economy as a Factor of Livability

Another factor that accounts for Montreal's great livability is its well-developed social economy. Social economy enterprises improve local quality of life by reinvesting in their community while stimulating the economy, strengthening the social safety net, and ensuring a better distribution of wealth. The province of Quebec is a world leader in the field of social economy. According to Gérin-Lajoie (2016), countries with a thriving social economy generally enjoy a greater distribution of collective wealth and a higher happiness index, two quality of life indicators that are higher in Quebec than in the rest of North America. The province's 0.31 Gini coefficient, lower than both English Canada's (0.34) and the United States' (0.45), indicates that a greater proportion of the province's population directly benefits from collective wealth (Gérin-Lajoie, 2016).

Social economy enterprises generally emerge in response to crises, when basic needs are unmet by both public and private sector entities. In the province of Quebec, the social economy was initially oriented towards insurance cooperatives and credit unions, but it is now more concerned with the community-based economic development. Today, Quebec is the Canadian province where cooperatives and not-for-profit organizations are the most active and gather the highest membership. In 2013, Quebec adopted its Social Economy Act to promote the development of such enterprises and support their contribution to the socioeconomic vitality of the province.

The social economy is a vital sector of Montreal's economic activity. The city counts 3,590 social economy establishments, which provide more than 60,000 paid jobs and generate annual revenues of over C$2 billion. The sector also mobilizes over 100,000 volunteers, or the equivalent of a third of total manufacturing employment. Overall, nonprofit organizations account for 79% of establishments, while cooperatives represent 20% (CES, 2017).

Montreal actively supports the development of collective enterprises, by injecting important sums in financial support to community entrepreneurs. In 2016, the city held the Third World Social Economic Forum, which attracted 1,500 participants from 330 cities in 62 countries to promote collaboration between social economy organizations and local governments, and foster social innovation, equitable growth, sustainable development, and the progress of participatory democracy.

Montreal's Uniquely Convivial Built Environment

Montreal's built environment is another factor contributing to the city's livability. Architectural historian Melvyn Charney (1980) described Montrealness as a uniquely human-scale form of urbanity, with a strong neighborhood identity, richly layered interstitial spaces, and a unique house form, the *plex*, that allows for great social mixing. Montreal can be described as a city of neighborhoods, and is constituted of 19 boroughs, each run by its own mayor and administered according to its own peculiar needs and reality. Recent decades have seen the emergence of very progressive public policies in boroughs such as Le Plateau and Rosemont-La-Petite-Patrie that include a public consultation process, the implementation of innovative sustainable development initiatives, and participatory budgeting.

Housing in Montreal is highly accessible, and the majority of Montrealers are renters. Rents are almost seven times lower than in New York, four times less than in London, and half as much as in Toronto (Garon & Stevanovic, 2014). The city invests substantial funds in the creation of social and community housing, whose costs are shared with the Government of Quebec and the Montreal Metropolitan Community.

Montreal's typical house form is the *plex*, a two- to three-story multifamily building (duplex or triplex) containing one self-contained flat on each floor. Each unit has its own street address and is directly accessible from the outside, often through an external staircase. Dating from the late 19th century, the *plex* is the constitutive element of Montreal's urban landscape (Legault, 1989). These high-density houses, adjoining on both sides, have given rise to the city's continuous street façade, with relatively uniform brick or stone house fronts, punctuated by twisting staircases and projecting balconies. Some *plex* neighborhoods like Le Plateau figure among some of the most densely populated residential areas in North America, reaching a density of up to 25,000 people per square kilometer (VdM, 2017b). Built on deep, narrow lots that abut onto a mid-block alley used as a safe environment to play or socialize, the *plex* also encourages social cohesion.

This house form is instrumental to the constitution of human-scale, mixed-use urban neighborhoods, as ground floor units, particularly those located on street corners, accommodate smalls shops, especially the iconic *dépanneur* or family-run convenience store that is an integral part of the city's landscape. The *plex* is highly conducive to social mixing in terms of household type, socioeconomic makeup, and form of tenure. It was created to grant middle-income family access to home ownership, as the owner-family occupies the ground floor and rents the top-floor units. Although many apartments have now been converted into condominiums, many residents remain tenants, and renters and owners of diverse income brackets continue to live side by side, often without knowing each other's economic status. In spite of the *plex*'s great flexibility in accommodating changes in household formation, through vertical and alleyside expansions or conversion into single-family cottages, Montreal is still struggling to keep families on the island. Every year, nearly 10,000 families leave Montreal for cheaper, newer, larger homes in the suburbs (VdM, 2017b).

Green Spaces and Parks as Factors of Livability

A great contributor to Montreal's livability is its abundant vegetation and vast network of parks, which range from tiny pocket spaces to large regional parks. All residential units in Montreal are located less than 500 meters from a public park. The city was built around Mount Royal—The Mountain, as locals call it—designed as a park in 1876 by Frederik Law Olmstead and which remains one of the city's great landmarks and a beloved year-round destination.

Montreal also has an impressive number of trees (over 1,200,000), mainly owned and maintained by the city and located in parks and along city streets. In recent years, the city has come to recognize this urban forest as an essential component of municipal infrastructure, which helps mitigate the impacts of urban density by creating microclimates, improving air quality, reducing noise, and controlling erosion. Trees and parks also have a positive impact upon the *heat island* effect, especially as the city increasingly faces heat waves as a result of climate change (VdM, 2012). The city adopted its Tree Policy in 2005 to develop and protect this public urban forest. Its ambitious Canopy Action Plan, initiated in 2012, aims to raise Montreal's canopy index by 25 percentage points before 2025, with the production of an additional 2,333 hectares of canopy, and the planting of 300,000 trees (VdM, 2012).

In recent years, boroughs like Rosemont-La-Petite-Patrie and Le Plateau have seized upon the opportunity of newly designed curb extensions to create expansive flowerbeds, with a striking visual impact that also adds porosity to an overly mineral environment and allows rainwater to return to the ground table. Many urban boroughs also support the resident-initiated conversion of back alleys into collectively managed green spaces. These projects are assisted by the Éco-quartier (eco-district) program, initiated in 1995 by the city to support citizens in a host of environmentally minded actions.

Montreal is also multiplying initiatives to promote urban agriculture, for which it has a long tradition in the form of community and collective gardens.[4] Recent urban agriculture initiatives include Urban Path, a nonprofit organization whose mission is to mobilize communities around social greening projects that promote environmental awareness and the socio-professional integration of youth. Garden Network re-naturalizes vacant lots in low-income boroughs. The citizen-initiated network Make Yourself at Home promotes urban agriculture by cultivating alleys, sidewalks, or street gardens. Lufa Farms, a private enterprise established in 2009, exploits unused rooftops throughout the city to build giant greenhouses and grow various organic food crops, which are sold at weekly markets and in home-delivered food baskets.

Mobility Patterns and Their Contribution to Livability

Mobility is an area where Montreal could improve upon its livability record. In spite of recent advances in terms of sustainable, active, and collective modes of transportation, Montreal remains entrenched in a car-centered culture. According to the City of Montreal (VdM, 2014), in 2014, 54% of trips were made by car, followed by public transit (34%), walking (8%), cycling (3%), and other modes of transportation (1%). In addition, over 50% of roadways and other spaces dedicated to transportation across the urban territory serve the needs of car drivers. Conservative residents and politicians often block proposals to reduce the space allotted to private automobiles, especially in terms of parking and a better sharing of the street. This is particularly the case when one moves away from central city boroughs.

Mobility patterns in Montreal have nonetheless been transitioning away from car-dependency. In 2015, the city publicly acknowledged that congestion costs—estimated at C$1.8 billion—were detrimental to its productivity and economic performance (CCMM, 2015). To address the issue, it launched a series of new public transit projects and set up Mobilité Montréal, a task force made up of 19 public and private sector organizations, to promote an integrated approach to the movement of people and the transport of goods within the metropolitan area.

Montreal's public transit system goes back more than 150 years. It consists of a metro network, a wide variety of bus lines, and a commuter train system. Montreal's Metropolitan Transport Service (STM) has recently vowed to adapt its services to people with reduced mobility, especially with the installation of elevators in some of its 67 metro stations, built without them in the 1960s. The STM also launched several projects to improve its transit offering and quality, including the deployment of reserved bus lanes, the gradual electrification of the bus network, the implementation of more spacious metro cars (AZUR), and the development of the iBUS application, enabling real-time tracking of lines on the network (STM, 2016). In addition, a new Metropolitan Electrical Network is in the works to connect the western part of the island to the metro system with a light-rail service. However, most service improvements are concentrated in the island's central and western boroughs, while the poorer north and east ends remain under-connected. Recurring promises such as the eastward extension of the metro's Blue line or the Pink line proposed by the city's new (2017) mayor have yet to materialize.

In recent decades, cycling has become a favorite alternative mode of transportation in Montreal. The city's favorable topography and the gradual shortening of the cold, snowy season have led a growing proportion of Montrealers to adopt cycling not only for recreational and exercise purposes, but for their daily commute as well. The city boasts a 788-kilometer bike lane network, used by 51% of the city's population (Vélo Québec, 2015). This constantly expanding network, to which 85 km of lanes were added in 2016 alone, places Montreal in second position among Canadian cities with the largest cycling networks (Vélo Québec, 2015). Montreal is the only Canadian city to have made the Top 20 Annual Copenhagenize Index, which recognizes the most bike-friendly cities in the world, and has featured in every edition of that compilation since 2011 (Copenhagenize, 2017).

Montreal has taken several concrete actions to make the city more bike-friendly, notably with the maintenance of bike lanes throughout the winter period, the creation of protected bike zones at key intersections, and the admission of bicycles on the subway during off-peak hours. Although Montreal has yet to draft a biking master plan which would help adopt bike-specific orientations throughout the island, its mobility plan now includes a new set of guidelines for the implementation of bicycle lanes.

Montreal has also developed an expertise in bike-sharing services, and has exported its system (locally known as BIXI) to dozens of cities around the world, including Melbourne, London, New York, Boston, and Washington, D.C. In 2008, *Time* magazine placed the system in 19th position in its ranking of the 50 best inventions of the year (Caplan et al., 2008). The continuous expansion of BIXI, implemented in 2009, has helped broaden the city's mobility options and enroll new cyclists. Nonprofit organizations such as Vélo Québec, which ensures the continuous promotion of cycling in Quebec, can also be credited for the improvement of biking conditions in the city (Vélo Québec, 2015).

Other innovative mobility options that contribute to Montreal's livability are the city's new electric taxi initiative and extensive car-sharing systems. Launched in 2015, Téo Taxi is an app-based taxi service with a fleet entirely made of electric cars that is rapidly transforming Montreal's taxi culture while offering a sustainable alternative to Uber. The city also enjoys a variety of car-sharing systems, which include Car2Go, Communauto, and Auto-mobile, whose membership is combined with the STM's bus and metro network. These different services remain largely concentrated in central city districts but are rapidly expanding to other sectors. Although they are privately run, the city has encouraged their development by providing reserved parking spaces and installing charging stations throughout the city, in the hope of reducing individual car ownership. In some boroughs, partnerships have been established to allow car-share users to park in areas reserved for local residents.

In 2006, Montreal adopted its Pedestrian Charter, a planning tool meant to promote walking as a mode of travel, particularly through a better sharing of public space. The recent Sustainable Development Strategic Plan 2016–2020 also places emphasis upon enhancing the city's walkability (VdM, 2016). As a result, a number of pedestrian-oriented policies were put in place, including the widening of sidewalks, the creation of neckdowns, reduced speed limits, the construction of protected rest areas (placottoirs, or chat rooms), and the conversion of existing streets into pedestrian or shared streets (VdM, 2016). Nonprofit organizations such as CRÉ-Montréal, Vivre en Ville, and Piétons Québec have helped stimulate a public discussion about a better sharing of streets in favor of vulnerable users.

Information Technology and Smart City Systems

A last ingredient that is contributing to Montreal's livability is the city's use of new information technologies to help improve public service delivery and communication with citizens. In 2014, Montreal set up its Smart and Digital City Office, responsible for implementing digital tools to tackle issues such as mobility, public services, housing, and economic development. The city called upon the creativity of institutional and private communities, as well as members of the general public to develop innovative ideas, which yielded dozens of projects (Montreal Smart City, 2017).

Among these, one of the most anticipated project is iBus, a multi-platform intelligent system that allows the management of the city's bus fleet in real time, in order to optimize services and to improve punctuality and regularity. Customer information will be disseminated on the STM website, iBus application, and Twitter at bus stops and on buses themselves. The system should help reduce crowding, inform customers of breakages and delays, ensure a better coordination with the subway and commuter train networks, and increase the safety of both customers and drivers (Montreal Smart City, 2017).

Other projects are tackling issues of traffic management and the mobility of people and goods, especially with regards to the security of pedestrians, cyclists, and people with reduced mobility. Geo-Traffic aims to deploy a dynamic cartographic database that will communicate the general state of all urban roadways in real time. This project will facilitate first responder interventions through dynamic traffic management and integrate data updates from multiple public transit users.

Other initiatives focus on parking management. Montreal is testing real-time parking data collection systems such as pavement sensors to provide up-to-the-minute information to guide motorists to available parking spots. A Dynamic Parking Signage System has already been set up to inform drivers about the availability of parking spaces in key urban districts, such as Quartier des spectacles and Old Montréal, in order to make traffic more fluid and reduce congestion caused by drivers looking for parking.

Other Smart City initiatives are designed to optimize direct services to citizens. For example, Info-Neige is a smart phone application that will provide snow removal information in order to minimize towing in areas where parking is temporarily banned and to improve the safety of snow loading operations. Info-Collections is another digital solution which will give citizens access to customized information on the collection of household waste, recyclables, green residues, and other refuse. It aims to make waste collection more efficient, to reduce the number of calls to the 311 municipal hotline, and to minimize the accumulation of uncollected waste on sidewalks. A notable project on the city's drawing board is the Digital Citizenship Identity Card, which would provide a secure access to all online municipal services and gradually replace the multiple access cards to the city's various public facilities, including public transportation, libraries, museums, cultural centers, etc. The Smart and Digital City Office is also developing partnerships with various telecommunications companies to help bridge the digital divide and provide free high-speed Wi-Fi access to the greatest number of residents and visitors (Montreal Smart City, 2017).

Yet another digital initiative is the development of Public Labs, located in the city's public libraries, to foster innovation and co-creation. These new incubators of creativity will turn public libraries into citizen service centers, spaces for experimentation, catalysts for collaboration, and facilitators in the acquisition of design thinking tools. The first Montreal Libraries Public Lab opened its doors in 2016 at the Benny Library in Notre-Dame-de-Grâce. Montreal has thus demonstrated a strong leadership position in its efforts to position itself at the forefront of the digital age and to be considered as a *Smart City* by making the city more user-friendly. However, this ambition has yet to be fully realized and the city is lagging behind in the concrete realization of many projects.

Conclusion: Montréalité as a Way of Life

This chapter sought to investigate some of the main factors behind Montreal's uniquely convivial character. It suggests that the city's high livability index is not only the product of innovative planning instruments that could be branded and exported as Montrealism, but depends upon a host of ingredients, which are rooted in both the past and the future and stem from unique historical, climatic, political, and social conditions. These factors have contributed to the remarkable level of adaptability, openness, and solidarity that have come to characterize Montreal. Over the last four centuries, the city has had to adapt to a harsh climate, to juggle with different cultural influences, and to struggle with changing economic conditions. To survive, its population relied upon community and solidarity networks, and its social engagement helped create a society without great social polarization, with a high tolerance for difference, respect for the arts, creativity, and innovation.

We thus propose to name the city's particular brand of livability and conviviality Montréalité, which reflects a particular way of life and a highly collaborative mode of thinking in the city that results from a mix of public programs, civil society initiatives, and citizen participation. The factors that make Montreal a safe, fun-loving, welcoming, and affordable city include a human-scaled built environment, a progressive socio-democratic political culture, a rich cultural heritage, and a vibrant use of the city's varied public spaces. While Montreal still faces a number of challenges in terms of aging infrastructure, faulty maintenance, and lagging services, and while its changing cultural makeup is also at the source of rising social and political frictions, it remains a city full of opportunities and resources, and a place where life is good for a majority of citizens.

Notes

1   Enrolled in the Master of Environmental Design program, these students participated in my graduate seminar on Environmental Design and Sustainable Culture in the fall semester of 2016. They include Marion Gosselin, Marine Fayollas, David Allard, Joseph Westres, Gabriel Bissonnet, Chloë Augat, Robin Carbonne, Samuel Rancourt, and Fayza Mazouz.

2   For example, there were only 23 murders in Montreal in 2016 for a population of about 2 million inhabitants. By comparison, Philadelphia, a similarly sized city, had 277 homicides the same year (SPVM, 2016).

3   For example, the Aéro Montréal cluster includes 215 companies employing more than 42,000 people and generating more than C$12 billion of economic activity, a significant portion of the province's GDP (Grappes Montréal, 2015).

4   Community garden members individually cultivate their allotted land parcel, sharing water access, tools, and rest areas. Collective gardens are composed of a single parcel gardened jointly by members who collectively select the species to cultivate, partake in the horticultural labor, and share the resulting crops.

References

Bloom, L. B. (2017). *Ranked: The 50 best cities for millennials to live right now.* Retrieved from www.forbes.com/sites/laurabegleybloom/2017/04/24/ranked-the-50-best-cities-for-millennials-to-live-right-now/#7c7df80e5692.

Caplan, J. et al. (2008). *Best inventions of 2008.* Retrieved from http://content.time.com/time/specials/packages/0,28757,1852747,00.html.

CCMM (Chambre de commerce du Montréal métropolitain). (2015). *Forum stratégique sur la mobilité urbaine et le transport intelligent.* Retrieved from www.ccmm.ca/fr/fs_transport_intelligent_0515/.

CES (Chantier de l'économie sociale). (2017). *Découvrez l'économie sociale.* Retrieved from http://chantier.qc.ca/decouvrez-leconomie-sociale/.

Charney, M. (1980). The Montrealness of Montreal: Formations and formalities in urban architecture. *Architectural Review, 999*(May), 299–302.

Copenhagenize. (2017). *The Copenhagenize bicycle-friendly cities index 2017.* Retrieved from http://copenhagenize.eu/index/.

Demographia. (2017). *World urban areas.* Retrieved from www.demographia.com/db-worldua.pdf.

Design Montréal. (2015). *Montréal ville UNESCO de design.* Retrieved from https://design-montreal.com/montreal-ville-unesco-de-design-0.

Dumont, F. (1993). *Genèse de la société québécoise.* Montréal: Boréal.

EIU (Economist Intelligence Unit). (2017). *The Global Livability Report.* Retrieved from www.eiu.com/public/topical_report.aspx?campaignid=livability17.

Garon, J. D., & Stevanovic, D. (2014). *Analyse du coût de la vie des ménages Comparaison entre Montréal et d'autres villes nord-américaines. Confédération des syndicats nationaux.* Retrieved from www.ledevoir.com/documents/pdf/comparaison_villes.pdf.

Gérin-Lajoie, F. (2016). *Le Québec, Champion Mondial de l'économie sociale. Institut de recherche et d'information socioéconomique.* Retrieved from http://iris-recherche.qc.ca/blogue/le-quebec-champion-mondial-de-l-economie-sociale.

Grappes Montreal. (2016). *Les grappes métropolitaines de Montréal.* Retrieved from http://grappes-montreal.ca/grappes-metropolitaines/les-grappes-metropolitaines-de-montreal/.

Handler, R. (1985). On having a culture: Nationalism and the preservation of Québec's patrimoine. In G. W. Stocking (Ed.), *Objects and others: Essays on museums and material culture.* Madison: The University of Wisconsin Press.

Legault, R. (1989). Architecture et forme urbaine: L'exemple du triplex à Montréal de 1870 à 1914. *Revue d'histoire urbaine, 18*(1), 1–10.

Mercer. (2014). *Worldwide cost of living survey 2014: City ranking.* Retrieved from www.mercer.com/newsroom/cost-of-living-survey.html.

Monocle (Producer). (2016, June 20). Quality of life survey: Top 25 cities [Video file]. Retrieved from https://monocle.com/film/affairs/top-25-cities-2016/.

Montréal International. (2013). *Le Grand Montréal. Le Pouvoir de vous faire réussir.* Retrieved from www.montrealinternational.com/wp-content/uploads/2013/10/Montreal-International-Facteurs-d-attractivite2013-2014.pdf.

Montreal Smart City. (2017). *A fruitful collaboration: Mid-term report.* Retrieved from http://villeintelligente.montreal.ca/en.

MUC (Montreal Underground City). (2017). Retrieved from http://montrealundergroundcity.com.

Olazabal, I. (2006). Le Mile-End comme synthèse d'une montréalité en devenir. *Les Cahiers du Gres, 6*(2), 7–16.

Port of Montreal. (2015). *A force for growth: Annual report 2015.* Retrieved from www.port-montreal.com/files/PDF/publications/2016-05-05_RA2015-interactif-EN.pdf.

Quacquarelli Symonds. (2017). *Best student city ranking.* Retrieved from www.topuniversities.com/city-rankings/2017.

SPVM. (2016). *À votre service. Rapport annuel 2016 du Service de police de la Ville de Montréal.* Retrieved from http://rapportspvm2016.ca.

STM. (2016). *Grands projets.* Retrieved from www.stm.info/fr/a-propos/grands-projets.

Stolarick, K., Florida, R., & Musante, L. (2005). *Montreal's capacity for creative connectivity: Outlook and opportunities.* Montreal: Catalytix.

Tourisme Montréal. (2017). *Tourism remains one of Montréal's most dynamic industries in 2017.* Retrieved from www.octgm.com/communiques/EN/Bilan-touristique-estival2017_Tourisme-Montreal.pdf.

Vélo Québec. (2015). *L'état du vélo à Montréal.* Retrieved from www.velo.qc.ca/files/file/expertise/VQ_EDV2015_Mtl.pdf.

VdM (Ville de Montréal). (2012). *Direction des grands parcs et verdissement. Plan d'action canopée 2012–2021.* Retrieved from http://ville.montreal.qc.ca/pls/portal/docs/PAGE/GRANDS_PARCS_FR/MEDIA/DOCUMENTS/PAC_JUIN_2012_FINAL.PDF.

VdM (Ville de Montréal). (2014). *Population de 15 ans et plus selon le mode de transport utilisé dans les déplacements domicile—lieu de travail.* Retrieved from http://ville.montreal.qc.ca/pls/portal/docs/PAGE/MTL_STATS_FR/MEDIA/DOCUMENTS/13H_MODES%20DE%20TRANSPORT%20VERS%20LE%20TRAVAIL_0.PDF.

VdM (Ville de Montréal). (2015a). *Le revenu disponible par habitant.* Retrieved from http://ville.montreal.qc.ca/pls/portal/docs/PAGE/MTL_STATS_FR/MEDIA/DOCUMENTS/FICHE%20REVENU%20DISPONIBLE.PDF.

VdM (Ville de Montréal). (2015b). *Comparaison du pouvoir d'achat dans certaines villes internationales.* Retrieved from http://ville.montreal.qc.ca/portal/page?_pageid=6897,67865570&_dad=portal&_schema=PORTAL.

VdM (Ville de Montréal). (2016). *Marche—Rues piétonnes.* Retrieved from http://ville.montreal.qc.ca/portal/page?_pageid=8957,99645644&_dad=portal&_schema=PORTAL.

VdM (Ville de Montréal). (2017a). *Montréal métropole culturelle.* Retrieved from http://montreal-metropoleculturelle.org/portal/page?_pageid=5017,15631571&_dad=portal&_schema=PORTAL.

VdM (Ville de Montréal). (2017b). *Profils sociodémographiques, recensement 2016.* Retrieved from http://ville.montreal.qc.ca/portal/page?_pageid=6897,68055570&_dad=portal&_schema=PORTAL.

Warin, T., Sinclair-Desgagné, B., & Van Assche, A. (2015). *L'économie du Québec 2015 Contexte et enjeux internationaux.* Montréal: Presses Internationales Polytechniques.

Chapter 2

MOST LIVABLE PITTSBURGH
Sabina Deitrick

Thirty years ago, Pittsburgh received the *Most Livable City* ranking from Rand McNally's *Places Rated Almanac*, 2nd edition (Boyer & Savageau, 1985). Many were surprised when, in the first Rand McNally edition in 1981, Pittsburgh ranked fourth among the most livable cities, but just a few years later—first? The guffaws didn't stop, reaching late night heights with coverage by Johnny Carson on NBC's The Tonight Show (Rotstein, 2010). After the initial reactions, the ranking did serve as a vehicle for others to recognize the changes that were taking place in Pittsburgh. Importantly, the noteworthy ranking also changed residents' views of their own city and region, occurring just a few years after the shuttering of many steel mills and manufacturing plants in the early 1980s. At that time, the region's unemployment rate topped 17% and tens of thousands relocated elsewhere.[1]

One could say that, by 1985, Pittsburgh's notoriety as the Steel City and Smoky City were part of its past, and livability came to mean more than steel jobs. The meaning of livability in post-industrial cities and regions shifts over different contexts over time. Pittsburgh's regional economy underwent tremendous industrial restructuring in the latter decades of the 20th century and regained economic stability through new growth sectors.

What made Pittsburgh livable? Over decades, major environmental improvements and policies were critical. In the 1950s, Pittsburgh enacted some of the earliest air and smoke controls to combat its smoky skies (Lubove, 1969). Later, after the shuttering of steel mills, redevelopment of brownfields also enhanced environmental conditions in the region (Deitrick & Farber, 2005). Slow growth has also created another constant for Pittsburgh's livability—affordability, broadly defined. In a region that grew slowly over the next three decades, it neither boomed in the late 1990s and mid-2000s nor busted in the Great Recession, and that story resonated globally (Kaufman, 2011). Continuing improvements in quality of life were evident in many spheres, and Pittsburgh picked up the *Most Livable* honor again in 2007 (Savageau, 2007) and scored *Most Livable* by *The Economist*'s ranking in 2014.

But is Pittsburgh *Most Livable* for everyone? Livability varies by social groups and race, and the understanding of livability is that it "means something different to different people" (Okulicz-Kozaryn, 2013, p. 433). This chapter will use data from a 2011 Quality of Life Survey conducted by the University of Pittsburgh Center for Social and Urban Research to examine livability and quality of life for different residents of Pittsburgh and Allegheny County. Specifically, how are community satisfaction and livability perceived by residents in the region, and how are views of quality of life related to different conditions in neighborhoods and communities? Do these subjective valuations differ by race and other socioeconomic conditions? Though Pittsburgh shines on many indicators of livability, collecting more recognition in recent years, this chapter contends that there are critical differences in livability among residents of Pittsburgh and Allegheny County. The quality of life survey results point to a protracted problem in the area, with African-American Pittsburghers reporting significantly lower levels of satisfaction on many indicators of livability than white residents. Pittsburgh's long transition as a post-industrial region has not been without many contradictions, as evidenced by the survey discussed. The chapter will conclude on what these local differences in quality of life and livability mean for Pittsburgh and what needs to improve.

Pittsburgh's notoriety in the lack of livability long preceded its livability rankings. The degraded condition of the coal, iron, and steel region was assured when Charles Dickens travelled through America in the 1840s and famously proclaimed Pittsburgh as "Hell with the lid lifted" (Steinberg, 1957). Over the next century, Pittsburgh's rapid and consuming industrialization accelerated, creating extensive problems in the urban environment. In 1907–1908, the Russell Sage Foundation pioneered the remarkable Pittsburgh Survey, one of the first in-depth, sociological studies of early 20th-century industrial America in a six-volume analysis (Greenwald & Anderson, 1996). By the time of the survey, Pittsburgh had become synonymous with urban industrial problems, and the Pittsburgh Survey was part pioneer of survey and social research and part "model" of social reform (Greenwald & Anderson, 1996, p. 6). Understanding the region in a large-scale social science analysis occurred again at mid-century. Building on the famous New York regional study,[2] a group of prominent economists, led by Edgar Hoover and Benjamin Chinitz, produced the Pittsburgh Regional Study, a four-volume report on the Pittsburgh region's changing economy and prospects for its future. The report underscored the uncertainty about Pittsburgh's core industries generating growth in the future (Pittsburgh Regional Planning Association, 1963). Pittsburgh had already begun losing its comparative advantages in its industrial structure, and employment in manufacturing was in decline by the mid-1950s (Jacobson, 1987).

By this point in the mid-20th century, through public and corporate leadership, Pittsburgh transgressed its projected decline through a new growth coalition, the Allegheny Conference on Community Development, formed by Pittsburgh Democratic Mayor David Lawrence and financier Richard King Mellon in 1943. Forged with urban renewal funding at the federal level, Pittsburgh redeveloped its central business district to shore up values and improve its environmental and built environment conditions (Lubove, 1969). The partnership worked hard to shift the old smoky city's hard scrabble, boilermaker image:

> Brawny Pittsburgh has always shouldered a heavy load as the industrial workshop of the United States. Its area has consistently produced about a quarter of the nation's steel, or more than the total output of Britain, Germany or Japan. Pittsburgh today is working even harder at something different. A former sooty eyesore, cursed by travelers and despised by local residents, it is excitedly rebuilding itself in a park like setting. It is showing the world, for if Pittsburgh can rebuild, any other artery-hardened city can do it too.
>
> (Steinberg, 1957, p. 1)

Pittsburgh's economic restructuring from steel and industry to service-led regeneration proceeded rapidly (Deitrick, 1999). In the late 1970s and early 1980s, deindustrialization occurred with plant closings, manufacturing job losses, and community disinvestment (Harrison & Bluestone, 1982), driven by the collapse of the region's steel industry in Pittsburgh. Jacobson presciently noted how Pittsburgh stood apart from other industrial regions:

> Although the process has been painful, especially for steel workers, Pittsburgh has effectively reshaped its manufacturing-dominated economy to one that is largely service oriented. In contrast, it remains to be seen how well other major cities, such as Detroit and Cleveland, will adapt to changes in the economic environment.
>
> (Jacobson, 1987, p. 38)

The rankings business has certainly grown in the years since Rand McNally was one of the only games in town with its *Places Rated Almanac*, and Pittsburgh landed on top (Boyer & Savageau, 1985). David Savageau, who developed the ranking with Rand McNally as the first publisher and continued his system through the years, commented that, "Neither I nor Rand-McNally could believe the response. The fierce partisanship in Pittsburgh was amazing. And Mayor (Richard) Caliguiri gave us the key to the city" (Majors, 2007). Twenty-two years later, with *Places Rated* continuing outside the Rand McNally banner, Pittsburgh again came out on top of the 379 metropolitan areas surveyed for the report. Over the nine categories measured for the most livable ranking, Pittsburgh failed to make the top 20 in any one category, but collectively emerged at the top in the 2007 edition (Majors, 2007).

Not all rankings have been so positive, however. On the other side of the rankings scale, more reflective of the city that it used to be than had become, the Pittsburgh region was the 8th most polluted city by particle pollution in 2017 and 17th for short-term particle pollution, earning the grade of F (failing) for ozone and particle pollution by the American Lung Association (American Lung Association, 2017). Despite its environmental leadership in the 20th century, the region failed to maintain its environmental improvements in the 21st. It also was a long-term *shrinking city*, with population loss in five decades (Beauregard, 2009). Many of the livability metrics discussed did not contend with inherent tensions in post-industrial Pittsburgh.

As Pittsburgh continues to transform itself as a post-industrial city and region and has just begun to reverse decades of population decline, it remains important for planners and policymakers to understand the people and parts of the regional economy experiencing lower quality of life than other residents and what is affecting those lower perceptions. As Thomas (2011, p. 1) notes, "race, ethnicity, and social-economic status are at the very heart of the dilemma facing shrinking cities in the U.S." In the next section, we analyze subjective survey results about quality of life issues and find that livability rankings are not necessarily a stand-in for subjective quality of life as captured by survey data (Okulicz-Kozaryn, 2013). Pittsburgh represents the contradictions in livability through comparisons of these subjective and objective measures.

In 2011, the University of Pittsburgh Center for Social and Urban Research conducted a large-scale quality of life survey of Allegheny County residents.[3] The survey was conducted by telephone sampling, with 799 surveys collected, including an oversample of African-Americans to ensure that geographical and racial distinctions could be significant (University Center for

Social and Urban Research & Pittsburgh Today, 2012). The survey sample closely matched Allegheny County measures on most socio-demographic measures (see Table 2.1).

The goals of the survey were to examine perceptions, attitudes, and behaviors related to quality of life through a number of subject domains.[4] Quality of life is affected by a broad range of conditions across human life and represented by residents' perceptions and attitudes about their environments (Marans & Stimson, 2011; McCrae, Stimson, & Marans, 2011). The Pittsburgh quality of life survey also offered the opportunity to provide detail on how quality of life is related to different socioeconomic attributes of respondents and respondents' neighborhoods and communities, with these subjective measures of quality of life compared—and contrasted—with the recognition Pittsburgh has received on objective livability indicators.

Survey results show strong differences in perceptions of neighborhood satisfaction by race, along with other key demographic features. These survey results illustrate the important distinctions between objective livability rankings and subjective quality of life and satisfaction survey results. While objective livability rankings place Pittsburgh in a good position, subjective survey measures reveal important differences among residents in their perceptions of quality of life in Pittsburgh.

The survey asked about changes in quality of life in the region over the previous few years. In a region that did not bust in the Great Recession, the responses to the first quality of life question showed similar results by race in a year coming out of the downturn. Respondents were asked whether quality of life in the region had improved, declined, or stayed about the same in the previous few years (see Table 2.2). Overall, only 28.2% of respondents felt that quality of

Table 2.1 Survey Respondents vs. Allegheny County Population (%)*

Variable		Allegheny County	Survey
Gender	Male	47.1	44.6
	Female	52.9	55.4
Age	18–29	21.2	21.4
	30–44	22.3	22.1
	45–64	35.6	35.5
	65+	20.9	21.0
Race	White only	83.8	81.5
	African-American only	11.9	15.4
Education	High school or less	40.2	30.0
	Some college	27.8	27.0
	Bachelor's degree	19.4	26.5
	Master's degree or higher	12.1	16.6

Source: Author.

Note
* The survey population was slightly more female and more highly educated than the general population in Allegheny County and, with the oversample, included a higher proportion of African-American respondents. These factors were controlled through weighting of survey results.

Table 2.2 Rating the Pittsburgh Region by Race of Respondent

Would you say that the overall quality of life in the Pittsburgh region has improved, declined, or stayed about the same during the past few years?

Race	Improved (%)	Declined (%)	Stayed the Same (%)
White (417)	28.8	25.4	45.8
African-American (316)	28.2	33.9	38.0
Total (772)*	28.2	30.6	41.2

Source: Author.

Note
* Includes "all others" (39) respondents.

life had improved over recent years. There was little difference between white and African-American respondents, with 28.2% of African-Americans rating that regional quality of life had improved over the past few years, compared with nearly 29% of white respondents. Conversely, a third of African-American respondents viewed the region's quality of life as declining, a higher proportion compared with a quarter of white respondents.

While respondents' views of overall changes in quality of life in the region showed some similarities between white and African-American residents, the differences between African-American and white respondents become more pronounced with a different set of quality of life questions focused on community and built environment issues:

1 Thinking about the overall quality of life in Southwestern Pennsylvania, how would you rate the region as a place to live? (5 points—Poor to Excellent)
2 How would you rate your neighborhood or local community as a place to live? (5 points—Poor to Excellent)
3 How would you rate the overall quality of public recreational areas in the region, such as parks, trails, or playgrounds? (5 points—Poor to Excellent)
4 How would you rate the conditions of other houses or buildings in your neighborhood? (5 points—Poor to Excellent)

Important differences by race emerged as questions focused on more specific issues of quality of life in Pittsburgh. Consistently across these measures, significant differences were found by race in how respondents rated various aspects of quality of life (see Table 2.3). In general, for those questions focused on community and environmental issues, white respondents, on average, had strongly favorable ratings of their communities and the Pittsburgh region, while African-American respondents, on average, were more likely to rate these quality of life indicators much lower.

One critical quality of life concern is ranking the Pittsburgh region as a place to live. For Allegheny County respondents, nearly half (48.7%) reported that the region was an excellent or very good place to live, while nearly a quarter rated the region as only a fair or poor place to live. This split, however, widens when race of respondent is considered, and the differences between

Table 2.3 Select Quality of Life Indicators by Race of Respondent, Allegheny County

Rate	Excellent (%)	Very Good (%)	Good (%)	Fair (%)	Poor (%)
Thinking about the overall quality of life in the region, how would you rate the region as a place to live?					
White	19.0	48.4	23.7	6.7	2.2
African-American	5.0	23.8	27.5	36.2	7.5
All	12.1	36.6	27.9	18.4	5.0
How would you rate your neighborhood or community as a place to live?					
White	25.3	36.8	27.1	7.3	3.5
African-American	9.0	15.4	34.6	25.6	15.4
All	17.1	31.1	26.8	16.9	7.7
How would you rate the overall physical or structural conditions of other houses or buildings in your neighbourhood?					
White	18.6	40.8	30.0	7.6	3.0
African-American	6.3	29.1	35.4	26.6	2.5
All	14.2	35.9	31.3	13.5	5.1
How would you rate the overall quality of public recreational areas in the region, such as parks, trails and playgrounds?					
White	23.7	40.3	26.2	8.1	1.8
African-American	15.2	26.6	21.5	21.5	15.2
All	17.7	32.5	27.2	14.9	7.8

Source: Author.

the views of white and African-American residents are substantial. Over two-thirds of white residents viewed the Pittsburgh region as an excellent or very good place to live, compared with just over a quarter (28.8%) of African-American respondents. For those residents who rated the region as a fair or poor place to live, the same deep divide between white and African-American respondents was evident, with just under 10% of white respondents ranking the region as a fair or poor place to live compared with 43.8% of African-American respondents.

The same sharp contrast between African-American and white residents was evident when respondents were asked to rate their neighborhood or community as a place to live. Again, just under a quarter of African-Americans rated their neighborhood or community as a very good or excellent place to live compared with 62.1% in the top ratings for white residents. The differences persisted for more negative ratings of respondents' community or neighborhood—41% of African-American respondents rated their neighborhood or community as a fair or poor place to live, compared with just 10.8% of white respondents.

These differences in perceptions of one's community or neighborhood by respondents' race occurred again when the survey asked respondents to rate the overall conditions of other houses or buildings in their neighborhood. The same distinct differences in the views of white and African-American respondents arose, and the differences were significant and substantial. Just 35% of African-Americans gave the other houses and buildings in their neighborhood a very good or excellent rating, compared with 64% of white residents, another sharp difference in quality of life perceptions.

For the final quality of life question, African-American respondents gave higher ratings for the quality of public recreation areas in the region than for any of the other quality of life questions. Rating overall quality of public recreational areas in the region, such as parks, trails, and playgrounds, found good to excellent ratings of 41.8% by African-American respondents, higher than African-American ratings on the other quality of life questions, but, nonetheless, ratings that were significantly lower than white survey respondents. Nearly two-thirds (64%) of white respondents reported good to excellent ratings on public recreational areas in the region. Conversely, over a third (36.7%) of African-American respondents rated recreational areas in the region as fair or poor, compared with just 10% of white respondents. Though recreational areas were viewed more positively by African-American respondents than the other quality of life questions, there was a sizeable number whose views were distinctly negative on public recreational areas in the region.

The results show significant and protracted differences in rating quality of life by a number of indicators by African-American and white respondents. These differences by race of respondent in subjective rankings of quality of life in the Pittsburgh region are consistent when age of respondents is considered. Survey analysis of the quality of life questions reveals even more pronounced differences by race when age of the respondents is added to the analysis.

When asked about rating the Pittsburgh region as a place to live, the differences between white and African-American respondents become greater when age is a factor (see Figure 2.1). In the 18–29 age group, 0% of African-American respondents rated the region as an excellent place to live, compared with 18.2% of white respondents. Combining the very good and excellent ratings, we find young white respondents viewed the region similarly to overall white respondents, 65.9% to 67.4% respectively. By contrast, just 26.8% of younger African-American respondents, aged 18–29, rated the region very good or excellent—just slightly lower than the average of 28.8% of all African-American respondents.

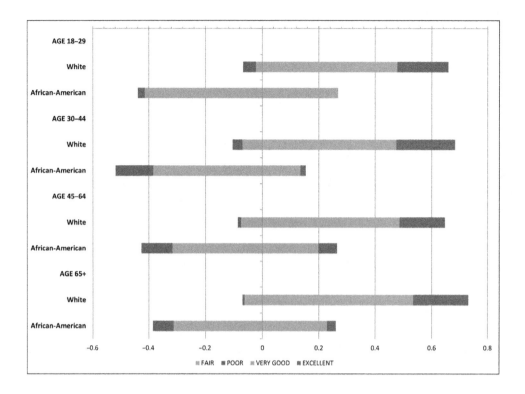

Figure 2.1 How would you rate the region as a place to live?

Source: Author.

The contrasts by age cohort and race were largest in the 30–44-year age group. Among African-American respondents, 51.2% rated the region as a poor or fair place to live, compared with just 10% by white respondents, and only 15.4% of African-American respondents rated the region as a very good to excellent place to live. African-American respondents aged 30–44 stood in contrast not just to white respondents of the same age group, but also other African-American respondents. It's not a part of the survey, but one possible explanation may be that many in this working age cohort had not only been adversely affected during the recession but also by Pittsburgh's slow post-recession recovery. Manufacturing, for instance, by 2012, had only recovered 15% of the jobs lost during the recession, compared with other Midwest regions recovering 50–100% of the manufacturing jobs they lost during the recession (Miller, 2012).

Similar differences by age and race are found in respondents rating their own neighborhood or community as a place to live. Over 40% of African-American respondents between 18 and 29 years of age rated their community or neighborhood as a fair to poor place to live, compared with only 16% of white respondents in that age group. Conversely, over 60% of young white respondents reported that their communities or neighborhoods were very good to excellent places to live, while only 17% of young African-Americans had the same community rating. Differences by race for these quality of life ratings extended through all cohorts, but they were not as strongly differentiated. White respondents across all age groups registered consistent good

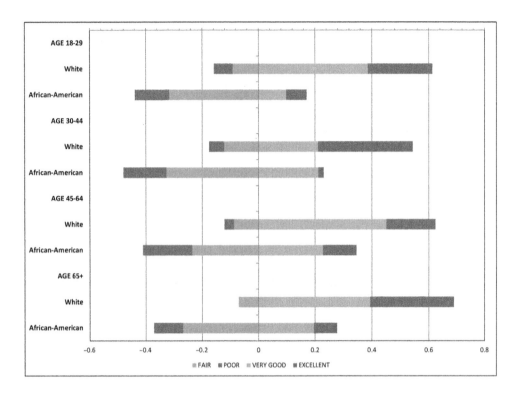

Figure 2.2 How would you rate your neighborhood as a place to live?

Source: Author.

to excellent ratings of their communities as a place to live, at or near 60%. Among African-Americans, there were greater differences across age groups, with African-Americans aged 45–64 years giving their communities or neighborhoods higher ratings than other age groups.

These results show the critical importance of differences in subjective ratings by greater demographic breakdowns. As Okulicz-Kozaryn (2013, p. 444) points out, "the best places to live … for the most part … depends on who you are." Neighborhood conditions in largely African-American neighborhoods within the city of Pittsburgh and nearby communities tend to have higher levels of property distress, vacancy, and tax delinquency than white-majority communities. Certainly, respondents' views of quality of life reflect different conditions in the built environment in which they live.

The final area of examination for comparing Pittsburg's livability rankings with subjective views from the quality of life survey show some interesting counters to the race divide in livability and subjective quality of life among Allegheny County residents discussed above. This concerns the measure of happiness. Happiness is a quality of life indicator that stood apart from the other quality of life measures discussed above. Happiness as a quality of life/livability measure attempts to understand how individuals' identity of themselves and their lives translates into life satisfaction or subjective wellbeing (Pfeiffer & Cloutier, 2016). The survey included a focus on personal happiness and satisfaction that shows that the differences between respondents' views on happiness contrasted with their views of the region's quality of life on built environment issues:

Taking all things together on a scale of 1 to 10, how happy would you say you are? (Scale from 1 to 10, very unhappy to very happy)

The mean score for happiness for African-American respondents and white respondents was identical, at 7.9 on a scale from 1–10. Happiness is certainly related to objective livability indicators and subjective quality of life measures, but the similarity between respondents makes the impacts of build environment less clear, perhaps, than other quality of life indicators. Does happiness stem from these or more from internal capacities and other social networks?

Finally, reflecting the quality of life questions about respondents' community and neighborhoods, in happiness, also, there are distinct differences by race and age cohorts (see Figure 2.4). White respondents, on average, are happier than African-American respondents at younger ages, ages 18–29 and 30–44, in Allegheny County. The difference between white and African-American respondents is greatest at the younger age group, 18–29, and these results show similarities between the happiness self-assessment and quality of life indicators. The difference with

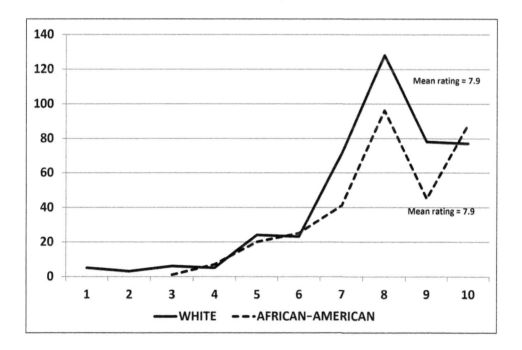

1 = Very Unhappy   10 = Very Happy

Figure 2.3 Taking all things together on a scale of 1 to 10, how happy would you say you are?

Source: Author.

the happiness indicator, however, is with older age cohorts and African-American respondents, who reported slightly higher self-assessments of their happiness than white respondents, with the mean scores across both the same. It would be difficult to assess the driver of these differences, but the literature is clear that happiness does not always align with other subjective quality of life measures. Pfeiffer and Cloutier (2016, p. 269) provide an extensive review of research on happiness related to neighborhood, or geographic drivers. Geographic drivers of happiness are less certain than individual traits and social relationships: "More heated is the debate on contributing factors in the body of literature on the geographic drivers of happiness" (Pfeiffer & Cloutier, 2016, p. 269). Respondents' assessments of their own happiness show some contrast with other quality of life indicators. The differences in happiness, however, do not negate the significant differences by race in the quality of life measures discussed.

The ratings business is complicated, but the subjective views of livability, as shown from results of the Pittsburgh quality of life survey, are equally complicated when aligning to livability composites drawn from objective secondary indicators. While Pittsburgh has garnered top livability ratings, demonstrating a long-term structural transformation from its industrial past to a 21st-century, post-industrial region, the transition continues. The differences between African-American and white respondents on the Pittsburgh quality of life survey brings forth the tensions in Pittsburgh in the region's continuing post-industrial transition and the inherent contradictions in post-industrial restructuring affecting residents in Pittsburgh and Allegheny

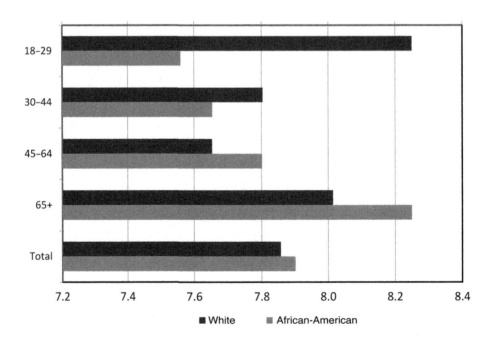

Figure 2.4 Taking all things together on a scale of 1 to 10, how happy would you say you are? Mean scores by race.

Source: Author.

County. When objective livability indicators are coupled against subjective ratings, the research here has found an extensive range of views, largely divided by race, and often age, as well. Most Livable Pittsburgh is an elastic term, and the survey results reveal an inherent contradiction in most livable being applied to all. The city and region may well be most livable for some, but not for all.

Notes

1   According to Fuguit and Beale's estimates, net migration from the ten-county Pittsburgh region was estimated to be a loss of over 227,000 between 1980 and 1990 (cited in C. Briem, June 2014, PEQ).

2   The Regional Plan of New York and Its Environs contained Volume One, *The Graphic Regional Plan: Atlas and Descriptions* (1959) and Volume Two, *The Building of the City*, 1931.

3   The full Pittsburgh Regional Quality of Life (QOL) survey extended to nearby counties, but the examination of factors by race was limited to Allegheny County. The Pittsburgh Regional QOL Survey conducted an oversample of African-Americans to be able to understand and statistically analyze differences by race. Of the original regional population, 91.8% of African-Americans resided in Allegheny County in 2010, the home county of the City of Pittsburgh.

4   The topic areas included: local neighborhoods, environment, government, arts, transportation, education, public safety, housing, economy, health, demographics, overall satisfaction with the region, and overall life satisfaction and happiness. This chapter draws on related quality of life indicators from the environment, housing, overall satisfaction, and happiness section of the survey.

References

American Lung Association. (2017). *State of the air*. Retrieved from www.lung.org/our-initiatives/healthy-air/sota/.

Beauregard, R. A. (2009). Urban population loss in historical perspective. *Environment and Planning, 41*, 514–528.

Boyer, R., & Savageau, D. (1985). *Places rated almanac* (2nd ed.). New York: Rand McNally.

Briem, C. (2008, December). Recessions and Pittsburgh. *Pittsburgh Economic Quarterly*. Pittsburgh: University of Pittsburgh Center for Social and Urban Research.

Deitrick, S. (1999). The post industrial revitalization of Pittsburgh: Myths and evidence. *Community Development Journal, 34*(1), 4–12.

Deitrick, S., & Farber. S. (2005). Managing brownfields as community assets. In F. Wagner, T. Joder, A. Mumphrey, Jr., K. Akundi, & A. Artibise (Eds.), *Revitalizing the city: Strategies to contain sprawl and revive the core*. Armonk, NY: M.E. Sharpe.

Greenwald, M. W., & Anderson, M. (1996). Introduction: The Pittsburgh survey in historical perspective. In M. W. Greenwald & M. Anderson (Eds.), *Pittsburgh surveyed: Social science and social reform in the early twentieth century*. Pittsburgh: University of Pittsburgh Press.

Harrison, B., & Bluestone, B. (1982). *The deindustrialization of America*. New York: Basic.

Jacobson, L. (1987). Labor mobility and structural change in Pittsburgh. *Journal of the American Planning Association, 53*(4), 438–448.

Kaufman, D. (2011). Second life Pittsburgh. *Monocle, 47*(5), 75–68.

Lubove, R. (1969). *Twentieth century Pittsburgh: Government, business and environmental change.* Pittsburgh: John Wiley.

Majors, D. (2007, April 25). Pittsburgh rated 'most livable' once again: After 22 years, back atop Places Rated Almanac. *Pittsburgh Post-Gazette.*

Marans, R. W., & Stimson, R. J. (2011). *Investigating quality of urban life: Theory, methods and empirical research.* New York: Springer.

McCrae, R., Stimson, R., & Marans, R. W. (2011). The evolution of integrative approaches to the analysis of quality of life. In R. W. Marans & R. J. Stimson (Eds.), *Investigating quality of urban life: Theory, methods and empirical research.* New York: Springer.

Miller, H. G. (2012, September 2). Pittsburgh's job growth isn't helping the unemployed. Retrieved from http://pittsburghfuture.blogspot.com/2012/09/pittsburghs-job-growth-isnt-helping.html.

Okulicz-Kozaryn, A. (2013). City life: Ranking (livability) versus perceptions (satisfaction). *Social Indicators Research, 110*(2), 433–451.

Pfeiffer, D., & Cloutier, S. (2016). Planning for happy neighborhoods. *Journal of the American Planning Association, 82,* 267–279.

Pittsburgh Regional Planning Association. (1963). *Economic study of the Pittsburgh region.* Pittsburgh: Pittsburgh Regional Planning Association.

Rotstein, G. (2010, February 27). 'Most Livable City' took its lumps over tag: No. 1 ranking in 1985 drew scorn from disbelievers. *Pittsburgh Post-Gazette.*

Savageau, D. (2007). *Places rated almanac: The classic guide for finding your best places in America* (7th ed.). Washington, D.C.: Places Rated Book, LLC.

Steinberg, A. (1957). The new city called Pittsburgh. The Reader's Digest Association, condensed from National Municipal Review, June 20, 1957.

Thomas, J. M. (2011, April). *Race, class and social conflict: Addressing the racial and social implications of urban shrinkage.* 110th American Assembly, Columbia University, April, Detroit.

University Center for Social and Urban Research and Pittsburgh Today. (2012). *The Pittsburgh regional quality of life survey.* Pittsburgh: University of Pittsburgh.

Chapter 3

LIVABLE STOCKHOLM
Stefan Lundberg, Tigran Haas, and Mats J. Lundström

Introduction

Stockholm was ranked 6th on the Economist Intelligence Unit (EIU) list of the world's most livable cities in 2012. The high ranking in 2012 was, among other things, because of the many green spaces in the center of the city. Criteria for the ranking include population density, air quality, connectivity, green space, and pollution concentration. Over 40% of the Swedish capital is composed of parks, lakes, and hiking trails. Since then, Stockholm's ranking has gone down, but it is still high, as Stockholm is a dynamic city with high ambitions. But ranking in all its might is nice, but livability, in the sense of people's everyday life, goes beyond ranking.

The city of Stockholm is growing, and expansion means possible conflicts when land, such as woods and parks, is transformed into housing areas or when high-rise buildings take the view away. The city of Stockholm has a high standard in its city and urban planning and gives a voice to those concerned. Still, the city has an issue with the housing situation. If you would like to buy an apartment, the price has gone up for several years now, especially in or around the central city. If you instead would like to rent an apartment, the situation is even worse; the building of tenant flats has been far too low, so the demand is greater than the supply. Some researchers argue that Sweden now represents "a monstrous hybrid" with clear signs of neoliberalization but with considerable regulatory framing still in place.

The early Swedish actions regarding sustainable urban development, initiated in the 1990s, were mainly focused on the environmental aspects of sustainability. Gradually, the social perspective has gained more attention in urban planning discourse and practice. The main drivers for this development are the increasing socio-spatial segregation and social unrest.

After World War II, the new urban planning did call for an expansion of the city based on a new suburban hierarchy with more or less independent satellite cities and associated smaller suburbs. The new suburbs, with modern housing, services, and workplaces, were located in a radial star pattern around the new subway and commuter trains.

When a ten-year-long *million homes program* ended in 1975, there was an oversupply of housing in Stockholm, especially in the newest large-scale multi-family housing estates. Despite high-quality and modern housing, these areas early on got a bad reputation. Alcohol and drug problems and other social problems were widespread in some suburbs, especially among the youth of the working class and immigrant population.

When the period of high modernism was over, attention was focused on the densification and conversion of brownfield areas in more central areas. As a reaction to the modernist suburban expansion and urban sprawl, urban development and planning were driven by a desire to create urban, vivid, and attractive neighborhoods.

In the new millennium, dialogue and cooperation are key process strategies to implement the goals of the city's Vision 2030 adopted in 2007. The main goals of the vision clearly connect to the concept of livability. Stockholm has become a more divided city, and the goals are now to make Stockholm a cohesive city, a city for all. The vision is good, and the future will show if the vision will come true. If so, that would truly strengthen Stockholm as a livable city.

Global Rankings

Stockholm was ranked 6th on the Economist Intelligence Unit (EIU) list of the world's most livable cities in 2012. Since then, Stockholm's ranking has gone down to 24th after the terror bomb in 2017. The EIU ranking has been performed every year since 2000. The EIU is the research and analysis division of The Economist Group, a sister company to *The Economist* newspaper. The high ranking in 2012 was, among other things, because of the many green spaces in the inner city. Criteria for the ranking include population density, air quality, connectivity, green space, and pollution concentration. Over 40% of the Swedish capital is composed of parks, lakes, and hiking trails. The EIU Annual Livability Ranking, which ranks 140 cities for their urban quality of life based on and assessed through 30 indicators in 5 categories is weighted as follows: stability (25%), healthcare (20%), culture and environment (25%), education (10%), and infrastructure (20%). One criticism of the ranking is that it does not take into consideration the cost of living in the cities. The differences are quite small in the top segment, but Stockholm is lagging behind in one important area: healthcare (87.5% in comparison with Melbourne at 100%, which is number one in these rankings).

As there are other rankings (Mercer, Monocle, etc.) with different results, how much attention should one put on such a ranking? What is this ranking all about? Dr. Barrett at the Royal Melbourne Institute of Technology quotes one of his professors, who claimed that these rankings are just designed to help multinational corporations determine what kind of relocation package they will offer to their professional staff who are seconded overseas. They are rankings for expats. So, for the citizens of Stockholm (and other cities), it is perhaps more valuable to look at the city and ask, is life in the city as good as it can be? If we, for example, look at the Happiness Index, what can it tell us about life in our own city? The Happiness Index is found in the World Happiness Report. For 2013 to 2015, Sweden, as a country, was ranked as the 10th happiest country in the world. The happiest people live in Denmark, followed by Switzerland, Iceland, Norway, and Finland. The result is based on roughly 3,000 respondents in each of more than 150 countries in the world. Based on a happiness ranking, Stockholm is among the world's ten best countries to live in.

The Economist Intelligence Unit (EIU) ranking is not about livability at all but is designed to help the human resource managers for transnational corporations determine the compensation paid to their mobile global talent. There is Mercer's Quality of Living Ranking and *Monocle* magazine's Quality of Life Survey. Vienna is the clear winner, with a strong showing in all three rankings (CityMetric, 2018). One of the areas on the World Happiness Report was about corruption in the

Table 3.1 Rankings

Mercer Quality of Life Rankings 2016	Monocle Quality of Life Survey 2016	EIU Livability Ranking 2015
Vienna	Tokyo	Melbourne
Zurich	Berlin	Vienna
Auckland	Vienna	Vancouver
Munich	Copenhagen	Toronto
Vancouver	Munich	Adelaide
Dusseldorf	Melbourne	Calgary
Frankfurt	Fukuoka	Sydney
Geneva	Sydney	Perth
Copenhagen	Kyoto	Auckland
Sydney	Stockholm	Helsinki

Source: Authors.

country. Respondents were asked, "Is corruption widespread throughout the government or not?" and, "Is corruption widespread within businesses or not?" The answers were binary. The happiest countries were basically very much equal in this area, except for Iceland, which stood out with a very low feeling of having widespread corruption in the country.

When looking at the Corruption Perception Index, Denmark, in 2016, had the highest ranking (90) together with New Zealand being least corrupt, as judged by the inhabitants in the countries, closely followed by Finland (89) and Sweden (88). So, based on happiness and corruption, it seems like Sweden and Stockholm (as the capital of Sweden) could be quite well off when it comes to livability. But livability in the sense of people's everyday life goes beyond corruption and is critical to the establishment of a sustainable community, if for no other reason than, if it is not present, people will not stay in the community.

The Safe Cities Index of 2017 examined 60 cities in the world and used four categories of security: namely, digital, health, infrastructure, and physical. This ranking is also produced by the EIU. Tokyo tops the overall rankings, closely followed by Singapore in 2nd position. The Japanese capital's strongest performance is in the digital security category, and it has risen seven places in the health security category since 2015. However, in infrastructure security, it has fallen out of the top 10 to 12th. Stockholm is ranked as number 8 on the list, and it is one of three European cities on the top 10 list. Zürich is ranked as number 10 and Amsterdam as number 6. When looking closer at the ranking, Stockholm is not in the top 10 when it comes to digital security but ranked as number 10 in health security. This category is not only about acute care and medical care but also about how the cities handle healthy urban environments in the form of traffic management schemes, the provision of green spaces, and other measures with an impact on health. Stockholm is ranked as number 4 in infrastructure security. The report points out the importance for a society to have a good and secure infrastructure, which means that cities have a responsibility to secure the safety of buildings, roads, bridges, and other physical infrastructure. The fire catastrophe in London was a reminder of this, according to the report. Lastly, in the personal security ranking, Stockholm is number 9.

Different ranking lists, for what they are worth for everyday life in the city, still give a hint of the fact that Stockholm is doing well and that the city of Stockholm can regard itself as having the basics in place to be called a livable city.

Vancouver, Canada has been ranked as one of the most livable cities in the world, and it comes out as number 3 in the latest Mercer 2017 ranking. The city of Vancouver has changed its city-planning concept and has rejected the highway and sprawled city model so common in North American cities. When quality of life and environmental concerns won out over a city model, based on a highway network, the city developed a livability agenda. The components of livability, as seen in the city of Vancouver are: protection of the environment; maintenance of a diverse economy; provision of accessibility through land use; delivery of services for residents and businesses; housing choices; balanced city budget; and involvement of citizens in planning and delivery. If this agenda is compared with the way the city of Stockholm is growing, they all fit in well with the way the city of Stockholm is handling its expansion and urban planning.

Livability and Beyond: Housing Issues

Planners, architects, urban designers, and policymakers concerned with creating or maintaining livable cities have long invoked *livability* as the major guiding principle for the investment and decision-making that shape the urban, social, economic, physical, and biological environment

Figure 3.1 Stockholm, Capital of Scandinavia. Scenic summer aerial panorama of Stockholm, Sweden, 2018.

Source: Stockholm City.

(Benzeval, Judge, & Whitehead, 1995; Hills, 1995; Pacione, 1982, 2003; Ruth & Franklin, 2014). In the Swedish language, there is no direct equivalent to the English terms *livable* and *livability*. In her study of the (mainly) American livability concept from a Swedish transportation planning point of view, Moa Tunström finds it quite similar to how the concept of social sustainability is used in the Swedish urban planning and development discourse, concerning key issues such as wellbeing, a functioning everyday life, integration, and justice (Tunström, 2014). However, livability seems to take a more short-term, pragmatic, and local point of view compared with the concept of social sustainability. It is a community and human-centered perspective, focusing on how planning can affect social conditions and quality of life. Furthermore, it highlights the importance of place and place-making based on the conditions and needs of the specific local community. Additionally, Tunström notes that the concept of livability also includes administrative and procedural aspects of planning, stressing the need of coordination and a more holistic perspective, including multilevel governance, cross-disciplinary planning processes, and the introduction of new participatory tools and integrative methods.

Despite the fact that Stockholm does well in different rankings, we can see that there are some difficult areas for the city of Stockholm to handle. The most difficult part in Stockholm for the moment is the housing situation. The deficit in housing has created a situation where the price for an apartment has risen to sky-high levels. Lind and Lundström (2007) argue that Sweden currently has one of the most liberal housing regimes in the world with very little state intervention, and they hypothesize that further policy changes after 2001 have continued to increase social polarization. Christophers (2013) argues that Sweden now represents a monstrous hybrid with clear signs of neoliberalization but with considerable regulatory framing still in place. He identifies increasing housing shortages due to the undersupply of rental units, along with escalating purchase prices, as the two biggest challenges that contemporary Swedish housing policy must overcome. The housing issue is a huge problem for Stockholm, and it makes the city less livable for those who look for a job in the city and cannot find a place to live. Each fall, the new students coming to the city to study are in a race to find somewhere to stay. Many find short-term solutions, while both studying and searching for a permanent apartment at a reasonable price.

Increased Focus on Coordination and Cross-Disciplinary Collaboration

Swedish national authorities and organizations, during the last two decades, have promoted and supported the development of more multilevel coordinated and cross-sectorial urban planning practices. In the 1990s and early 2000s, the National Urban Environment Council, known for its Agenda for the City, was advocating for and promoting municipalities to focus on place-making, social meetings, and urban qualities, which required more coordination and less silo thinking. In the early 2000s, several national campaigns and projects were initiated to support coordination between the transport and urban planning sectors. One example is the National Board of Housing, Building, and Planning's campaign, Town Planning instead of Transport Planning and Urban Planning (Boverket). Another is the new national transport planning guidelines Transports for Attractive Cities (TRAST), a call for local governments to coordinate planning efforts in various sectors and to support urban development with people and place quality in mind rather than vehicles and transport infrastructure. Furthermore, national research and development projects were initiated in the mid-2000s and carried through to the early 2010s to develop new knowledge and build new capacity among local authorities in order to coordinate sectoral planning and urban planning.

Sustainable Urban Development in Sweden: Environmental to Social Focus

The early Swedish initiatives and actions regarding sustainable urban development initiated in the 1990s were mainly focused on the environmental aspects of sustainability. The most famous examples are the Bo01 housing exhibition, and the following urban redevelopment of the Western Harbor in Malmö, and the Hammarby Sjöstad development in Stockholm, both initiated and planned in the 1990s and implemented from around 2000 and still running.

The government's initiative, the Delegation for Sustainable Cities, supported urban development projects focusing on both environmental and social sustainable development.

Gradually, the social perspective has gained more attention in urban planning discourse and practice. The main drivers for this development are the increasing socio-spatial segregation and social unrest. One example of the growing interest for the environment as well as socially sustainable urban development is CityLab (2015), the Swedish equivalent of REEAM Communities (Building Research Establishment Environmental Assessment Method), or the U.S. Green Building Council's Leadership in Energy and Environmental Design (LEED ND). The Swedish Green Building Council, in collaboration with many urban development actors, runs CityLab.

Post-War Era Planning and Urban Development

While similar methods have also sprung up, such as Greenstar in Australia and CASBEE in Japan, BREEAM and LEED are the main methods currently in use. After World War II, the housing shortage was high in Stockholm. With inspiration from Anglo-Saxon planning approaches such as neighborhood units and the County of London Plan, a new era in Stockholm's urban planning was launched.

The new urban planning approach called for an expansion of the city based on a new suburban hierarchy with more or less independent satellite cities and associated smaller suburbs. The new suburbs, with modern housing, services, and workplaces, were located in a radial star pattern around the new subway and commuter trains, what we today call TOD, Transit-Oriented Development. Hökarängen, Gubbängen, and Årsta are examples of more small-scale suburbs in southern Stockholm, which were planned and built in the 1940s based on the neighborhood unit principles.

Eventually, these new suburbs became larger because of the retail industry's desire for a larger population or customer base, and the buildings were increasingly adapted to large-scale industrial construction. In the 1950s, a pearl string of new suburbs was built along the northern subway line (Vällingby, Blackeberg, Grimsta, Råcksta, and Hässelby), where Vällingby, with its center, served as a satellite city and regional center for the neighboring smaller suburbs.

When the ten-year-long government initiative *million homes program* ended in 1975, there was an oversupply of housing in Stockholm, as well as in most of Sweden, especially in the newest large-scale multi-family housing estates. Despite high-quality modern housing, services, and good public transportation, these areas, early on, got a bad reputation. Alcohol and drug problems and other social problems were widespread in some suburbs, especially among the youths of the working class and immigrant population (Hall, 2009).

The Post-Modern Reaction

When the period of high modernism was over and the large-scale suburban expansion came to a halt, attention focused instead on the densification and conversion of brownfield areas in more central areas, such as the South Railway Station (1980s); Hammarby Sjöstad, a former industrial area (1990s); and St. Erik, a hospital area (1990s). As a reaction to the modernist suburban expansion and urban sprawl, urban development and planning was driven by a desire to create more urban, vivid, and attractive neighborhoods.

The main strategy in the city's Comprehensive Plan 1999 was to develop Stockholm in a sustainable way and to build the city inwards: to manage and improve the city already built, reuse already claimed land, and preserve and develop the green structure and the character of Stockholm. The plan points out a number of development areas for 60,000 new homes, mainly in the old industrial and port areas, such as Liljeholmskajen, Lindhagen, Hagastaden, and Stockholm Royal Seaport.

At the same time, the regional Public Transport Company planned to expand the Crossway Line, a light-rail line linking the inner suburbs and public transport stations, to allow travel by public transport between the suburbs without having to travel through the bottlenecks in central Stockholm. The first phase, connecting Gullmarsplan and Liljeholmen, was opened in 2000, and the extension to Hammarby Sjöstad opened two years later.

Planning and Urban Development in the New Millennium

Most of the development areas designated in the 1999 plan were planned and built during the first decade of the new millennium, while others started in the 2010s. Compared with earlier developments in Stockholm, the new urban areas have considerably denser urban structures, too dense, according to some critics, especially regarding Hagastaden.

Sustainable Livable Communities I: Hammarby Sjöstad (Hammarby Waterfront)

Hammarby Sjöstad is a district south of the inner city, a pioneer sustainable urban development known all over the world for its environmental endeavors, systems thinking, and its urban and green qualities. It was actually divided in two parts on each side of the Hammarby Lake. The northern part, built in the early 1990s, was located on Södermalm, which is a part of the inner city. The general public sees only the southern part to be Hammarby Sjöstad. Planned in the 1990s on brownfield land with the aim to create a new city district, it includes the best parts of the inner city's urban qualities and the suburb's light and green outdoor spaces. The politicians had the planners make it more urban, since this was supposed to be the Olympic Village, as Stockholm was bidding to host the Olympic Games in the summer of 2004. The new district was planned with very ambitious environmental goals. The city didn't get the Olympics, but it kept some of the environmental amenities when developing the new district.

Since the opening in 2000, it has attracted thousands of urban professional tourists. Hammarby Sjöstad is a flagship project used for branding Stockholm as an attractive and sustainable post-industrial city and was an important feature when Stockholm was appointed as the very first European Green Capital in 2010. However, Hammarby Sjöstad has been criticized from a social point of view as being an attractive but socially segregated enclave for the white, well-off, upper-middle class. It is supposed to be fully built in 2020, with 25,000 inhabitants and 150,000 square meters of workspaces (Marcus, Balfors, & Haas, 2013).

The Walkable City, Strategic City Plan (2010)

The Walkable City is the popular name of the Stockholm Strategic City Plan of 2010. The comprehensive plan of 2010 continues the 1999 plan's strategies of densification in respect to Stockholm's historical and natural assets. However, it places greater emphasis on linking the city's districts, focusing on strategic nodes and creating a vibrant urban environment. The need for a denser city and better integration and connection between districts are important starting points for the city plan. The five urban development strategies of the city plan, intended to create sustainable urban growth, are: continue to strengthen central Stockholm; focus on strategic nodes; connect city areas; and create a vibrant urban environment.

Urban sustainable development (green and ecological) is today seen as one of the key elements towards unlocking the roadmap for a sustainable and resilient built environment. One

Figure 3.2 Hammarby Sjöstad, June 2016.

Source: Ola Ericsson (Stockholms Foto); Sustainable Livable Communities II: Norra Djurgårdsstaden (Stockholm Royal Seaport).

feature of urban sustainability is the increased interest in developing sustainable (ecological showcase) urban districts. For many of these developments, guiding sustainability documents are developed to frame future goals (Holmstedt, Brandt, & Robèrt, 2017).

Sustainable Livable Communities II: Norra Djurgårdsstaden (Stockholm Royal Seaport)

The Hammarby sustainability model was based on technology and ideas from the 1990s, and eventually other cities were catching up. A new flagship project was needed in order to keep the sustainable city brand of Stockholm (Haas, Littke, & Wells, 2017). In 2009, the city of Stockholm decided to make Stockholm Royal Seaport, the new designated area with an environmental profile, to become the new model of sustainable urban development in Stockholm. This was called Hammarby Sjöstad 2.0, "A global showcase for sustainable urban construction and design, where innovative environmental technology and creative solutions are developed, tested and presented" (Metzger & Rader Olsson, 2013, p. 80).

The brownfield area, situated quite close to the city in a beautiful setting between the Baltic Sea and the unique Royal National City Park, is being converted into "an attractive and vibrant neighborhood with at least 12,000 flats and 35,000 new jobs" (Stockholm Royal Seaport, 2018). The first 700 apartments were built in 2012, and construction is expected to continue until 2025. The former gas works will be transformed to accommodate various art and culture attractions.

The urban development is based on four overall targets: climate (fossil-fuel-free by 2030, climate change adapted); ecology (resource management and a green structure that supports ecosystems); social (vibrant city that serves its people and enables sustainable choices); and innovation (catalyst for innovation and environmental technologies supporting economic sustainability) (Shahrokni, Årman, Lazarevic, Nilsson, & Brandt, 2015).

Stockholm Royal Seaport has been praised for its environmental ambitions, but as in the case of Hammarby Sjöstad, there have been concerns about the area being a socially enclosed enclave for the well-off, upper-middle class. The attractive location, combined with high costs for soil remediation of the former industrial land, has led to high housing prices in the area (Haas et al., 2017).

Vision 2030

The three main goals of the vision clearly connect to the concept of livability. The first goal is a city that is innovative and growing, versatile, and full of unique experiences. The second goal of Citizens' Stockholm is an accessible, safe, urban region with no physical or social barriers. The goal focusing on being innovative and growing stresses the need of being competitive in the global market. The third goal, being versatile and full of unique experiences, enhances Stockholm's unique combination of top-class education and business opportunities and unspoiled nature at the doorstep that will continue to attract international visitors.

The densification of the existing city is evolving over time. In addition to major transformation projects on brownfield areas, the city is densified by less extensive densification projects in existing districts. The densification takes place mainly in the quiet central suburbs, but in addition, the outer districts or suburbs begin to become densified as well. An important part in this densification process is the so-called Stockholm model, which began to be used in the 1990s following the extensive Swedish financial crisis, when few developers dared to build.

The Stockholm model, as somewhat simplified, is a developer-driven planning process where developers propose smaller land areas where they want to build, and then the city will develop a detailed plan for this development. However, this approach continued in the 2000s and 2010s, although the market situation is now the reverse compared with the 1990s. Presently, the housing market is skyrocketing.

The Stockholm model has been criticized because it is considered by many to be too project-oriented and lacking a holistic perspective without taking into account how the project affects the city and the city districts. For some years now, the City Planning Office has had 14 special area planners with special responsibility for coordinating the spatial planning and urban development in its district area, together with residents, businesses, and the other departments within the city administration.

Recent Urban Planning: Increased Focus on Social Sustainability

In 2015, the city of Stockholm committed to reverse the trend towards a more divided Stockholm. One of the city's four main goals is to make Stockholm a cohesive city. The vision is a socially sustainable city with good living conditions for all, where the wellbeing of inhabitants

Figure 3.3 The Royal Seaport, vision by Mandaworks AB, 2014.

Source: Mandaworks AB.

grows in tandem with the city, and everyone has the opportunity to realize their lives through studies and work, a city where all Stockholm citizens are given access to vivid and safe habitats (City of Stockholm, 2016).

In the same year, the city appointed the Commission for Socially Sustainable (Bremberg, Slattman, & Alarcón, 2015) with the task of analyzing differences in living conditions in Stockholm and proposing measures for an equally and socially sustainable city. The Commission was working on four development areas: democracy and security, work and income, housing and urban environment, as well as education and training. Its work ended in December 2017.

In its first report, *A Stockholm of Differences 2015*, the Commission notes that there are major socioeconomic differences between the different city districts of Stockholm. It concerns health, employment, education, and income levels, and this pattern is reinforced over time. As the proportion of long-term unemployment and the number of households with long periods of social security subsidies increases, it is harder to get out of long-term exclusion. The gaps in income and the socioeconomic segregation in the city are growing.

Today, average income in the richest district is four times as high as in the poorest. Twenty-five years ago, the difference was just over twice as high. In addition, segregation has a more pronounced ethnic character, which means that people of different backgrounds do not meet each other as often in everyday life. The possibility for socioeconomically weak groups to choose area and housing has fallen in recent years as the number of apartments for rent has decreased, especially in attractive areas. Childhood conditions of growth differ significantly in different parts of Stockholm. Families living in financial vulnerability are found mainly in the city's outer suburbs, built in the 1960s and 1970s, under the so-called *million homes program* (Bremberg et al., 2015; City of Stockholm, 2016).

At the same time, the health situation among Stockholm inhabitants has improved in several ways, and Stockholm is an attractive city with strong population growth. However, access to the city's attractive qualities, such as a wide range of urban activities, public spaces for recreation and social encounters, diversified labor markets, and expanded public transport, is lower in the city's socioeconomically weak neighborhoods. It also applies to the experience of security.

During the first decade of the 21st century, social trust in the city of Stockholm has increased but varies considerably between different districts, with the lowest trust in areas with low educational levels. The Commission believes that the unevenly distributed living conditions between different groups and areas can change. Through early investments in Stockholm's young inhabitants, it is possible to make profits in the longer term, both for individuals and for the city and for society as a whole (Bremberg et al., 2015; City of Stockholm, 2015).

In a report on housing and urban environment (Bremberg et al., 2015), the Commission raises the city's two main urban development challenges, namely, housing shortage and spatial segregation. In planning, social perspectives must be included throughout the planning process, and the social intentions should be clearly stated in the plans. The report proposes special efforts on selected profile projects for socially sustainable urban development to promote knowledge and method development. Physical investments will strengthen attractiveness and counteract spatial segregation and may be coordinated with efforts that stimulate local employment. Furthermore, the Commission highlights the central role of the comprehensive plan. The current 2010 comprehensive plan, the Walkable City (City of Stockholm, 2010), is proposed to be developed and promote the development towards a city where more people meet each other in

Figure 3.4 Stockholm aerial image, business region, 2018.

Source: Stockholm Data Parks.

everyday life, increased flows throughout the city, as well as identify urban development measures for neighborhoods that today are spatially segregated (Dahlin, 2016).

The work on anchoring a new comprehensive plan for Stockholm was in progress in 2016 and 2017. In order to get a better understanding of the children's perspective in the city's development, the city has focused on children and youth. Among other things, the City Planning Office has employed a planner with special responsibility for children and youth. The comprehensive planning was run as an inclusive process with broad representation so that children's and young people's thoughts also give impetus to the forthcoming plan. The plan is expected to be adopted by the city council in the near term.

Vision 2040

The new vision, adopted in 2017, Vision 2040—A Stockholm for Everyone, is a promise to all residents to give equal opportunities (Stockholm City Council, 2015), which means that wherever people live in the city, it should be possible to get to work and to school with good communication, there should be access to quality squares, parks, and green areas, and there should be public and commercial services.

The new vision consists of four main goals: a Stockholm that stands united (a cohesive and accessible city, equal opportunities for children, affordable housing, secure elderly life, and gender equality); eco-smart Stockholm (prioritizing green transport, increased use of renewable energy, and non-toxic environments); financially sustainable Stockholm (easy access to jobs, education, and housing); democratically sustainable city (promoting human rights, combating discrimination, and guaranteeing all inhabitants equal rights and opportunities).

The new comprehensive plan is based on Vision 2040. The plan comprises four objectives for urban development: a growing city that is attractive, has high growth rates regarding housing and community functions for all, as well as good accessibility for personal and corporate development opportunities; a cohesive city in which it is easy to move between different districts and everyday meetings among people with different backgrounds and urban environments are accessible to everyone; a good public environment with a diversity of identity-rich neighborhoods with living neighborhood centers, good living environment, and good access to urban qualities and safe, well-designed public environments; and a climate-smart and robust city with effective land use and transport-efficient urban structures that contribute to increased accessibility, reduced climate impact, and limited resource consumption. This would be resilient urban structures and technical systems.

The comprehensive plan includes a development strategy that is intended to be used as a tool for urban planning and for making priorities in order to make urban development steer towards the vision of a city for everyone. It is intended to be adopted in 2018, and it has four parts:

1   The attractions of the inner city should be a resource for the entire city: denser structures around the inner city and gradual growth outward.
2   Four main areas are designated for redevelopment (outer suburbs from the 1960s and 1970s).
3   All city districts need value-added additions to secure housing and sustainability goals.
4   Planning and urban development must be based on a holistic and long-term sustainable development perspective.

Conclusions

The discussion above highlights the following five issues at the intersection of socioeconomic and environmental dynamics as critical in defining and shaping livability, having direct relevance to Stockholm. As conceptualized by Ruth and Franklin:

> Firstly, the history of architecture and planning abounds with well-intended examples, the plans of visionaries, master plans—efforts to create livability that have proven ephemeral at best; secondly, the concept of livability has received growing attention, and ever more data are collected and synthesized on the urban condition but theoretically grounded models that can help planners and decision-makers scope out the potential *livability implications* of alternative investments in infrastructures and institutions are missing; thirdly, infrastructures and institutions are usually long-lived and difficult to change. Yet urban systems characterized by rapid demographic, socioeconomic, and environmental changes must be increasingly flexible to adjust to unforeseen and often unforeseeable future conditions; fourthly, growing national and global interconnections among cities gives them new market opportunities and a broader knowledge base for action. It also creates the danger that adverse impacts on a select set of cities ripple through to affect others; fifth, and finally, diversity is both the scourge and banner of livability. It is the banner or hallmark of livability in the sense that diverse economies, populations, and responses to social and environmental challenges strengthen cities and make them more resilient and, arguably, more livable.
>
> (Ruth & Franklin, 2014, pp. 10–11)

When we look at some livability rankings of cities in the world, Stockholm comes out quite well. To get a closer look at Stockholm we have discussed livability in relation to some urban development areas in Stockholm, for example Hammarby Sjöstad and Stockholm Royal Seaport. A common problem is the lack of socioeconomic integration and affordable housing in new urban development areas.

Stockholm has a long history of planning schemes and visions that we briefly present in the text. We don't have any good Swedish term for *livable city*; the best resemblance we can find in the Swedish discourse is social sustainability.

Since the 1990s the city has been focusing on environmental sustainability, but gradually the social perspective has gained more attention in urban planning discourse and practice. This was basically due to the increasing socio-spatial segregation. In 2015 the city appointed a Commission for Socially Sustainable Stockholm (Bremberg et al., 2015) with the task of analyzing differences in living conditions in Stockholm and proposing measures for an equally and socially sustainable city. The city had noticed an ongoing trend towards a more divided city and wanted to change this for the better.

Stockholm's example of livable (ecological) communities such as Hammarby Sjöstad and the Royal Seaport reminds us of the fact that these large-scale green showcase regeneration projects are still in their embryonic phases and will need time to be fully evaluated. These Stockholm-based projects are still in development, as well as others in Europe, such as Hafen City. Currently they all share generic dullness and uniformity in form. Maybe in time, as urbanism requires a longer timescale than architecture, they will be perceived positively and hopefully become more dynamic through the way that people use the space.

Built Environment for Children—The Stockholm Experience concluded that Stockholm is considered by some as one of the few role models of child-friendly cities in Europe (Jing, 2015) and is widely recognized for its leadership in sustainable urban development, highlighted by being named the first European Green Capital in 2008 (Freeman & Tranter, 2011).

Recently, the influx of immigrants has risen and the pressure on the societal systems is greater. The terror that has struck several cities in Europe has come to Stockholm as well, but the citizens of Stockholm are not afraid. They keep on going in very much the same way as they have always done. To Stockholm's citizens, it is an attractive and livable city.

References

Benzeval, M., Judge, K., & Whitehead, M. (1995). *Tackling inequalities in health*. London: Kings Fund.

Bremberg, E., Slattman, H., & Alarcón, P. (2015). *Skillnadernas Stockholm, Kommissionen för ett socialt hållbart Stockholm (A Stockholm of differences)*. Stockholm: City of Stockholm, Executive Office.

Christophers, B. (2013). A monstrous hybrid: The political economy of housing in early twenty-first-century Sweden. *New Political Economy, 18*(6), 885–911.

City of Stockholm. (2010). *The walkable city plan: Stockholm city plan*. Stockholm: City of Stockholm.

City of Stockholm. (2015). *Stockholm—the first European Green Capital*. Stockholm: City of Stockholm.

City of Stockholm. (2016). *The city of Stockholm's annual report 2016: A Stockholm for everyone.* Stockholm: City of Stockholm.

CityMetric (2018). Retrieved from www.citymetric.com/politics/forget-rio-its-time-urban-livability-olympics-2349.

Dahlin, Å. (2016). *Från delad till enad stad: Översiktsplanering för social hållbarhet (From divided to unified city: Comprehensive planning for social sustainability).* Stockholm: Stockholm Stad.

Freeman, C., & Tranter, P. (2011). *Children and their urban environment: Changing worlds.* Oxford: EarthScan.

Haas, T., Littke. H., & Wells, W. (2017). Creating green space in the compact city: A Swedish perspective on a global issue. In J. H. P. Bay & S. Lehmann (Eds.), *Growing compact: Urban form, density and sustainability.* London: Routledge/Earthscan.

Hall, T. (2009). *Stockholm: The making of a metropolis (planning, history and environment series).* London: Routledge.

Hills, J. (1995). *Inquiry into income and wealth, Vol. 2.* York, England: Joseph Rowntree Foundation.

Holmstedt, L., Brandt, N., & Robèrt, K-H. (2017). Can Stockholm Royal Seaport be part of the puzzle towards global sustainability? From local to global sustainability using the same set of criteria. *Journal of Cleaner Production, 140*(1), 72–80.

Jing, J. (2015). *Built environment for children: The Stockholm experience.* KTH—Royal Institute of Technology and White Architects.

Lind, H., & Lundström, S. (2007). *Bostäder på marknadens villkor (Housing on market terms).* Stockholm: SNS Förlag/Publishers.

Marcus, L., Balfors, B., & Haas, T. (2013). Sustainable urban fabric: The development and application of analytical urban design theory. In J. Metzger &. A. Rader Olsson (Eds.), *Sustainable Stockholm: Exploring urban sustainability in Europe's greenest city* (pp. 71–101). New York: Routledge.

Metzger, J., & Rader Olsson, A. (Eds.). (2013). *Sustainable Stockholm: Exploring urban sustainable development in Europe's greenest city.* New York: Routledge.

Pacione, M. (1982). The use of objective and subjective measures of quality of life in human geography. *Progress in Human Geography, 6*(4), 495–514.

Pacione, M. (2003). Urban environmental quality and human wellbeing: A social geographical perspective. *Landscape and Urban Planning, 65,* 19–30.

Ruth, M., & Franklin, S. R. (2014). Livability for all? Conceptual limits and practical implications. *Applied Geography, 49,* 18–23.

Shahrokni, H., Årman, L., Lazarevic, D., Nilsson, A., & Brandt, N. (2015). Implementing smart urban metabolism in the Stockholm Royal Seaport: Smart city SRS. *Journal of Industrial Ecology, 19,* 917–929. doi:10.1111/jiec.12308.

Stockholm City Council. (2015, October 19). *Vision 2040: A Stockholm for everyone.* Stockholm: Stockholm City Council.

Stockholm Royal Seaport. (2018). Retrieved from www.stockholmroyalseaport.com/.

Tunström, M. (2014). Livability på svenska: Kunskapsutveckling kring livability som begrepp, politik och praktik i svensk transportplanering (Livability in Sweden: Knowledge development around livability as a concept, politics and practice in Swedish transport planning). *Trafikverket, 177,* 42.

Chapter 4

LIVABLE SEOUL: VILLAGE COMMUNITY BUILDING
Ji Hei Lee

Introduction

Village community building has been a key planning policy of Seoul to enhance the livability since 2012. Seoul, the capital city of South Korea, with a population of over 10 million, has experienced unprecedented progress in economy and urban development for the past 50 years. Seoul has been constantly striving for more livable communities. This chapter seeks to explore the background of this policy, including the meaning of livability for Seoul residents, and examine how the policy works. The rationale of the policy and remaining issues will also be discussed.

Background

In South Korea, '마을' (Ma-ul), meaning a village, used to be the basic unit of locality where residents felt a sense of belonging and identity to the past. After Seoul experienced rapid urbanization for the past 50 years, it was rare to see Ma-ul in Seoul. Like other metropolitan cities, people living in Seoul seem to enjoy the amenities. For the past five years (2012–2017), the Global Power City Index (Institute for Urban Strategies, 2017) has ranked Seoul in 6th place, behind London, New York, Tokyo, Paris, and Singapore. The index evaluates and ranks the major cities by their comprehensive power to attract creative people and business enterprises from around the world, taking into account factors such as economy, research and development, cultural interaction, livability, environment, and accessibility (Institute for Urban Strategies, 2017).

Since 1960, Seoul has achieved an exponential economic growth, often called the Miracle of Han River, which can be witnessed through the dynamic changes in urban economy and built environment over the years. Until the early 1990s, the central government had taken a strong leadership role in providing infrastructure and redeveloping the dilapidated areas. However, the top–down decision-making process in urban redevelopment has often caused conflicts and resistance from residents and communities. Since the early 1990s, a more decentralized and bottom–up approach has been sought in the decision-making process and translated into planning policies and development projects.

Around the early 2000s, the paradigm of urban development and planning shifted from urban renewal to urban regeneration. The urban regeneration approach has somewhat resolved a major drawback of the previous approach, that is, a lack of public participation throughout the process. However, people have become slowly aware and have experienced that both approaches do not necessarily result in their improved quality of life. Issues still remain outstanding: lack of childcare for working parents; decreasing job opportunities for young adults; increasing rates of suicide and divorce; social isolation; and overly competitive social and working environments. Public awareness was raised that there should be a new approach to deal with local issues.

In the early 1990s, several area-based community groups were voluntarily formed in Seoul to tackle community issues, and they have become the basis of grass-root community-building movements. The grass-root community-building movements were spotlighted for their creative ways of solving issues, and they gradually spread across the nation. In early 2000, community building ended its 'urban movement' status and was officially adopted as a mainstream, key urban policy by the central and local government authorities in South Korea. Seoul is now at the forefront of this community development policy and implementation. To support the resident-led community development, the Seoul Metropolitan Government attempted to formulate the policy framework and translate it at different scales.

In 2012, Seoul set out the Village (Ma-ul) Community Building ordinance and established the Seoul Community Support Center (SCSC) to support communities and distribute resources. At present, the Village Community Building is the core urban policy of Seoul for community livability, which has been in effect across all districts of Seoul.

Livability for Seoul Urbanites

Livability is a relative concept that measures how residents perceive and feel satisfied with their living environment. Various indexes on livability and quality of life are published annually by different organizations, which are useful in comparing the quality of life across different cities. Some indexes only reflect expatriates' point of view, not that of the long-standing residents of the community. Others include the residents' perceptions, but they still fail to reflect the local context, culture, and prominent issues of society, which may question the validity of weighting each factor constituting livability. Livability needs to be understood and perceived on the basis of local, social context. In this regard, it is worth noting what is meant by livability for people living in Seoul at present.

A recent study (Cho & Hwang, 2014) conducted a survey on livability in six metropolitan areas of South Korea, in which half of the participants were the residents of Seoul. This study found that among various factors constituting livability, young married couples most valued basic life infrastructure (e.g., secure jobs and housing prices), families with kids and young adult children ranked social support infrastructure the highest (e.g., quality of education, security, and healthcare). Middle-aged couples and older adults highly valued natural landscape infrastructure (e.g., weather, landscape, cleanness of air, and water) and cultural infrastructure (e.g., culture and leisure facilities, diversity of cultural activities, and places for social interaction). These findings imply that livability does not hold the same meaning for different people, at least by different age groups and characteristics of households.

Policy Rationale: Social Interaction through Third Places

The rationale behind the Village Community Building is basically to promote social interaction through creating *third places*. An informal public gathering place, a third place (Oldenburg & Brissett, 1982), has been recognized as a hub for the social vitality of a community. The first place is home, the second is workplace, and the third place is where you spend your leisure time outside your home (Oldenburg & Brissett, 1982). It is a meeting place, i.e., a place to socialize and hang out with friends and neighbors. People usually perceive community as the presence or provision of amenities, common meeting places, resources, and facilities in neighborhoods (Baum & Palmer, 2002).

When there are opportunities for everyday informal face-to-face contact, casual social relationships (i.e., weak social ties) are developed and maintained (Granovetter, 1983; Greenbaum, 1982; Skjaeveland & Garling, 1997). After experiencing repeated casual contact, neighbors become acquaintances, engage in social activities, or develop friendships (Kweon, Sullivan, & Wiley, 1998). Even casual social relationships, or weak ties, are important contributors to social support (Henning & Lieberg, 1996; Guest & Wierzbicki, 1999). Positive social functions and the health benefits of third places have also been recognized (Rosenbaum, Ward, Walker, & Ostrom, 2007). Therefore, it is important for residents to have places in their local area, outside their home, that enable them to meet and interact. Social interaction through third places underlies the policy of the Seoul Village Community Building.

Policy Overview: Village Community Building

In 2011, Seoul set out the Village Community Building ordinance to support village community building in Seoul. In 2012, the Seoul Community Support Center (SCSC) was established in the form of a public–private partnership, which is an intermediate support organization to support resident-led communities (Seoul Community Support Center, 2013). Basically, once a few neighbors collectively propose a community project for their neighborhood and submit the project application, the SCSC evaluates the submitted applications and provides financial support for the implementation of the selected project.

Other major roles of the SCSC involve monitoring funded projects, free training and consulting, improving governance, and doing research to develop policies.

The SCSC is not the only support organization. In the Village Community Building policy framework, the main support organizations include the Seoul Metropolitan government, the Seoul Community Support Center, autonomous district authorities and district community centers. Table 4.1 outlines the role of each organization. Projects vary in size, theme, and support procedure. According to a recent policy evaluation report (Ahn & Gu, 2017), between 2012 and 2015, Seoul supported 3,442 community projects with 43 billion South Korean Won, involving 72,000 participants. Examples of the community projects include community enterprises, parents' community, community media, community libraries, book cafés, cafés for the youth, and art production studios.

In 2012, the city of Seoul launched a five-year comprehensive plan to promote and support building village communities, targeting to expand the number of community projects to 975 and

Table 4.1 Community Governance System

Governance System	Roles
Seoul Metropolitan Government	• Managing institutional systems of communities in Seoul • Operating projects by theme • Campaign targeting citizens
Seoul Community Support Center	• Research on policies of Seoul-type communities • Supporting autonomous districts to lay the foundation • Discovering community activists
Community centers in districts	• Community-Agenda Network • Outreach counseling • Training residents and community activists
Autonomous districts	• Outreach Community Center • Participatory budgeting • Ordinance on supporting • Citizen autonomy

Source: Seoul Community Support Center (SCSC), 2013a.

foster 3,180 community activists by 2017 (Seoul Metropolitan Government, 2014). The key aims of the comprehensive plan are as follows (Seoul Metropolitan Government, 2014):

•   to support resident-led community planning
•   to foster community activists who can lead community projects
•   to build a community space/facility within a ten-minute walking distance
•   to support resident-led community activities and projects
•   to support the economy of the village community.

The aims are mainly focused on creating shared spaces or programs for childcare, local economy, energy-saving/efficiency, and wellbeing. In comparison with projects driven by urban renewal and urban regeneration, the spatial scale of projects under the village community development scheme is usually small (e.g., part of a building, site, or neighborhood). It does not deal with typical large-scale developments (e.g., where, when, how to provide housing, retail, office, and major urban infrastructures).

In the comprehensive plan, the capacity building of marginalized groups is stipulated as one of the key goals. It aims to strongly promote participation from young graduates, retirees, members of low-income households, and females. Interestingly, a recent survey of the policy performance conducted in 2015 reveals that 70% of the total participants in the village community projects were middle-class females aged between 30 and 40 (Ahn & Gu, 2017).

Table 4.2 Key Community Projects by Themes

Project by Theme	Aims/Examples
Energy independence project	To achieve energy independence through energy saving and energy production Example: Solar installation, insulation or LED replacement, and publicity activities
Media project	To provide community broadcasting/media education and support to help people to communicate with their neighbors Examples: Education on media, activation of network, support for the establishment of resident-led media
Art studio project	To support the creation of spaces for culture and art where residents can operate voluntarily and anyone can participate Examples: Art craft education, production studio, cafe, and shared community space
Co-parenting project	To help neighbors learn how to raise children and to solve childcare problems Examples: Co-parenting, development and experience programs, parent education, talent donation, second-hand shop for childcare goods and toys, etc.
Multi-family residential community project	To support a pleasant apartment community through social interaction among neighbors Examples: Programs for conflict resolution and life-sparing, local festivals, education center for residents, and programs for reducing maintenance expenses
Community enterprise project	To support community-based enterprises to utilize community assets and to create more job opportunities
Community planning	To identify and share problems people feel in their daily lives, centering on the administrative districts, and select local issues through resident general meetings
Community and school networking	To provide local eco-education based on cooperation of residents, teachers, students, and parents
Community center renovation	To identify and utilize the underused space of existing community centers for the use of residents by engaging residents in its conceptualization, design, and management
University and community network	To support students to be self-determined as members of the community

Source: Seoul Community Support Center (SCSC), 2013a.

Discussion

Overall, the Village Community Building process, in which residents identify their own needs and issues and plan and lead the project, with financial support of the government, can be viewed as collaborative planning and micro-planning (in terms of spatial scales) to improve community livability. Village Community Building is still undergoing its experimental stage, thus it is not the appropriate time to evaluate the performance of policy implementation, governance, and outcomes. However, the following are a few of my reflections on the underlying concepts of this policy.

First of all, it's necessary to go back to the question, why and to what extent do Seoul urbanites need a village community? At the conceptualization stage of this policy framework, discussion, consensus building, and possibly a referendum should have been held to discuss the concept of village community among various groups. A community is defined as members of a community sharing a particular geographical locality, identity, and interest (Parker & Doak, 2012). The city of Seoul has set a target number of communities to be created and allocated a significant amount of budgets for supporting the community projects.

It is questionable whether community can be created from this government-led directive. It takes time for communities sharing similar identities and interests among themselves to emerge and grow. In addition, consensus on the needs and interests of community members is essential. A large sum of taxes has been used for place-making initiatives for community facilities and programs that promote social interaction among residents. For some, social interaction with neighbors may be important, while others want improved amenities.

Another consideration involves the contribution of Village Community Building to the planning system. The transition from the government-led, top–down approach to resident-led, bottom–up approach is a natural phenomenon as a society grows more mature in democracy and civic awareness. The latter approach seeks both growth and community empowerment. For example, neighborhood planning in the UK was introduced in 2011 through the Localism Act. It aims to decentralize power and resources, to enable residents to decide what, where, and when to build in their own neighborhoods. Despite its efficacy of community empowerment, it is a very lengthy process from planning to community referendum. Moreover, it risks potential "NIMBYism" (not in my back yard).

In contrast, the Village Community Building approach is based on the grant application, thus the process is relatively straightforward and less time-consuming. However, the process does not delegate the functions and authorities of the existing planning system. In addition, the scope of residents' participation is only confined to place-making and programming for certain areas such as shared spaces, childcare, art, and welfare. Sadly, it does not function as a remedy to the potential conflicts and outcomes of urban renewal scheme and the early phases of urban regeneration approaches.

Another issue is whether the community enterprises and facilities can be sustainable without further funding by the government. Many of the community enterprises created and funded by this policy scheme generate marginal profits, as the sole purpose of these community enterprises is not to maximize profits. The city of Seoul has been pumping seed-money into many community projects over the past few years. The initial costs, as well as the operation and management costs, should be taken into account at the initial stage of selecting these community projects.

Lastly, planning activities and development projects have not been free from allegations of links to political and personal interests. To curtail or mitigate these potential links, it is crucial to maintain transparency in the implementation and governance of these planning activities and projects and to build and maintain a database to monitor and evaluate project processes and outcomes.

References

Ahn, H. C., & Gu, A. (2017). *Analysis and implication of community support program in Seoul.* Seoul: The Seoul Institute.

Baum, F., & Palmer, C. (2002). "Opportunity structures": Urban landscape, social capital and health promotion in Australia. *Health Promotion International, 17*(4), 351–361.

Cho, S. N., & Hwang, E. J. (2014). A comparative study on conditions of a livable city. *Social Sciences Research Institute, 30,* 235–267.

Guest, A. M., & Wierzbicki, S. K. (1999). Social ties at the neighborhood level: Two decades of GSS evidence. *Urban Affairs Review, 35*(1), 92–111.

Granovetter, M. (1983). The strength of weak ties: A network theory revisited. *Sociological Theory, 1,* 201–233.

Greenbaum, S. D. (1982). Bridging ties at the neighborhood level. *Social Networks, 4*(4), 367–384.

Henning, C., & Lieberg, M. (1996). Strong ties or weak ties? Neighbourhood networks in a new perspective. *Scandinavian Housing and Planning Research, 13*(1), 3–26.

Institute for Urban Strategies, The Mori Memorial Foundation. (2017). *Global power city index yearbook 2017.* Retrieved from http://mori-m-foundation.or.jp/english/ius2/gpci2/index.shtml.

Kweon, B., Sullivan, W. C., & Wiley, A. R. (1998). Green common spaces and the social integration of inner-city older adults. *Environment and Behavior, 30*(6), 832–858.

Oldenburg, R., & Brissett, D. (1982). The third place. *Qualitative Sociology, 5*(4), 265–284.

Parker, G., & Doak, J. (2012). *Key concepts in planning.* London: Sage.

Rosenbaum, M. S., Ward, J., Walker, B. A., & Ostrom, A. L. (2007). A cup of coffee with a dash of love: An investigation of commercial social support and third-place attachment. *Journal of Service Research, 10*(1), 43–59.

Skjaeveland, O., & Garling, T. (1997). Effects of interactional space on neighbouring. *Journal of Environmental Psychology, 17*(3), 181–198.

Seoul Community Support Center. (2013). *Community governance system.* Retrieved from www.seoulmaeul.org/programs/user/eng/introduction.html.

Seoul Metropolitan Government. (2014). *Seoul village community comprehensive plan.* Retrieved from http://gov.seoul.go.kr/files/2012/09/505fe52fcc3801.77363403.pdf.

Chapter 5

THE LIVABLE CITY IN THE CONTEXT OF DEPOPULATION IN JAPAN
Fumihiko Seta

Two Different Characteristics of Japanese Cities

When we apply the context of community livability referred to by Wagner and Caves (2012) to Japanese cities, an important characteristic of Japanese national and urban structures should be initially taken into account.

Japan consists of a number of large metropolitan regions and other provincial areas. Tokyo and Osaka metropolitan regions, whose populations are each more than 10 million, have a rich network of public transportation. Most of the people living there usually move by railways. Commercial areas are full of people walking in and around districts. Most residents do not have a car. If they have one, they use it only on the weekend. Thanks to the large population, private railway companies have been mostly financially independent from the central and local governments (Kato, 2000). They are operated on the revenue from passengers, most of whom are commuters from suburban areas to central business districts. In each district, along railways, walkability is basically well maintained through equipping rail stations with small and medium retail shops including convenience stores and supermarkets. Restaurants, bars (Japanese Izakaya), and some other commercial and public facilities are also located on and near the station. People use the commercial streets and urban services whether or not they use the trains. Community livability can be seen in these two metropolitan regions, although it is not the same as in the U.S. or other countries.

On the other hand, provincial regions have different characteristics. Urban structures are quite dispersed and almost all of the people use cars for various purposes, including commuting. Town centers, which once had most of the commercial and business functions in a city, were negatively impacted by suburbanization from around the 1990s. Most vibrant commercial functions moved to suburban areas and relocated in shopping malls and roadside zones in suburban areas. Shops along commercial streets of town centers closed their shutters and became known as *shutter town*. Former livable communities almost died or at least changed drastically in order to survive. The communities are now far from walkable. While the basic infrastructure and facilities are in place, it has negatively impacted the mobility of those who do not have cars. Minors and elderly people without a driver's license have trouble to go and buy something by themselves. And moreover, the use of buses for transportation is not satisfying to the residents.

Because of both motorization and depopulation in provincial cities, local bus companies tend to reduce or abandon their routes, and it leads to reduced passengers and vice versa. Although the local government supports these companies, both institutionally and financially, they have not provided a good alternative.

Influence of Aging and Depopulation

The aging rate of Japan is already the highest in the world. As of 2017, 27.3% of the population is over 65 and 13.3% is over 75 (Cabinet Office, Government of Japan, 2017). The rising aging rate often leads to the discussion of the loss of the workforce, an increase in welfare costs, and the deterioration of the pension system and the crisis of public finance derived from these individual factors. The vibrancy of communities is diminished in aging communities, since more and more residents become inactive and disappear from community activities and chores. Serious mobility problems for aged people, who do not have a car or driver's license in rural and suburban areas, come to be located more and more in villages and suburban housing complexes. Villages and housing complexes whose aged population is more than half are called *critical villages* (Genkai Shuraku) or *critical housing complexes* (Genkai Danchi).

The aging rate is higher in provincial regions than metropolitan areas, mostly due to the outflow of the younger generation. Though the birth rate tends to be higher in towns and villages in provincial regions, than in metropolitan regions, the population continues to be aging since the absolute number of young females, who are expected to bear children, decreases. The Masuda Report, which was released in 2014 by a private think tank headed by Hiroya Masuda, ex-Minister of Internal Affairs and Communications and now a guest professor at the Graduate School of Public Policy of the University of Tokyo, pointed out the problem and showed a list of municipal governments that could vanish within 30 years, based on the projection of population of these young females. The report defined *disappearing municipalities* as municipalities, most located in provincial regions, whose female population aged 15–40 will be diminished by half by 2040.

The aforementioned problems of vibrancy and mobility in rural and suburban areas are accelerated by depopulation following the aging process. Depopulation causes the decrease of demand of any local public and private services, including retail and passenger transport. Private services that become financially unsustainable, in sparsely settled or scattered areas, are diminished and finally abolished or substituted by public services or self-help. This imposes more burdens on public resources and finances, and other resources of the communities.

Demographic changes from urbanization, due to growth and shrinking, causes further problems for the maintenance of various public facilities such as libraries, community centers, sports facilities, and welfare centers. Given urbanization, especially in the latter half of the 20th century, municipalities in Japan continued to equip public facilities on their own, and the central government provided financial subsidies for the construction. Now, after several decades, many municipalities face renewal or reconstruction of these facilities. However, the demand of these facilities is not what it once was, due to depopulation. Most of the municipalities have started to introduce methods of facility management, which are based on advanced trials of municipalities in the U.S.

When we consider the community livability in a depopulating society, like most cities in Japan, the treatment of both the present and future livability of the community, which often conflict with each other, should be taken into account. The investment to enhance vibrancy in depopulated areas sometimes contradicts sustainability of the entire city and municipalities. Under the condition that the birth rate has stagnated and the rebound of the population is not expected in most regions, careful community planning and locational strategies for maintaining and enhancing livability are essential.

Many academicians and practitioners already compare and refer to countermeasures against depopulation in some depopulating cities in the Rust Belt in the U.S. or Eastern Germany. Some municipalities try to introduce methods such as land banking, or Rueckbau (Mallach, Haase, & Hattori, 2017). But the important difference of Japan, in comparison with these countries, is that depopulation is unavoidable in the long term because the Japanese government has been reluctant to invite foreign immigrants into the country. The percentage of the foreign population in Japan is much lower (1.6%) than the U.S. (7.0%) or Germany (9.3%) in 2013 (OECD, 2018), even when one counts those so-called *old comers* who came from Korea and China more than half a century ago. Livability for the future, in each Japanese city and community, should be planned based on the long-term depopulation and the reduction of any kind of services or infrastructure.

Depopulation in Megacities

Tokyo forms by far the largest metropolitan region and keeps its strong incentives to attract people by meaningful economic policies and the agglomeration of both companies and universities. Recent government statistics showed that the jurisdiction of Tokyo Metropolitan Government (TMG) and surrounding prefectures (a local government area), namely, Kanagawa, Chiba, and Saitama, invite population inflow from other regions. Tokyo's strength has been said to be derived not only from the absolute agglomeration of population and activities, but also from the concentration of public and private entities like the central government, headquarters of domestic companies, international firms, and megabanks. The share of functions of universities and research institutes in Tokyo metropolitan region is also high in Japan.

Osaka metropolitan region, the second largest in Japan, includes the big cities of Kyoto and Kobe. It is not as economically strong as Tokyo. Its regional economy has recovered recently by the revival of the national economy and the rapid growth of some specific industries, namely tourism from surrounding Asian countries. Osaka continues to struggle economically as it lacks some important national functions that Tokyo has. Asian countries like South Korea and Taiwan have harmed regional industries like electronics. Several municipalities in Osaka, which are located along important national corridors, have a strong inflow of people because of a better local economy. However, if you leave the corridor, the population decline is quite severe.

The Osaka metropolitan region can be regarded as the first megacity to lose population. The common definition of a megacity is one that has a population of 10 million and their population increases almost continuously. Now, more and more megacities are located in developing countries. But in Eastern Asian countries, whose birth rates are far lower than the standard to maintain the population, provincial cities and megacities are aging at a rapid pace and will depopulate in the near future. The Osaka metropolitan region is such an example and thus has become the first depopulating megacity in the world.

Livability for Depopulating Megacities

Most of the characteristics of a livable of community in a metropolitan region will be weakened because of aging and depopulation. Railway companies will suffer from rapid decrease of passengers, most of whom are commuters, and some of the suburban lines will be at risk of

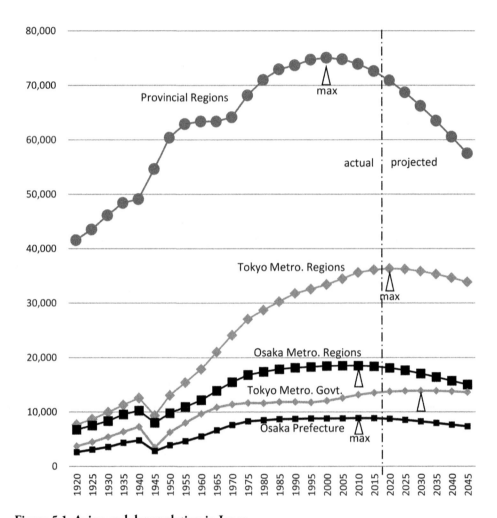

Figure 5.1 Aging and depopulation in Japan.

Source: (actual data) The National Census of Japan. (Projection) National Institute of Population and Social Security Research (2018).

Notes

1   Tokyo Metro. Region includes the jurisdiction of Tokyo Metro. Government, Kanagawa, Saitama and Chiba prefectures. Osaka Metro. Region includes those of Osaka, Kyoto, Hyogo and Nara prefectures.

2   Provincial region consists of the other prefectures than Tokyo Metro. Government and seven prefectures shown above. Population of Okinawa prefecture is not included during 1945 and 1970, when it was occupied by the U.S.

abolishment (Funabashi, 2018). The suburbs of Japanese cities, including those in the Osaka metropolitan region, have sprawled based on loose land use regulations and as a result have formed a relatively dispersed physical structure for communities (Sorensen, 2002). While those officials in Osaka have maintained relatively higher density in order to maintain the demand for public transport, depopulation will gradually affect the financial condition of private companies who operate public transportation.

Suburban areas in the metropolitan regions in Japan and in Asia, which have been developed following the inflow of population and investment, are at a turning point due to the new reality of demographic changes. Under the scenario that population will continue to be aging and depopulating for the long term, how should we define livability? And how can we find the ways to realize the new type of livability under depopulation? The next section describes some typical examples found in a far suburban city in the Osaka metropolitan region, Iga City.

Struggle for a Livable City in a Shrinking Megacity

The Situation of Iga City, Mie Prefecture

Iga City, in Mie prefecture, is located 60 km east of the city center of Osaka. The jurisdiction area was originally developed with a town center, small villages, paddy fields, and small forests. Iga has been famous as a cradle of ninjas—spies in the medieval times in Japan. Following the progress of modernization and urbanization, especially after World War II, several areas of Iga City developed as places for commuters to commute to Osaka. Workers in the city and cottagers came from the Osaka metropolitan region. Land and housing prices continued to surge until the early 1990s, when the economy started to decline. People working in Osaka had no other choice but to buy a plot or a house far from their working places, most of which were in the city center. The rapid surge of land prices also stimulated the speculation of real estate and many people bought plots without considering any purposes for the land. Iga City had more than 40 small and medium housing lots mostly supplied by real estate developers.

But after the economic decline, the long-term economic recession started. Because of the decrease of land prices, many houses in the near suburbs or even in the city center became affordable for commuters. As a result, demand for the land in the far suburbs like Iga City drastically decreased and many plots became derelict, leaving some residents who had already started to live there with significant problems. The population of Iga City increased until the 1990s and counted 101,527 persons in 2000. Years later, it started to decrease, and in 2015 it was 90,581 persons. Those older than 65 made up 31.6% of the total population.

Phenomenon Caused by Depopulation

Presently, many vacant lots can still be seen. And more people are now in housing complexes than in existing villages or towns. Most of the land in these complexes was bought in the process of expansion of the Osaka metropolitan region but many houses or buildings have not been constructed. Most of these complexes are located in out-of-the-way places and are inconvenient to access from the town center or train stations. The conversion from housing to other purposes to factories or warehouses is not easy in terms of location, land use regulation, and the existence

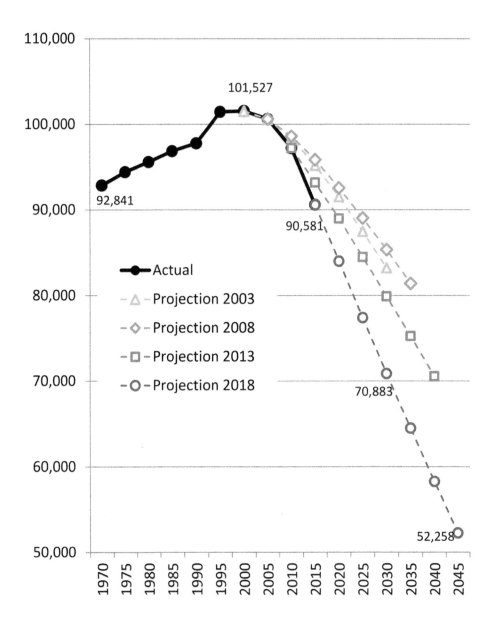

Figure 5.2 Projection of depopulation in Iga City.

Source: (actual data) The National Census of Japan. (Projection) National Institute of Population and Social Security Research (2003, 2008, 2013, 2018).

of residents. Most of the vacant lots are neglected. Not only are weeds present, but also decades-old trees can be seen. It's like a small forest. In some lots, illegal dumping is also a problem.

Development regulations in suburban regions in Japan are very loose, as discussed earlier. There is little power by urban planners to prohibit dividing lots or imposing beneficiary liability on existing landowners and real estate developers, which is unlike the U.S. The balance between demand and supply is hardly controlled by the municipalities. As a result, it has created large numbers of vacant lots.

On the other hand, each municipality is mostly obliged to supply necessary public services such as water, road maintenance, and garbage collection. It is a significant burden for a municipality to supply these services to so many scattered areas.

Aging and depopulation will deteriorate this situation over time. Municipal revenue will be decreased both in terms of citizen tax and real estate tax. Aging will affect the number of workers and taxpayers. Real estate tax, which is calculated on land price, will decline following the trend of depopulation. The decrease of population density, because of sprawl and depopulation, will increase inefficiency. The increase of the aging rate and the absolute number of aged people will raise welfare costs.

Maintaining Livability by Reducing Urban Facilities for the Future

Related to urban and regional planning, depopulation in cities in metropolitan regions means the reduction of various facilities and services that were once provided. The number and amount of public facilities and services should be, generally speaking, in proportion to the population who need to enjoy them. In the depopulation phase, plans should describe how to reduce the supply of facilities and services.

Private facilities like shops, cafes, restaurants, or supermarkets, which sell commodities and supply services for the people living there, will gradually disappear following the reduction of demand, partly by their own intention and partly by the unwilling closure of business or bankruptcy. This situation will lead to the reduction and in some cases the elimination of shopping districts and squares, creating considerable inconvenience for residents.

On the other hand, public facilities like libraries, cultural centers, community centers, gymnasiums, welfare centers, etc., are largely operated or subsidized by public organizations, thus these facilities tend to stay in place even under the depopulating scenario. Under the depopulating phase, efficiency of public facilities and infrastructures will gradually diminish unless the municipality intentionally tries to make the reductions. Inefficiency of public facilities and infrastructures will bring about severe financial problems for the municipalities and its residents.

Given depopulation, public facilities and infrastructure will need to be reduced. This will be difficult as legal trials to reduce them usually face negative responses and the strong opposition of residents. Some critics might say that these people are narrow-minded and focus only on their own interests; they don't consider the overall condition of the city, including finances and demographic changes. Overall, it is difficult to find an appropriate solution to deal with people who are left after facilities and services are diminished. Some people move from an inconvenient place where many services are diminished, but the elderly and poor often cannot move and the municipalities have to supply services in another way.

Iga City, which had once experienced public financial difficulty in the age of rapid urbanization, tried to find a way of reducing public facilities. The practical goal was to reduce the floor of public facilities by 30% until 2045. The ratio is calculated by 20% decrease of population in the target year multiplied by 1.5 times higher floor rate of public facilities per capita in comparison with the average of Mie prefecture, to which Iga City belongs. The city considered the

Figure 5.3 A housing complex filled with many vacant lots.

Source: Author.

amount of floor and demand for public service and found a way to restructure. Public facilities, which are identified as those to be abolished, are in most cases not sufficient to survive a large earthquake or are already too old for rehabilitation. Public services such as lending books, supplying rooms for various activities, or answering general inquiries on public services were to be transferred to other entities that will remain.

To respond to various opinions for the new policies, including opposition to the abolishment of public facilities, Iga City held workshops in selected towns and villages in order not only to acquire the response of people but also to try and think through solutions with them. A draft report was made for discussion. The composition of the draft and workshops for residents were implemented by the city and a steering committee that consisted of academicians and representative citizens.

Though the interim draft was posted on the website of the city, most of the participants did not know the policy to radically reduce public facilities. Thus, they were astonished by the initial presentation by public officials. But after their understanding of the situation of depopulation and severe public finance, not all, but most of the people started serious constructive discussions for the future of their towns and villages after some public facilities were reconsidered.

Their opinions are in part related to the actual shape of livability. Although the citizens admit the reality of aging and depopulation, they are eager to consider ways to keep their towns and villages healthy and salient. Some participants worried about the decline of livability caused by abolishment of some important public facilities and loss of places where people get together and enjoy various activities. However, some other participants pointed out the loss of livability because of inefficient and costly maintenance of public facilities. Public officials and committee members insisted that the residents should enhance the livability of towns and villages by utilizing remaining public and private facilities.

As a result, most of residents supported the contents of the interim draft in every workshop and the public hearing. The interim draft was finally completed as the final plan, and the local parliament approved the plan almost unanimously.

In the overall process of making the plan, livability in the future is not clearly defined. Participants of workshops tried to imagine a brighter future for their towns and villages, given the reality of an aging and depopulating situation. Some put a stress on mutual cooperation among residents. Some others insisted on activating remaining public facilities for various activities.

At the present time, towns and villages in Iga City still maintain their original ties from long ago, and community policies of the city support various activities held there. Several spontaneous activities by residents, such as crime prevention, town cleaning, watching for neighboring aged people, or mowing activities, have already started with the support of the city. It has also activated other community activities including traditional festivals. Livability in the near future will be centered on these kinds of community activities and enhanced by public organizations.

Figure 5.4 A workshop on facility management held in a district of Iga City.

Source: Author.

The future of such things happening will be tempered by the reality of the impacts of aging and depopulation. It is estimated that the population will become half in about 35 years. Then most community activities will not be maintained as they are now, and public support will not be expected because of shrinking public finances.

Summary

Many cities in the Osaka metropolitan region are already following in the path of Iga City. Most private and public services will become ineffective following the decrease of population and its density. Infrastructure, which the local government has the responsibility to build and maintain for residents, will also face restructuring due to severe financial difficulties. Communities will become smaller with vacant housing, shops, etc., which will cause many problems for those that remain.

Provincial cities have already had such a phenomenon due to earlier severe aging and depopulation. Residents there rely less on newly established facilities and services like those in metropolitan areas. They have for many years lived traditional lifestyles and have community ties continuing across generation to generation. Even if they are changed by modernization and urbanization, the people in provincial cities and towns can still lean on existing systems.

But the lives of most of the metropolitan people, especially those who come to residential complexes following strong economic development, depend on public facilities, infrastructure, and services that were built in the phase of urbanization and population increase. Now, the people in the peripheries of the depopulating metropolitan regions face a real test of will to adjust to the new phase. First Osaka will be impacted, and then most of the East Asian mega-cities will suffer from the same or more serious situation described above.

It is the personal view of the author that the long-term strategy for livability in the depopulating phase needs a two-tier approach. In the short term (first tier), it is useful and important to enrich community ties and activities to maintain or even enhance community livability even in the aging and depopulating phase. Nevertheless, while the standard of 65 years old is the threshold of aging, many people are still active. After retirement, most people can and still want to work for their communities. Thus, their experiences and skills will be useful in various fields of community activities.

However, in the long run (second tier), community ties will confront clear limitations, since aging and depopulation will further proceed and activities maintained by communities will diminish because of absolute lack of manpower. In order to prepare for the situation, radical measures will be needed. As examples, moving people to more dense areas to increase the efficiency of services, merging communities, and towns and even cities to create the appropriate amount and density for the supply of necessary public services. In addition, discussion should take place on regional collaboration and cooperation in order to find ways to address ongoing issues and concerns.

Lastly, technological advances and applications to tackle these problems must be explored. Advancement of home delivery services, mobile catering, and the introduction of automated driven cars will radically affect strategies for maintaining and enhancing livability in depopulating cities and towns.

In conclusion, Osaka and the country of Japan have major issues to contend with. Only time will tell the outcome.

References

Cabinet Office, Government of Japan. (2017). *Annual report on the aging society.* Retrieved from www8.cao.go.jp/kourei/whitepaper/index-w.html.

Funabashi, Y. (Ed.). (2018). *Japan's population implosion: The 50 million shock.* New York: Springer.

Kato, S. (2000). Development of large cities and progress in railway transportation. In *A history of Japanese railways 1872–1999.* Tokyo: East Japan Railway Culture Foundation (EJRCF).

Mallach, A., Haase, A., & Hattori, K. (2017). The shrinking city in comparative perspective: Contrasting dynamics and responses to urban shrinkage. *Cities, 69,* 102–108. Retrieved from http://dx.doi.org/10.1016/j.cities.2016.09.008.

OECD. (2018). "Elderly population" (indicator). doi: 10.1787/8d805ea1-en (Accessed April 6, 2018).

Sorensen, A. (2002). *The making of urban Japan.* London and New York: Routledge.

Wagner, F., & Caves, R. (Eds.). (2012). *Community livability: Issues and approaches to sustaining the well-being of people and communities* (1st ed.). New York and London: Routledge.

PART II

URBAN AND REGIONAL PLANNING ISSUES

Chapter 6

HOW ASHEVILLE, NORTH CAROLINA, HAS LEVERAGED LIVABILITY AS AN URBAN DEVELOPMENT STRATEGY
Elizabeth Strom and Robert Kerstein

"Rundown and shabby, with store displays, facing on narrow, dirty sidewalks, swags of utility lines, and intersections that are difficult to navigate" (Chase, 2007, p. 182), was how a 1968 Tennessee Valley Authority report described downtown Asheville. Although the city had flourished as a late 19th-early 20th century vacation spot, by the 1960s the area was failing to attract residents, investors, or many visitors. While tourists still came to the area for the mountains, Asheville's urban core had few attractions.

By the turn of this century that had changed, evidenced not only by increases in tourist visits and resident population and by changes to the central city built environment, but in the string of accolades found among the arbiters of place in the popular media. Today one finds Asheville highlighted on all kinds of best lists, including those aimed at travelers (Lonely Planet, 2016); for retirees (CNN Money, 2010); and for all seeking a high quality of life in a mountain setting (Carmichael, 2016).

The city's turnaround, which has centered on embracing and marketing its livability, has grown out of a confluence of forces. Asheville's location and history have provided inherent advantages for development in an era that prizes natural amenities, a historically significant built fabric, and claims to authenticity. Political and civic leaders have taken steps to shape urban development to build on these advantages. In recent years, however, key leaders have become more concerned about the pace and uneven benefits of growth, and some of the city's newest initiatives focus on managing growth and broadening its beneficiaries. In both local discourse and policy initiatives, civic and political leaders have expanded their idea of a livable community from one almost entirely centered on amenities and culture, to one where equity and inclusion are equally important goals.

After several decades of population stagnation, Asheville has been growing since the 1990s, and its growth has been fueled by in-movers attracted to the area's natural and created amenities. The city was home to 53,583 in 1980 (a decline from its 1970 total), but in 2016 was estimated to have a population of 89,121, a striking 66% population increase. The city is predominantly white (76% as of 2010). Once 20% of the city's population, African-Americans made up just 13.4% of the population in 2010. This reflects both a small absolute loss of African-American residents and the influx of a large number of white in-movers.

On average Asheville isn't a wealthy city, with a median income of $43,354, which is below the median income for North Carolina ($46,556) and for the U.S. ($51,939). Low median incomes are, however, combined with a high level of education. In 2015, 46.4% of Asheville residents held bachelor's degrees, compared with 28.4% across the state and 29.8% across the U.S. These numbers suggest a high degree of polarization between an educated and affluent population and a struggling population (the 17.5% poverty rate also exceeds those of the state and nation).

Mountain Air as Nineteenth-Century Livability Amenity

Although the *livability* language is relatively new, in fact tourism-focused places like Asheville have long distinguished themselves with an emphasis on a high quality of life. In the 19th century, when Asheville first emerged as a resort area, its appeal sprang from its natural amenities. Asheville's first tourist boom was as a health resort, drawing patients to convalesce at its sanitaria, and upper-middle-class and wealthy city dwellers to find relief from summer heat. Many of Asheville's most prominent civic leaders and investors of the late 19th and early 20th century were industrialists and professional class denizens who came to the area for recreation or recuperation and ended up making Asheville either a full- or part-time home. Thanks to these amenity-seeking in-movers, by the 1920s the city had a downtown with well-designed hotels and shops, a civic center, and a park system.

Asheville's early growth was fueled by the existence of an elite that could leave work behind, staying in Asheville for long periods of recuperation or summer recreation. Today's growth and development is in part attributable to a similar population, or at least its modern equivalent. Twenty-first-century America has a growing cohort of people who remain active and healthy long past retirement and can afford to seek out retirement locations based entirely on lifestyle amenities, in which Asheville is rich. Also, new information technologies produce an expanding number of workers who don't need a fixed location. These would include freelancers of varying kinds, but also a growing number of employees who work remotely. Asheville's livability makes it an attractive destination for such workers.

Livability as a Planning Goal

Planning efforts in Asheville frequently center on the effort to build and nurture a high quality of life. John Nolen, a student of Frederick Law Olmstead, Jr., drew up the city's first comprehensive plan in 1922. Nolen had been brought in at the behest of several prominent business leaders who were among the outsiders who had gravitated to Asheville and who wanted their new home to be attractive to other elites as well as lucrative for investors (Frazier, 1998). The plan sought to rationalize the development of this rapidly growing city, with a mix of real estate boosterism and a concern for the quality of public spaces. Much of the historic contour of the downtown grew out of his vision.

After a boom period in the early and mid-1920s, Asheville suffered a real estate and financial collapse that predated the national crash of 1929. In the following decades, during which the city found itself constrained by crushing municipal debt, there was little in the way of planning, development, or investment, especially for the increasingly dormant downtown.

The city's debts were paid off by the mid-1970s, after which one found the stirrings of strategic planning and redevelopment. Interestingly, Asheville's current downtown revival can be traced back to a development that didn't happen. A 1979–1980 plan to raze 11 square blocks of the downtown, including a number of historic buildings, in favor of a mega-block enclosed mall was promoted by the city's version of a *growth coalition* as the last best hope to revive the city center. Already, however, a small but determined group of retailers, artists, and preservationists had burrowed into the historic core. Because the mall plan required public funding, it was put to a referendum in 1981 and defeated. This was significant for two reasons. First, the defeat left blocks of the historic core undisturbed. Second, the anti-mall campaign mobilized previously disparate interests into a new coalition pushing for a downtown of preserved buildings, locally owned businesses, and the arts (Strom & Kerstein, 2017). The formation of a local Historic Resources Commission around the same time led to the creation of several designated historic districts and enforceable preservation guidelines.

Since then, comprehensive planning for the city as a whole and master planning for the downtown have become more common practice. In 2002 the city's staff created a Center City Plan whose focus was improved livability and quality of life to support the development of what was still a struggling urban core. Livability was listed as a goal of downtown planning efforts; strategies to realize this goal included: a full range of consumer goods and services; improved physical infrastructure along with safety and cleanliness; improved mobility with a better pedestrian environment; and more transit options.

That same year, the city undertook a new comprehensive planning effort reflecting an improved outlook, and emphasizing smart growth strategies that would increase prosperity while maintaining a high quality of life. The principle of livability appeared in a section on historic preservation (restoration of existing built environment promotes livable communities), as well as in sections on land use and transportation, where the development of sidewalks and greenways are linked to improved livability.

An even more ambitious downtown plan was developed in 2009 after months of public meetings and stakeholder input; it was adopted by the City Council in 2010. This plan offered specific recommendations and action items that were later incorporated into city planning codes. Here, livability appeared less as an aspiration and more as a characteristic that the city had and would have to work not to lose. "It is essential that Asheville retain the special attributes central to its soul—creative, artsy, walkable, funky, fun, full of great restaurants, locally-owned, and offering an outstanding quality of life" (City of Asheville, 2009, p. 15).

There are, as of this writing, two ongoing planning efforts in Asheville; both consider the importance of livability, but this concept in now defined in new ways. A new comprehensive plan, for the year 2035, evokes a *livable* built environment that centers both on mobility and design quality. Its main livability concerns are found in a section titled *Welcoming Strategies for Livability and Equity* that focuses less on aesthetics and consumption, and more on the importance of distributing amenities equally across communities and encouraging opportunity and participation from places and groups that have had less of these.

The Asheville City Council also, in 2016, began to develop its own strategic plan, with a 2036 target year. The term livability still appears in this most recent document, but here too the emphasis is on diversity and equity, suggesting a new approach where quality of life means not simply having nice things for residents to enjoy, but to ensuring equal access to these nice things and opportunities to participate in civic life. Its goal of achieving "a well-planned and livable community" is articulated as such:

Asheville's unique character is reflected in our land use, preserved in our historic structures, and honored when incorporated in new development. Thoroughfares are lined with
thriving businesses mixed with residential and office uses, and neighborhoods are socioeconomically diverse with a range of affordable housing choices. Open spaces, parks,
greenways, community gardens, and edible landscapes are abundant throughout the city.

By 2036, according to this plan, the city should reach the point that "cultural diversity and
social and economic equity are evident in all that we do" (Daffron, 2016).

A Livable Downtown for Residents and Tourists

Efforts to redevelop and manage the urban core have highlighted the inherent conflicts in the
idea of livability and how it is implemented by planners and civic leaders. A revitalized downtown has generated new residential options, expanded hotel capacity, and created countless
retail, gastronomy, and cultural spaces. But the very success of these endeavors can also lead to
a host of problems that threaten the quality of life these efforts have created. This section considers three interrelated areas in which public, business, and civic sector actors have worked
toward a vibrant but livable downtown, and why these gains could be precarious.

Preserving the Urban Fabric

Asheville's claim to livability has been integrally connected to the preservation of its art deco-era
downtown. As noted earlier, much of that preservation was accidental, tied to the city's mid-
20th-century stagnation and later to the defeat of the mall bond referendum.

Since then, the preservation of the downtown has been key to revitalization efforts. Led
by a public Downtown Office, as well as civic leaders who were often investors in historic downtown properties or owners of small businesses, a preservation-focused downtown development
coalition emerged. The renovation of 1920s-era office buildings into condominiums with street-
level commercial space as well as the redevelopment of an old Woolworth building into a warren
of crafts galleries, called Woolworth Walk, set the tone for this new downtown. The restoration
of the Grove Arcade, built in the 1920s as an elegant market but repurposed, during World War
II, as nondescript federal office space, provided an important anchor for the city center.

Programming the space with craft fairs and community festivals also helped increase
downtown foot traffic.

With the Grove Arcade and dozens of other renovations under way by the 2000s, the
basic task of bringing in investment and activity had been quite successful, but a new set of challenges arose. Downtown Asheville had become such an attractor for residents and tourists that
there were new pressures from investors to build at greater heights and densities. For some, this
new investment threatened what was attractive about the city—its relatively low-rise profile and
easy-going street life. Planning regulations did not give clear guidance about building heights or
uses (the plan adopted in 2010 would address that), leading to hard-fought political battles over
development proposals.

The years of the Great Recession reduced development pressures, but since 2013 interest
has picked up, with particular focus on hotel development. New hotel development since 2009

is likely to triple the city's downtown hotel space (Burgess, 2016). The increase in hotel rooms, of course, then prompted a new push from the hospitality industry to fill those rooms. (Barrett, 2014b), and in 2015, the Buncombe County Board of Commissioners approved a tourist tax increase from 4% to 6% (Patrick, 2016; Lunsford, 2014). One can imagine an ongoing cycle in which hotel development leads to expanded marketing to increase overnight visitors, which then leads to more hotel development. Tourists can be a huge boon for a community, bringing in the wealth that sustains dozens of art galleries, restaurants, and boutiques. But research suggests that communities can face a tipping point after which tourists become a drain on resources and a threat to resident quality of life (Strom & Kerstein, 2015). One finds increasing pushback against downtown development generally and hotel development in particular. The 2015 city council electoral cycle featured discussion of hotel proliferation and its impact on quality of life, and led to the defeat of one incumbent seen as insufficiently critical of new development. The city council has also pushed for increased power to review new hotel development proposals.

Keeping it Real: Fighting against the Generic

Studies of urban tourism note the tendency of popular visitor destinations to move toward a kind of sameness, with a familiar but monotonous set of amenities anchored by chain retailers and restaurants (Judd, 1999). For Asheville stakeholders, avoiding that homogenizing trend is a high priority. Among the city's downtown interests, authenticity is closely tied to livability.

The quest to remain authentic can be found in several areas. The movement to preserve an older built environment, discussed above, in part grows out of a desire to maintain a built fabric that is linked to the city's past. The strength of the area's *buy local* advocacy is another indicator of the importance of authenticity. Downtown Asheville includes very few chain retail stores or restaurants, and that is not a coincidence, as the downtown leadership has made support for independent business a core goal. Their success in this regard is in part linked to the 1920s-era building footprints: these have created relatively small commercial space, which make them less attractive to national or global chains.

In addition, however, downtown property owners have valued the local nature of down-town businesses and, at least in some instances, have consciously kept rents at levels that are not prohibitive for existing or prospective local business owners. In the few instances in which chain retailers have come to downtown, the parent companies have agreed to design concessions that ensure their stores fit into their surroundings (Byrd, 2015). Hotel developers seeking approval for new projects have learned that agreeing to lease commercial spaces only to independent busi-nesses can help gain approval with a city council that is likely to support *buy local* approaches. As a result, Asheville is among the rare American cities where local bookstores, coffee shops, and shoe stores continue to flourish.

Healthy independent retail is associated with vibrant streetscapes. Asheville has a lively street music scene, and in the warmer months, downtown's Pritchard Park draws hundreds of people to a Friday night city-supported drum circle. Both the drum circle and the street performers, however, are greeted with ambivalence by some, seen as once genuine expressions of local creativity that have become too predictable (Fausset, 2015). Indeed, a downtown summer festival that had been a signature event for some 30 years, the Bele Chere festival, was abandoned when it grew too big and began to include too many outside vendors and performers. Once it stopped functioning as an emblem of local flavor, the city council was less inclined to pick up the growing tab. Fewer commercial festivals and celebrations continue to be found in the downtown area.

Supporting Culture

The Asheville region claims a strong connection to a long tradition of crafts production. Although Asheville was never part of a highbrow cultural circuit, lacking flagship museums, or established concerts halls, the region has roots in a strong vernacular culture. Indigenous crafts, from *mountain music* to traditional handicrafts to moonshine distilleries, have defined this region.

Wealthy visitors at the turn of the last century recognized that the hand-woven shawls and hand-hewn butter churns that were everyday items in the region's households would be seen as much desired art objects in urban homes, where nostalgia for pre-industrial artisanship ran high. They encouraged the rebirth of handicrafts in mountain communities, spurred by the sale of these items to visitors (Starnes, 2005). During the Great Depression, both the federal government and philanthropists invested in the production of traditional culture. The sale of local cultural artifacts to promote tourism has been characteristic of the region since the early 20th century (Starnes, 2005).

Thanks to these traditions an infrastructure is in place to support new generations of crafts practitioners, including several craft schools founded in the 1920s and 1930s, to mountain music festivals and crafts guilds. This provides a small comparative advantage to Asheville as it has competed for contemporary *creative industries*. One now finds clusters of visual and performing artists in the downtown and, most notably, in the nearby River Arts District.

Similarly, Asheville has benefitted from the broader search for authentic cultural practices in its emergence as a center for farm-to-table cuisine as well as one for craft brewing. Asheville's promoters have quite consciously cultivated a restaurant culture based on locally sourced seasonal foods, and strong connections between farms and restaurants, very loosely associated with indigenous cooking traditions. Of course the true authenticity of today's local food culture is a bit suspect—Long (2010) notes that true mountain cooking would probably not be welcomed by today's diners, and that the jalapeno grits she finds on a downtown menu would probably not be appreciated by traditional mountain cooks.

A proliferation of microbreweries and indeed an entire beer making and drinking industry has emerged in Asheville, although beer production is not particularly native to this area. It is nonetheless framed as part of the narrative of authentic cultural practice. Hayward and Battle (2018) note several reasons Asheville has proven to be fertile ground for this niche industry, including its strong *buy local* culture, its association with craft culture, and cultural tourism. The first microbrewery was developed in the 1990s, with an entrepreneur using Asheville as his location because he happened to have a summer home there, which is quite consistent with the establishment of most Asheville cultural and civic innovations dating back to the 1880s. Others were helped with financing from Public Interest Projects, a unique Asheville institution that is part philanthropy and part venture capital fund and has supported a wide range of Asheville's cultural and small business infrastructure (Strom & Kerstein, 2017). The development of the city's reputation as a magnet for beer aficionados has had larger payoffs as well. Two national brewers known for their small batch craft beers have chosen Asheville for regional production and distribution centers, creating jobs and, with brewery tours and performance spaces, new recreational destinations. Hayward and Battle (2018) see this as a good example of areas in which tourists and residents can benefit equally, thus reducing the possibility that tourism-generated growth comes at the expense of resident quality of life. Of course the entry of these national breweries into Asheville, along with the sale of the city's pioneer microbrew Wicked Weed to Anheuser-Busch InBev, demonstrates the difficulties of promoting economic development at sufficient scale to support an employment base while also maintaining the area's buy local ethos.

Equity in the Livable City

As Asheville has attracted new residents and tourists, concerns about equity, affordability, and engagement have become more salient. At first, the critical voices challenging the city's development trajectory came primarily from advocacy groups such as Just Economics of Western North Carolina, but increasingly other city and county leaders have become more engaged with efforts to create opportunities for more residents of what remains a very poor region.

Despite the many positive population and economic indicators and the city's growing reputation for natural and cultural amenities, the persistence of poverty and growing inequality are cause for concern. Much of that concern centers on the relatively high housing costs given the region's low wages. With demand fueled by retirees and second-home purchasers, studies have continually shown the city to have high housing prices and rents relative to wages. Studies of Asheville's housing markets have continually found high rents relative to income and high percentages of *cost-burdened* residents, paying over 30% of their income for rent (Frankel, 2015; Rohe, Cowan, Rodriguez, & Zambito, 2009). A significant homeless population also speaks to the dearth of affordable units (Byrd, 2013; US Conference of Mayors, 2013). Asheville has earned the dubious distinction of being rated one of the nation's fastest gentrifying cities by the website realtor.com (Boyle, 2017).

The city's African-American population has in particular experienced few of the benefits of recent improvements. African-Americans have high poverty rates, are overrepresented among public housing tenants, and have had little voice among Asheville's loosely knit governing coalition (Postelle, Forbes, Millard, & Sandford, 2008). The 2005 election of Terry Bellamy as the city's first African-American mayor, and attention to a languishing affordable housing project in the heart of the pre-urban renewal African-American community, contributed to a perception that more inclusion was possible. But the chasm between the educated, well-off, mostly white population that has moved to Asheville for its quality of life, and the less educated population of those, many African-American, struggling to survive in low-wage jobs, grows larger.

For the city's leadership, livability has come to mean greater attention to these inequalities. Local government tools are limited. North Carolina is not a home rule state, and an increasingly conservative state legislature has been loath to give cities authority to carry out equity measures associated with progressive urban governance (Graham, 2017). Nonetheless, concerns about both low wages and the dearth of affordable housing were reflected in city council elections in both 2015 and 2017. All candidates for local seats in the 2017 election prioritized the need for affordable housing, with one noting, "affordable housing is essential to the livability of our community"; another noted that "if Asheville wants to maintain its character, it must be a place that people of all means can afford to live" (Burgess, 2017a).

Where possible, elected officials have sought to use the carrots of public subsidies and approval of new development to encourage below-market-rate housing construction. Since the economic recovery, approvals for financial incentive packages and development code variances have sometimes been tied to community benefit agreements with a focus on affordable housing, with private development projects in the River Arts District and the downtown area including some mix of *workforce housing* and contributions to the city's Housing Trust Fund (Barrett, 2014a; Burgess, 2016, 2017c). At the same time, city and county officials have shown a willingness to use their limited funds to support nonprofit affordable housing developers, but they are unable to keep up with the demand for lower-cost units, with long waiting lists for new projects and for the county's Housing Choice Vouchers (Walton, 2017).

Housing affordability is, of course, closely connected to the problem of low wages that is endemic to tourism-dominated economies. As is true in many regions, city and county economic development officials try to attract higher-paying employment with marketing and targeted subsidies (Boyle, 2014). There are also efforts to improve the wages in existing industries. In 2007, the city council adopted a living wage ordinance for city employees and later extended it in phases to cover the workers of companies that receive city contracts, and Buncombe County followed suit in 2012. Just Economics of Western North Carolina has established a voluntary certification program for businesses agreeing to pay a living wage, and at least one major hotel developer has agreed to meet those standards in exchange for city development approvals.

In addition to addressing housing deficits and economic opportunity, Asheville's City Council has also taken steps to ensure greater diversity among those benefitting from the city's amenities, and better access for the city's African-American community. As noted above, the Council's 2036 strategic plan sees livability and inclusion as deeply intertwined. After adopting that strategic plan, and in response to a study showing racial disparities in traffic stops in addition to a police shooting of a black resident, the city hired its first equity and inclusion manager, who was given the mandate of reviewing all city agencies through an *equity lens* with hiring, purchasing, public safety, and citizen engagement among her early priorities (Burgess, 2017b).

Conclusion

With its breathtaking setting in the mountains, its temperate climate, and its tradition of artisanal cultural production, Asheville is well positioned to attract those seeking quality-of-life amenities, and its leadership has crafted a city center that functions well as the center of this region. Their success, however, has left many residents behind, facing low-wage jobs and rising housing costs. Asheville had earlier been associated with a strong urban core and vibrant cultural life, but the leadership of this politically progressive community has begun to recognize the need to provide opportunities to all segments of the population.

References

Barrett, M. (2014a, August 26). Asheville Council oks incentive for RAD Loft Project. *Asheville Citizen-Times*. Retrieved from www.citizen-times.com/story/news/local/2014/08/26/asheville-council-oks-incentives-rad-lofts-project/14658605/.

Barrett, M. (2014b, June 4). Downtown Asheville popularity fuels hotel plans. *Asheville Citizen-Times*.

Boyle, J. (2014, February 22). Asheville area workers face dwindling income. *Asheville Citizen-Times*.

Boyle, J. (2017, January 24). Asheville gentrification pace makes top 10 list. *Asheville Citizen-Times*.

Burgess, J. (2016, December 24). Asheville downtown hotel boom to break $187M. *Asheville Citizen-Times*.

Burgess, J. (2017a, September 26). Asheville election: Candidates talk about their plans for affordable housing. *Asheville Citizen-Times*.

Burgess, J. (2017b, July 20). Asheville hires city's first equity manager to focus on race. *Asheville Citizen-Times*.

Burgess, J. (2017c, June 16). Sixty-four apartments, half below market rate, coming to Asheville downtown. *Asheville Citizen-Times*.

Byrd, C. (2013, May 28). No place like home: Child watch tour emphasizes the need for affordable housing. *Mountain Express*.

Byrd, C. (2015, July 25). Asheville businesses fight to keep big chains out. *Asheville Citizen-Times*.

Carmichael, M. (2016, January 25). *Why Asheville is one of the one hundred best places to live.* Retrieved on October 6, 2017, from https://livability.com/nc/asheville/real-estate/why-asheville-is-one-of-the-top-100-best-places-to-live-in-americalivability.

CNN Money. (2010, October 6). *Best places to retire.* Retrieved October 6, 2017, from http://money.cnn.com/galleries/2010/real_estate/1009/gallery.best_places_retire.moneymag/22.html.

Chase, N. K. (2007). *Asheville: A history.* Jefferson, NC: McFarland & Co. Publishers.

City of Asheville. (2009). *Asheville downtown master plan.* Retrieved from www.ashevillenc.gov/Departments/EconomicDevelopment/ProjectsInitiatives.aspx.

Daffron, V. (2016, May 19). The road ahead: Asheville launches comprehensive planning process. *Mountain Express.* Retrieved from https://mountainx.com/news/the-road-ahead-asheville-launches-comprehensive-planning-process/.

Fausett, R. (2015, May 16). With this many buskers in Asheville, a discordant note was inevitable. *New York Times.* Retrieved from www.nytimes.com/2015/05/17/us/with-this-many-buskers-in-asheville-a-discordant-note-was-inevitable.html?_r=1.

Frankel, J. (2015, January 20). Study highlights Ashveille housing challenges. *Mountain Express.* Retrieved from https://mountainx.com/news/study-highlights-asheville-housing-challenges/.

Frazier, K. D. (1998). Outsiders in the land of the sky. *Journal of Appalachian Studies, 4,* 299–316.

Graham, D. A. (2017, March). Red state, blue city. *The Atlantic.* Retrieved from www.theatlantic.com/magazine/archive/2017/03/red-state-blue-city/513857/.

Hayward, S. D., & Battle, D. (2018). Brewing a beer industry in Asheville, North Carolina. In S. L. Slocum, C. Kline, & C. T. Cavaliere (Eds.), *Craft beverages and tourism, Volume 2: Environmental, societal, and marketing implications* (pp. 171–193). London, New York, Shanghai: Palgrave Macmillan.

Judd, D. R. (1999). Constructing the tourist bubble. In D. R. Judd & S. S. Fainstein (Eds.), *The tourist city.* New Haven, CT: Yale University Press.

Lonely Planet. (2016, December). *Lonely Planet's best in the US 2017.* Retrieved on October 6, 2017, from www.lonelyplanet.com/usa/travel-tips-and-articles/lonely-planets-best-in-the-us-2017/40625c8c-8a11-5710-a052-1479d276e336.

Long, L. M. (2010). Culinary tourism and the emergence of an Appalachian cuisine. *North Carolina Folklore Journal, 57*(1), 4–19.

Lunsford, M. (2014, June 6). Double Crown owners to open bar in downtown Asheville. *Asheville Citizen-Times.*

Patrick, D. (2016, July 28). Buncombe County hotel tax revenues up to $17.5 million. *Asheville Citizen Times.*

Postelle, B., Forbes, D., Millard, H. L., & Sandford, J. N. (2008, August 6). A house divided. *Mountain Express.* Retrieved from http://mountainx.com/news/community news/080608a_house_divided/.

Rohe, W. M., Cowan, S. M., Rodriguez, D. A., & Zambito, P. (2009). *A long way from home: The impacts of a limited supply of workforce housing in the Asheville metropolitan area.* Chapel Hill, NC: Center for Urban and Regional Studies, University of North Carolina at Chapel Hill. Retrieved from http://research.unc.edu/files/2012/11/BuncCty-Report-rev-100616.pdf.

Starnes, R. D. (2005). *Creating the land of the sky: Tourism and society in western North Carolina.* Tuscaloosa, AL: University of Alabama Press.

Strom, E., & Kerstein, R. (2015). Mountains and muses: Tourism development in Asheville, NC. *Annals of Tourism Research, 52,* 134–147.

Strom, E., & Kertstein, R. (2017). The homegrown downtown: Redevelopment in Asheville, North Carolina. *Urban Affairs Review, 53*(3), 495–521.

United States Conference of Mayors. (2013). *Hunger and homelessness survey: A status report on hunger and homelessness in America's cities.* Retrieved from https://endhomelessness.atavist.com/mayorsreport2016.

Walton, B. (2017, June 9). Report: Decent housing out of reach for many Buncombe workers. *Asheville Citizen Times.*

Chapter 7

THE TRANSFORMATION OF SEATTLE
Mark Hinshaw

O ver the last 15 years, all three of the largest cities in North America's Pacific Northwest— Vancouver, B.C., Seattle, Washington, and Portland, Oregon—have garnered kudos from many sources. They have consistently been placed in the top five of lists such as the most livable, the most walkable, the most transit friendly, most bikeable, best places to visit, and best places to start a business. This has not always been the case. Until the 1980s, all three cities were pretty lackluster. They were garnering no acclamations. This has been a remarkable change; I can think of no other three closely spaced cities in North America that have experienced such a dramatic shift.

The coastal region between Portland and Vancouver, B.C., is sometimes referred to as *Cascadia*, for the Cascade Mountain range that lines the east edge of all three. The region shares a number of attributes. It is politically liberal and has been for some time; there is a high tolerance for alternative lifestyles, a high regard for the role of government, and voters consistently approve progressive ballot measures for things such as marriage equality, elevated minimum wage, and the commercial sales of cannabis. For many people who have chosen to move to Cascadia over the past few decades, it is an area that is very livable.

Cascadia still exhibits some aspects of the frontier; after all, it was the last area to be settled on the continent. It continues to attract an independent, pioneering type of personality that is unrestrained by an entrenched set of institutions. Most people in Cascadia place a high collective value on public transit, public parks, museums, community centers, and schools—generally the common goods in which all citizens have a stake. There is little hesitation to fund these social goods with higher taxes. There is a collective sense of shared responsibility to ensure that the region continues to be livable.

Finally, Cascadia demonstrates a high regard for environmental protection. Strong laws preventing the filling of wetlands and despoiling of shorelines and watersheds have been in place for many years. There is a long-term, very consistent set of attitudes that eschew outward development in favor of saving forests and preserving farmlands. Each city within Cascadia has delineated a sharp line in the regional landscape where development may and may not occur. For many years, it has been virtually impossible to penetrate those boundaries with subdivisions, shopping centers, or industrial parks. Generally, many people see the merits of compact and connected communities.

I shall leave it to my colleagues in Portland and Vancouver to describe their transformations.

This story is about Seattle—how it came to evolve into a dynamic, culturally rich, highly livable city. While the most dramatic change has occurred fairly recently in time, it is useful to look at a few foundational roots to see their origins—at least of white settlement patterns. I certainly do not wish to minimize Native American history, which is important and still a major factor in the regional culture. But the contributions of first peoples, as well as early explorations by both the Spanish and British, is a subject in itself.

The Old Seattle—the first 100 years

The settlement of Seattle started in the mud—literally—in the mid-1800s. A settlement was formed on a small finger of dry land that was surrounded by broad tidal mudflats. The settlement would be occasionally inundated by salt water from Elliott Bay at extreme high tides. The mudflats impeded the use of sailing ships, disturbed the use of outdoor toilets, and just plain stank of dead fish. So when the first Seattle of wood frame buildings caught fire in 1889 and burned to the ground, the city was quickly rebuilt—12 feet higher and out of masonry. As the years passed, most of the tide flats were filled in, first with railroad trestles careening every which way, then later with buildable soil. And sometimes with not so buildable soil. Subsequent earthquakes have revealed that folly, especially in buildings that were constructed without reinforcing steel.

Strong unions centered around maritime commerce, and resource extraction became the basis for an eventual left-leaning political orientation. While no significant battles took place around Seattle, people died in riots associated with the socialist Industrial Workers of the World union, nicknamed the Wobblies. Chinese laborers, who helped bring transcontinental railroads to the city's doorstep in the 1880s, were almost kicked out of town by an angry white mob that found the ethnic group a convenient scapegoat for the social ills of the time. This potentially embarrassing civic moment was saved by the even-tempered voice of John Harte McGraw, who was rewarded for his courage later by subsequently being elected governor of the state.

Out of the stewpot of people seeking to make their fortune in the Alaskan Gold Rush of the 1890s, emerged a city that, while not exactly polished, began to feel urban. Although Seattle was not immune from racism, there was a collective entrepreneurial spirit that welcomed many different cultures, from Scandinavian fishermen to Italian laborers to Japanese merchants.

But the region has rarely been a hotbed of racial strife. The one tragic exception was the forced internment of Japanese-American citizens after the invasion of Pearl Harbor in the early 1940s. By federal decree, hundreds of families were sent to inland camps and lost businesses and homes in the process. The Nihonmachi, an established neighborhood of Japanese families and stores, was all but wiped from the map.

For several decades after World War II, Seattle was a rough and tumble port town, laced with various bases for the U.S. Navy with a waterfront lined with long docks for steamships from all over the world. Up until the mid-1970s, the presence of commercial and military shipping was profound. The 1970 film *Cinderella Liberty* with James Caan and Marsha Mason accurately portrayed First Avenue, near the waterfront, as a red light district packed with saloons, X-rated theatres, hookers, drunks, pool halls, and pawnshops. Roving pairs of MPs walked the street, ready to haul off brawling sailors still in uniform. The Lusty Lady, the last holdover strip joint of that era, finally closed a few years ago. Today, that part of town is now a tony district filled with pricey clothing stores, expensive hotels, condos, and elegant restaurants.

Seattle would not be the city it became without mentioning Boeing. Consisting of several massive plants first building wartime bombers then state-of-the-art commercial aircraft, the company is immense. With its tens of thousands of engineers, assembly workers, contractors, and suppliers, it made Seattle a company town for decades. The company's precipitous crash in 1970 sent shock waves through the city, with thousands of people departing. The city was almost eviscerated and could have been an early version of Detroit today. Although Boeing's impact has lessened since the moving of its corporate headquarters to Chicago and the recent rise of tech companies large and small, Boeing's presence is still formidable.

The New Seattle

One could mark the start of the New Seattle by the rapid rise of Microsoft in the late 1980s. Indeed, in some quarters, Seattle and Microsoft now are almost synonymous. Ironically, perhaps, Microsoft has almost no presence in Seattle itself. Following the examples of hundreds of corporate headquarters all over the country, Microsoft began in the suburbs and remains in the suburbs with an array of vast campuses so expansive that they justify their own transit system. Nonetheless, Bill Gates put Seattle on the map of international commerce, workplace tools, and technological innovation. It has stayed there ever since.

However, there were a host of watershed moments that preceded Microsoft, which were transformative in their impact. First, Pike Place Market was saved from demolition in the early 1970s from the forces of urban renewal that ravaged many other cities. In the years since, the market has been not only fully restored but has expanded beyond its original boundaries to encompass a district not unlike Covent Garden in London. This effort, led by a relentless and passionate citizen activist and architect, Victor Steinbrueck, saved the soul of the city. Pike Place Market is a multi-block, multistory collection of locally owned produce vendors, fishmongers, restaurants, and unique shops, as well as dense housing. It continues to be revered by the public. Indeed, in the late 1970s voters passed a bond issue to save the market again by taxing themselves to buy up farmlands in the county to prevent them from ever being developed.

At about the same time, two other critical initiatives occurred right during the height of the Boeing Bust of the 1970s. The State of Washington adopted an Environmental Policy Act (SEPA), along with the Shorelines Management Act (SMA). Together, both of these pieces of legislation slowed the wave of rampant, outward development that was starting to stretch to the foothills of the mountains—a pattern that had already occurred in the Los Angeles basin. SEPA required virtually all forms of development, whether public or private, to examine and reveal their impacts—environmental, cultural, and social. Only California has a similar piece of comprehensive statewide legislation that has such a profound effect on changing the course of development and making it responsible for its impacts. For Seattle, this meant that the future was secured from significant competition from suburbs. (The Metro area certainly saw many suburban cities, but only one—Bellevue—has taken on a truly competitive role.)

The second watershed event that sent Seattle into a different direction was the voter-approved Forward Thrust bond issue. Proposed by a passionate and persuasive activist, attorney

James Ellis, Forward Thrust provided a huge influx of funding to build a broad panoply of public works. Concurrently, a regional agency was formed to provide transit and build sewage treatment plants that cleaned up the increasingly toxic waters of Puget Sound. That this tax increase on property was approved during the Boeing Recession was indicative of a resolve to not let Seattle die a slow death of attrition. It was also a vivid demonstration of Keynesian economics—using strategic public investments to rebuild the economy.

Between the mid-1980s and the mid-1990s, Seattle's livability was affected by several other significant initiatives. By then, it had already established a solid record of neighborhood planning with at least a dozen neighborhood commercial centers strengthened by both master plans and targeted public investments. The year 1985 capped those efforts with a comprehensive and bold downtown plan that was enacted together with a set of laws governing development. Different densities for various districts, incentives for public spaces and housing, and design standards regulating urban form were set forth. While this led to an increase in development, the pace was slowed by a downturn in the local economy that left numerous buildings un-built or built but unoccupied. One completed but empty tower was eventually purchased by the city for administrative office space for pennies on the dollar.

By the late 1980s, the relatively low cost of Seattle real estate, as compared with California, was discovered by Californians. Some people sold a home in southern California and bought two in Seattle. Land prices and home prices shot up steeply. Houses would have potential buyers waiting in their cars with agents outside homes for sale to see if the deal being negotiated inside fell through. People made offers without contingencies, without inspections, and for offers well over asking price. The real estate industry went wild with a kind of gold rush frenzy. Within a matter of a year, Seattle went from being a city with comparatively affordable housing to one with not much affordable housing.

Long-time locals were furious. *Don't Californicate Seattle* was a common bumper sticker. License plates from that state seemed to be everywhere, and the resentment was intense. By the end of the 1980s a grassroots citizen initiative was put on the ballot that called for Draconian growth controls and proposed a state board that could overturn local zoning permits. An example of how extreme it was (although in fine print) was the requirement that no one who owned property could be appointed to the board. The initiative was widely predicted to pass, given the exasperations of existing residents.

The state legislature recognized the lighting rod that rapid growth could be and quickly responded with its own measure that was not as extreme. (As a way of context, Washington State is dominated, population wise, by the cluster of liberal cities around Puget Sound, while the vast majority of the state's area and towns are very conservative. There has been a long-standing debate about government control versus laissez-faire policies.) There was a striking agreement to adopt a Statewide Growth Management Act. The promise made to voters was that the GMA would be adopted if the citizens' initiative was rejected at the ballot box. The initiative failed.

What was adopted was a system that gave cities and counties broad discretion as to how to carry out the legislative framework. Crafting the Growth Management Act (GMA) involved first looking at other states like Oregon, Hawaii, and Florida to learn from their laws. There was little interest in a *top–down* approach like Oregon's. On the other hand, general policies such as in Florida were unacceptable. Adopted in 1992, the GMA was homegrown and involved some brilliant components.

First, rural counties that had experienced little growth were exempted from the act. Effectively, that eliminated a massive potential objection by farmers, ranchers, and small conservative towns. While attempts to abolish the Act have been made since adoption of the GMA, none has been successful.

Second, the Act required that the high-growth cities and counties declare which lands were environmentally sensitive and off limits to development. Third, local jurisdictions had to adopt urban growth boundaries based on reasonable estimates of growth, and moreover, they had to agree to them with their adjacent neighbors. This eliminated competing or conflicting zoning across adjacent city limits.

Fourth, it was expected that any unincorporated land inside the growth boundaries would be annexed to an existing city or incorporated into a new city. These areas would be provided with a full complement of urban services. Lands outside the growth boundary would remain as rural, agricultural, or forestry. In more than 25 years since they were mapped, there has been virtually no significant expansion of the urban growth boundary around Seattle.

It took a few years for the effects to occur, but the GMA effectively reversed the typical course of real estate values. Land inside the boundaries gradually became much more valuable, compared with that outside. Regional state-appointed boards would receive requests for changes from cities or property owners, but generally the principles were held fast. Meanwhile several citizen groups, such as 1000 Friends of Washington (now known as Futurewise) closely monitored every appeal case to make sure no movement away from the growth management approach slipped through the cracks. Some counties were even admonished by the board for attempting end-runs. One county resisted GMA altogether until the governor at the time threatened to deny them transportation funds.

It was a wild initial period of years, with lawsuits, counter ballot measures, and petitions by some areas to secede from GMA-required counties. After a few years the fussing died down. Elected councils got with the program, sometimes blaming GMA to angry constituents. The real estate industry, which pretty vigorously opposed the Act, changed their tune when they realized that a lot more money was to be made from urban land values. And school districts and utility districts re-programmed funds for inward infrastructure rather than outward. All this took years, with lots of hand-wringing and contentious public meetings at the local level. And it took a while for some people to fully realize that GMA meant more development in their vicinity, not less, since farmland, forestlands, and wetlands were now off-limits. Some people, even in relatively dense Seattle, still do not buy into this philosophy.

Despite the exemption for slow-growing counties, the GMA applies to 29 of the state's 39 counties, which collectively have around 85% of the population. The state government's role has been relatively modest, particularly compared with the powerful central land use board of neighboring Oregon. It is presumed that local governments will comply with the many administrative rules of the statute, and the state only reviews policies and codes for compliance.

The most important function of the state in the GMA is to issue population targets to be accommodated by each county and city. Local jurisdictions could not decide whether to accommodate development, only how they would do so. And their progress would be monitored.

Seattle embraced the Growth Management Act with a particular zeal. It translated the concept of directing growth to areas with services into a reorganization of its Comprehensive Plan. Adopted in the mid-1990s, the concept of guiding density and public investments into

Urban Villages continues up to the present day, albeit with some changes now being contemplated. New forms of zoning regulation have since been developed, which has created a considerable amount of infill development throughout many areas of the city.

The Urban Villages strategy calls for different intensities of development depending on transit access, transportation, and proximity of shops, services, and restaurants that can be reached by walking. There are several urban centers of regional impact, such as downtown and the University of Washington area. There are more than a dozen villages that are more locally oriented, many connected by bus, light rail, and streetcars.

One of the regulatory tools that set Seattle apart from other North American cities is Neighborhood Design Review. There are seven boards appointed by the mayor and confirmed by the city council. Each board must comprise a balance of residents, representatives of the design community, and professionals in real estate or development. This ensures both expertise and a range of voices. Meetings are public and the boards receive considerable input from residents.

Although they are not empowered to reduce density or building height, they can approve *departures* from certain numerical standards in the land use code. These are granted in exchange for public amenities or design improvements. The boards also must follow adopted design guidelines in accordance with state case law. Public testimony is limited in time so that the boards can deliberate expeditiously. And no testimony about subjects such as traffic impacts or reducing basic development entitlements is heard. The boards are not empowered to alter basic allowable intensity, despite the wishes of some neighborhood activists. The influence of these bodies has been profound on the form of the city over the past 20 years. Some developers claim the process is unpredictable, but only a handful of projects have ever been denied. The mode of deliberation emphasizes recognizing the context, collaborating with the community, and providing public benefits.

Another initiative that has affected Seattle's livability is the growing network of public transportation. The city began this approach with a network of safe, clean, predictable buses. This was enhanced by the building of a visually striking transit tunnel under downtown to expedite transit movement unimpeded by other vehicles. In addition, the city has also placed severe limitations on the amount of parking associated with development. This has made the choice to drive quite costly, as parking rates have increased dramatically given the constrained supply. Consequently, more than half of daily commuters do not arrive in single-occupant vehicles. Many younger workers do not even own cars, and the parking requirement in some zoning districts has been eliminated altogether.

The investment in the bus system has gradually expanded to include a panoply of choices in public transportation. Since the late 1990s, a regional transit authority—Sound Transit—has been busy building multiple light rail lines, two heavy rail commuter train lines, and a network of express buses. The city has complemented these with two operating streetcar lines and with a third under construction. With respect to bicycles, the city converted a major street through downtown to incorporate a protected and signalized bike lane. Recently it invited three bike-share companies to provide high-tech rental bikes that can be picked up and left in any public location.

Despite the relatively high levels of taxation, businesses with global impact have been sweeping into the city. There is no truth to the claim that many restaurants have closed in the wake of the $15 per hour minimum wage. To the contrary, more restaurants have opened, and some now pay their employees more than the minimum and offer good benefits. Costco has been a model for years of a socially progressive business model. Nordstrom has been a paragon of socially enlightened retailing for decades. Weyerhaeuser, the timber resource giant, moved its headquarters from a classic suburban location into the hard-core center of the city. Expedia has done the same.

And there is Amazon. Like Microsoft, Amazon was a *garage venture*. It has become such a merchandising leviathan that it is fast eclipsing Walmart and is essentially putting Sears out of business. The collection of numerous buildings that make up the current headquarters occupy 3 million square feet of space, and the company has another 3 million under construction—mostly in towers. Most of its employees prefer to live within walking or cycling distance; this has caused its own boom in dense urban housing.

Although Amazon is not solely responsible for the boom in apartment construction, they have contributed to it with a workforce of tens of thousands of young workers. Over the last two years, there have been over 60 construction cranes in the central city, putting up dozens of 30–40-story residential towers. Even so, there is still a shortfall in housing supply across all points in the spectrum. The resultant rapid increase in rental rates has spurred a kind of backlash to Amazon.

Whether or not that was the reason, Amazon's demand for space has been so voracious that it will be building a second base of operations in another North American city. Many people are relieved that the super-heated housing market might soon be cooling a bit as a result. As a company, Amazon is unique in many different ways, not the least being its collective team-oriented structure. It deliberately did not build a campus. Its many buildings are distributed throughout a wide portion of the central city. Moreover, it keeps its image modest. None of its buildings have a corporate logo, at least that you can see from a distance. Jeff Bezos has become a local (as well as international) icon, along with other local billionaires like Bill Gates and Paul Allen.

For many locals it is difficult to believe that out of the top five wealthiest people in the world, each with a personal worth above $55 billion, two of them are in Seattle. Gates now has his own private global health organization with a stunning set of buildings in the city center. Paul Allen, further down the list, has contributed huge sums of his wealth to local museums, theaters, transit, parks, and stadiums. His soccer team, the Seattle Sounders, is building compact European-style soccer fields, gratis, throughout the city, including low-income areas.

Seattle has numerous nonprofit housing providers that build and manage thousands of units below market housing values. Another powerhouse nonprofit is the Seattle Parks Foundation. Headed by an irrepressible executive director, Thatcher Bailey, the Parks Foundation has garnered contributions from corporations and individuals throughout the city to add to public funds for parks. Seattle has had a long tradition of local wealth donating to projects and programs that benefit the public as a whole.

Many private philanthropic organizations have contributed immensely to the arts, environment, and livability. Seattle now attracts vast numbers of young, highly educated people from countries and cultures across the globe. Microsoft also contributes to this phenomenon, not because it is in Seattle (which it's not), but because many Microsoft workers want to live in a dynamic city with sports teams, culture, music, and unique restaurants.

To be fair, Seattle has made some major mistakes. Huge ones. Money-wasting ones. Mistakes that would have been scandals in some other cities. But in a sort of strange combination of

Scandinavian and Asian reticence, we have kind of swept them under the civic rug. No one talks about them anymore. The principals have disappeared. Potentially revealing documents might exist somewhere, but no one wants to look very hard. It's like having a couple of embarrassing uncles who embezzled the family fortune.

Mistake #1: The Seattle Commons

Initially suggested by a long-time columnist for the *Seattle Times*, a number of influential people fell in love with the idea of building a huge central park just south of Lake Union on the north edge of downtown.

Paul Allen funded the effort, which involved the formation of a private planning group that would also buy property from owners of parking lots, warehouses, car dealers, and vacant buildings. Spend money they did. Millions. Trouble was they did not collect enough money to actually build it. That money was to come from a voter-approved ballot measure. Which failed, twice. Years were wasted. To provide the initial funds, Paul Allen declared the property that was acquired as collateral. When the plan fell apart, Allen was instantly the largest landowner in the city. Since then, his real estate company has built a wholly new neighborhood on that same land.

Mistake #2: The Monorail Fiasco

For some unexplainable reason, many Seattleites are absolutely mesmerized by the idea of a monorail as the solution to transportation issues. One of those people was a part-time taxi driver who set up a *build a monorail* petition table on random street corners. It was kind of a local joke until a few people got suddenly serious, set up a Monorail Development Authority, and got an initiative passed for millions to fund the planning and design as well as to buy right of way.

The authority had a huge, well-paid staff, dozens of costly consultants, and a small army of purchase agents buying property. There was even a catchy logo of a cute monorail train with the phrase *Rise Above It All*. Construction plans were drawn up to build the thing; everything was readied to get permits. Then, the authority's chief business manager realized they had made a major error in the math that showed how tax on annual car tabs would pay for it. A major mistake in the numbers revealed it would be grossly underfunded. That weekend the executive director and authority chair both left town. Not long after the mistake was discovered and displayed in headlines, the project went back to the voters. They rejected it by a wide margin. However, the initial tax increase to pay for the planning, design, and land purchases had to legally be added to car license renewals for years. This was civic foolishness on a grand scale. Somewhere in a dark vault somewhere—picture the end of the first Indiana Jones movie—there is an enormous crate of construction drawings that will never be used.

The Next Seattle

Currently, there are several big initiatives that will shape Seattle in the next couple of decades. Sound Transit is embarking on a massive expansion of the light rail network that will stretch its network north, east, and south. This is a game changer for the region and Seattle as its main hub. It will influence the form and intensity of development for a long time to come.

The city is also looking at light rail extensions to two sectors of the city—ironically, the very same that the failed monorail project was meant to serve. This will dramatically increase the ability of people to use transit to reach their workplaces as well as recreational destinations.

Finally, the city is in the process of implementing an agreement with the development community to increase the supply of affordable housing. Developers would be responsible for contributing to the solution in a significant way, no matter what type of development they do. The agreement also suggests major changes for density in the neighborhoods. Increasing density near single-family areas always makes some people completely crazy.

Seattle, in my view, is still a true frontier town. Albeit in the 21st century.

I want to express appreciation to Joe Tovar, FAICP, who reviewed an early version of this piece. Joe has been a great colleague and a true leader in planning throughout Washington State.

I want to thank Greg Hanscom and Joe Copeland for their years of support as publisher and editor of *crosscut*, a daily online magazine of culture, politics, and development in the Pacific Northwest. I thoroughly enjoyed my stint as a contributing writer. My articles commenting on changes in Seattle can be found at crosscut.com.

For 12 years prior to joining *crosscut*, I wrote a monthly column in the *Seattle Times*. For anyone wishing to see those pieces, they can be found in the online archives for the newspaper.

Chapter 8

TORONTO: A LIVABLE CITY/ REGION

David Amborski and Ray Lister

Introduction

Toronto is the largest city in Canada and the ninth largest metropolitan area in North America. Located in the province of Ontario, the city has a population of 2.7 million people, and the population of the region, the Greater Toronto Area (GTA), is 6.2 million people. This is expected to increase by 115,000 people per year mainly due to immigration as the city is a key gateway city. This increase may result in an anticipated population of 3.4 million for the city and 10.1 million for the region by 2041.

Toronto is a livable city. Partially as a result of this, people are drawn to the urban entity of Toronto, as well as to the region as a whole. This chapter will discuss the number of positive aspects of the Toronto region that make it a desirable place to live, as well as the challenges the city will face moving forward. While Toronto looks to remain an attractive place to live for both inhabitants and newcomers, these challenges must be addressed if governments wish to maintain Toronto's status as a *Livable City*.

The chapter will first provide a historical perspective of the government structure of Toronto to understand the nature of the city. Following sections will then examine the three components—good governance, good planning, and fiscal health—which are important conditions for a livable city. This will allow for a more complete examination of Toronto's ranking as a livable city as seen from the perspective of both external organizations and those found within the city itself. A discussion of key themes and how metrics in these evaluations relate to Toronto follows, in addition to an examination of external analysis of Toronto as a livable city. Finally, some areas of concern in regards to Toronto's future will be discussed.

Historical Perspective

In discussing Toronto as a livable city, it is necessary to discuss the definition of Toronto as its political boundaries and regional context has changed overtime. In the context of this chapter, Toronto refers to the broader region centered on the actual physical city of Toronto. As a result, data and analysis may relate to the actual city of Toronto, or in some cases the broader regional planning concepts like the Greater Toronto Area or the Greater Golden Horseshoe. This region

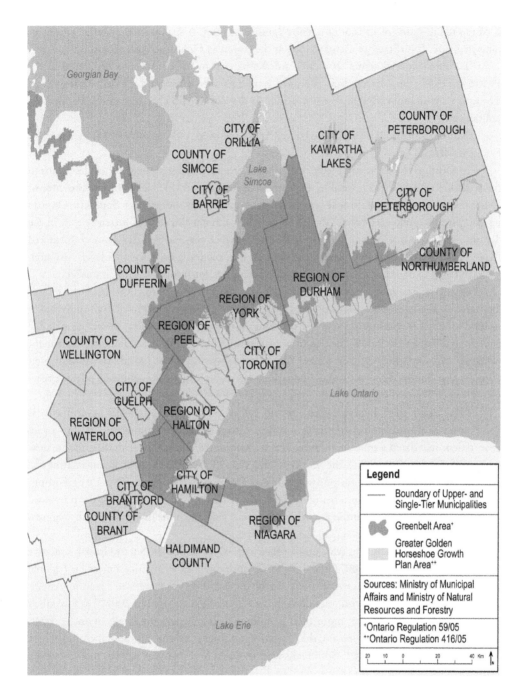

Figure 8.1 Map of the Greater Golden Horseshoe, Ontario.

Source: Author.

is connected in terms of its economy, jobs, housing market, transportation systems, and planning structure. It is therefore useful to look at the region as a whole to gain perspective.

Toronto's governmental structure gained attention in North America beginning in the 1950s. In 1954, the Metropolitan Toronto Act came into effect and created Metropolitan Toronto, then an innovative government structure that garnered the attention of academics and politicians.

A number of applications in the United States followed, most notably in Minneapolis-St. Paul and Miami-Dade.

In addition to the creation of Metropolitan Toronto, there have been other alterations to the structure of municipal governments in the Toronto region. In the 1970s the Province of Ontario created several additional two-tiered governments in the broader Southern Ontario region, where Toronto is located. These two-tiered government structures currently exist in the Toronto region outside the city of Toronto. The province also enacted the Toronto Centered Region Plan in 1970, the first provincial initiative into planning on a regional level. Although the plan failed to be implemented, it did create a template for future planning initiatives.

As the region grew, population growth increased in the suburbs outside of the city of Toronto. In the late 1980s the provincial government, under the Liberal Party, undertook a number of studies relating to potential planning initiatives in the region, as well as possible government reorganization. While this continued through 1990, the formation of a government headed by the Ontario New Democratic Party meant these initiatives stalled. The ensuing government then initiated the Greater Toronto Task Force, an initiative to address a possible reorganization of Toronto's governmental structure. It completed its background work in 1996.

Once again, the initiative stalled with the formation of a new provincial government, as the Progressive Conservatives returned to office. After a short delay, however, the provincial government mandated a number of municipal reforms in the late 1990s, including the amalgamation of municipalities across the province (Sancton, 2000). This included amalgamating the six local municipalities that previously constituted Metropolitan Toronto. The city of Toronto as it is now conceived came into being in 1998. It was also around this time that the provincial government initiatives for planning on a broad regional level, with the inspiration of the regional or statewide Smart Growth theme in the United States.

The Liberal government, which took office in 2003, modified the Smart Growth initiative with their Places to Grow (2007) plan for the Toronto region that identified areas for regional growth. This plan, which was awarded the Burnham award by the American Planning Association, was meant to work in conjunction with the Greenbelt Act passed in 2006. The Greenbelt Act, in contrast, encompasses more than 2 million acres of environmentally sensitive areas, including the Oakridge Moraine and the Niagara Escarpment, around Toronto, identifies where new development is prohibited. Both plans were initiated for a ten-year period, and set out the broad plan for development in the region. In 2017, these plans were revised at the end of their ten-year mandate after significant public input, detailed review, and consultation.

As seen in this brief historical review, government structure and the planning have evolved significantly in the Toronto region since the 1950s. Planners came to look at the region as a whole as it increasingly became linked by a regional transportation system of highways, commuter transit, and local transit systems, as well as by the labor market.

Three Key Components of Successful Urban Areas

There are three elements essential to a livable city. These are good governance, good urban planning, and financial capability. Good governance refers to both having an appropriate structure of government for its size and responsibilities, as well as good leadership, hopefully developed through a democratic culture. Good planning requires responsible planning legislation, reliable professional technical skills, and a culture of planning in the public interest. Finally, fiscal capacity is necessary to fund the infrastructure needed to support growth and services to support a good quality of life.

These three conditions are met in the Toronto region. It benefits, initially, from its location in Ontario and in Canada, which has stable, democratic governments that generally work together quite well. In Canada, the British North America Act (1867) assigns the responsibility for local governments to the provinces. Consequently, all legislation for local governments, such as the Municipal Act, the Planning Act, and the Municipality of Metropolitan Toronto Act, are enacted by the Province of Ontario. Ontario's Municipal Act also promotes a *weak mayor system* where the power is vested with council collectively, and the mayor exerts influence through their leadership skills. This does not mean they lack influence. In a number of Toronto region municipalities, including the City of Toronto, cities have benefited from the strong leadership skills of their mayors. Toronto has also benefited from a strong tradition of public participation in its planning process, encouraging shareholders to engage in the planning process. The Ontario Planning Act requires public meetings as part of its approval process for planning documents.

In terms of good planning, the region has also been fortunate. Policymakers made urban planning a consistent theme since World War II, influenced by British and American experience and planning traditions. The first Planning Act was passed by the Government of Ontario in 1946 (Hodge & Gordon, 2013). Governments have also been consistent in the need to monitor planning in the province in response to changing needs. Ontario legislation requires municipalities to prepare Official (Master) Plans and review them every five years. There is also a comprehensive approval process required for the development of greenfield sites for urban use. Larger-scale planning initiatives have also been undertaken in the region, as seen with the Toronto Centered Region Plan (1970), the Greenbelt Act (2006), the Growth Plan (2007), and the development of Toronto's Waterfront. Planning for transportation on a regional level has also been a key concern and priority, resulting in the creation of Metrolinx in 2006.

Municipalities in the Toronto region have also been fortunate in terms of economic growth. This, in addition to prudent legislation, has meant planners have had the fiscal capacity to follow through on their plans for the region. Ontario municipalities are not overly indebted and are fiscally stable. Stringent provincial legislation requires municipalities to approve balanced budgets. In addition, the province controls both the magnitude and the nature of debts incurred by cities through the issuance of debentures (Ontario Municipal Act). This has ensured municipalities have a good credit rating, pay low interest rates on debt, and therefore have borrowing capacity when required. This is an important situation given all municipalities, with the exception of the City of Toronto through the City of Toronto Act, are limited in their taxation authority, with having only taxing authority for the property tax.

Municipalities can, however, raise *own-source revenue* through imposing user charges. From the end of World War II through the beginning of the 1990s, the senior levels of government were integral partners in funding growth-related infrastructure in Canada. However, as federal and provincial grants were curtailed, municipalities began to make use of development charges to finance growth-related capital costs. Development charges, user fees, and other exactions became an important component of funding growth-related capital costs for new development in the Toronto region (Altus Group, 2018).

Livable City: Rankings and Evaluations

Toronto has gained a significant reputation internationally as a livable city. Analysts from *The Economist*, Global Livability Report, NUMBEO, Quality of Life Index, and Mercer, among others, have ranked it positively. Toronto was listed 4th in *The Economist*'s 2017 Livability survey, which is based on five categories: stability, health care, culture and environment, education, and infrastructure (Economist Intelligence Unit, 2017a). NUMBEO, which claims to have the world's largest contributed database regarding information on world living conditions, uses a broader and more comprehensive set of metrics. In 2017 it ranked Toronto 44th in global livability. Finally, there is the Mercer report, which ranked Toronto 17th in 2017. Although all these indices use different sets of metrics and weigh categories differently, this sample demonstrates that Toronto's reputation as a livable city stands out internationally. It is also interesting to look at how local organizations evaluate the livability of Toronto. Two notable examples stand out. The Toronto Region Board of Trade last published its Scorecard on Prosperity in 2015 (Toronto Region Board of Trade, 2015). It reflects the Board of Trade's interest on measuring the economy and its ability to attract labor by comparing Toronto with 23 other international metropolitan areas. It ranked Toronto 5th on its 2015 scorecard. The Toronto Foundation is a not-for-profit whose annual report, Vital Signs (2018), uses a number of metrics to analyze inequalities in Toronto. Rather than compare the city with other metropolitan areas, this report tracks performance over time on a number of metrics. These include arts and culture, environment, transportation, housing, health and wellness, income and wealth, learning, safety, and a grouping of leadership, civic engagement, and belonging. The report is thus able to provide feedback on issues related to livability in Toronto over a period of time, and aims to affect policy to improve livability. The focus is on aspects of inequality that require the attention of policymakers and to help direct donors to areas of need (Toronto Foundation, 2018).

In addition to the above organizations that have provided positive comments regarding Toronto's status as a livable city/region, the following section will provide some rankings that have been reported on specific themes that contribute to livable cities.

Key Themes for Livable Cities

There are a number of key themes or metrics that appear in the various evaluations of livable cities. These appear in terms of intercity comparisons and the self-evaluation of cities by local organizations. A number of these themes are discussed below in the context of Toronto as they contribute to the reputation of Toronto as a livable city/region.

Jobs

Livable cities exhibit healthy job creation and growth. The Toronto Census Metropolitan Area (CMA) produces 20% of Canada's overall gross domestic product (GDP), significantly more than Vancouver or Montreal (Statistics Canada, 2017b). Also, according to the documentation in the most recent Provincial Growth Plan, the GDP generated by the region is greater than 25% of the Canadian total. This makes Toronto and region the economic driver of the country, with the most highly educated workforce in the OECD (Toronto Global, 2017). Employers are drawn to Toronto because of its educated population, high quality of livability, and its rank as one of the top ten tax-competitive cities in the world (KPMG LLP, 2016).

Workers within the Toronto CMA are employed in many industries. In 2017, the share of jobs was highest among the following four industries: wholesale and retail trade (16%), professional and technical services (11%), finance and insurance (11%), and healthcare (10%) (Statistics Canada, 2017a). The Toronto region is also working to attract more jobs in the tech industry through a recent Amazon HQ2 bid. It has captured global attention for its work with Sidewalk Labs, a sister company of Google, and while this has raised questions about the future of livable city building, tech, and privacy, it also represents a potential shift in city-building technologies.

The changing nature of work in turn changes the spatial needs of employers, as many positions become hyper- or semi-mobile (Shearmur, 2018). Toronto is working to adapt to this new reality. In December 2013, Toronto City Council adopted Official Plan Amendment 231, which contained new economic policies and designations for employment areas. OPA 231 seeks to preserve the employment lands in Toronto, which have been encroached upon by mixed-use development and residential uses. The amendment was approved by the Province of Ontario in July 2014, though remains under appeal at the Ontario Municipal Board (City of Toronto n.d.a).

The education system and educational opportunities are an important input for the well-educated workforce in the Toronto region. This supports the job market as well as the opportunity for upward mobility of individuals. It begins with a good primary, secondary, and post-secondary education system in the Toronto area that is part of the broader provincially regulated and funded system. The provincial regulations and funding attempt to ensure a relatively uniform quality of education for students at the primary and secondary school levels across the province.

Consequently, this is also true for the Toronto area. Toronto's highly educated workforce reflects the fact that the region has five universities and seven community colleges, some of which have multiple campuses. It is also noteworthy that all these institutions are public institutions with tuition fees regulated by the province. Undergraduate fees are less than CDN$10,000 per year. In addition, there are financial aid packages available for eligible students in the province with special support for students from low-income households.

Transit

The Greater Toronto Area is home to a vast network of transportation systems that carry residents to their many destinations. This reflects the role transit plays in building livable cities.

Equitable and affordable access to transit increases livability in an urban context. It plays a key role in creating places for community interaction and in revitalizing neighborhoods and downtown cores. It also supports opportunities for local economic development, the shaping of growth patterns in a city, and the comfort of communities (Project for Public Space, 1997). For Toronto this also means the incorporation of cycling infrastructure and walking trails throughout the city.

Public transit has a long history in Toronto, beginning in 1849 with four horse-drawn coaches. The rapid growth of the region meant, however, that there has not always been a cohesive or well-funded approach to the issue. This changed when, in a 1946 referendum, property owners in the City of Toronto voted 90% in favor of funding the Yonge Street subway line (Levy, 2015). The line opened in 1954, beginning the 'golden age' of transit expansion in Toronto, which lasted into the 1980s (Levy, 2015). This expansion was enabled by provincial government funding of capital projects and operating subsidies. The demands of Metropolitan Toronto, however, put a strain on the public transit system as suburban interests forced it to expand to less dense areas without the use of zoned fares. Further, a period of disinvestment in public transit followed the 1987 recession (Levy, 2015). This culminated in 1995, when, under Michael Harris's Progressive Conservatives, the provincial government cancelled both capital and operational subsidies to the Toronto region.

Regional transportation planning in Toronto, however, has recently seen a period of reinvestment. Metrolinx, established by the Province of Ontario in 2006, allowed for a more comprehensive view of the transportation needs of the Greater Toronto Area. The agency released the region's first transportation plan, the Big Move, in 2008, which garnered a CAD$30 billion investment in rapid transit infrastructure for the region and produced nine transit projects (Metrolinx, 2018). Most recently its strategic plan for transit investment in the region, 2041 Regional Transportation Plan for the Greater Toronto and Hamilton Area, looks to future development.

Cycling infrastructure also makes up an important component of our transportation system. The City of Toronto has been slowly expanding the cycling network, as have nearby cities such as Ajax, Mississauga, Burlington, Brampton, Hamilton, and Whitby. The safety of vulnerable road users such as pedestrians and cyclists is also an increasing concern. The City of Toronto has recently adopted a Vision Zero Road Safety Plan that focuses on reducing collisions that result in death or serious injury, and which shifts focus to enhancing safety policies (City of Toronto, 2017c). The implementation of infrastructure, such as dedicated and protected bicycle lanes, is also being developed to ensure enhanced safety for all of those on Toronto's roads.

Healthcare

Toronto benefits from a strong universal healthcare system delivered through the Ontario Health Insurance Plan (OHIP), and which has been governed by the Provincial Ministry of Health since 1972. The universal healthcare system helps ensure quality of care for all its residents, regardless of income levels, and is a key contributor to overall livability in the region. The OECD rates Ontario 8.4/10 for health, placing it in the 78th percentile of global wellbeing. This ranking is based on life expectancy and age-adjusted mortality rates (OECD Regional Wellbeing, 2016). The coverage provided by OHIP has been enhanced in a number of ways. In

January 2018, the Ontario Liberal Party introduced OHIP+: Children and Youth Pharmacare. Under this program, everyone in Ontario under the age of 25 is eligible to receive prescription medication at no charge (Office of the Premier, 2018). This is in addition to the Trillium Drug Program, which allows people with high prescription costs and low household income to pay CAD$2 or less for each prescription (Province of Ontario, 2018).

Funding for healthcare is a key issue in the upcoming 2018 provincial election. Ontario's growing and aging population, along with relatively low funding per capita for healthcare by the province, is causing a shortage of hospital beds (Ontario Health Coalition, 2011). In Toronto, the municipal government provides nearly 25% of funding for the Toronto Public Health agency, which promotes healthy environments and communicable disease control, and prepares for clinic responses to emergency need for mass immunization (Toronto Public Health, 2016). Its staff members also advise the Toronto Board of Health on decisions related to public health policy. For example, the Board of Health approved three Supervised Injection Services in Toronto to combat the high number of overdose deaths brought on by fentanyl and to limit the spread of HIV and hepatitis C (Toronto Public Health, 2016).

In addition to health care provision, Toronto has a growing body of health researchers. The University Health Network (2017) has produced over 3,700 publications and is a leader in biomedical research. This is in addition to institutions such as the Wellesley Institute, which is a Toronto-based think tank that focuses on urban health.

Multiculturalism

Toronto is the most diverse city in the world (City of Toronto, 2017a). Thirty-nine percent of the Toronto region and 51% of the City of Toronto is foreign-born (Toronto Global, 2017). It has been suggested that over 90 languages and dialects are spoken in Toronto. The City of Toronto recognizes that diversity and inclusion are fundamental to the success of the city. It envisions Toronto's future as one where "multiculturalism is celebrated and cultural diversity supported" (City of Toronto, 2015). This diversity has been leveraged by Toronto Global, a multilevel regional partnership, in their response to Amazon's HQ2 Request for Proposal process (2017). In the proposal, they highlight Canada's immigration policy and Toronto's regional context as a means of "future-proofing" the employment base for the region (Toronto Global, 2017). Multiculturalist policy at the federal level has been embraced and expressed at the municipal and regional levels.

This does not negate the fact that multiculturalism is a contested term in the Canadian context. Multicultural policies have been criticized for encouraging the cultural consumption of dance, dress, and dining while failing to meaningfully address the dimensions of racial and social inequality present in Canadian society (Nakamura & Donnelly, 2017; Srivastava, 2007). Others have argued that multicultural policy focus on constructing new forms of citizenship for immigrants to Canada and, while imperfect, the policies have been a positive step forward in expanding Canadian identities (Kymlicka, 2010; Clarke, 2009). These challenges are especially evident given the often times inconsistent approach to implementing multicultural policies. Although implemented at higher levels of government, municipalities are not given an official mandate to implement multicultural policies—this accounts for varied policy responses at the municipal level (Fincher, Iveson, Leitner, & Preston, 2014).

In the Toronto context, each of these perspectives holds weight. While Toronto's governing structures see multiculturalism as a strength, they are also becoming more attentive to the structural racism experienced by people with diverse backgrounds. Difference is celebrated and commodified, and steps towards inclusion are taken by both activists and municipal government. For example, in the Toronto CMA, the population of self-identified black people increased by 10.15% between 2011 and 2016. In relation to this, the City of Toronto (2017a) has developed, along with stakeholders, the Toronto Action Plan to Confront Anti-Black Racism. This Action Plan is a five-year plan with 22 recommendations and 80 actions to address anti-black racism in five areas: child and youth development, health and community services, job and income supports, policing, and community engagement.

Culture

Toronto is home to a thriving arts and culture scene that helps make it a livable city. The City of Toronto has several strategic plans related to the arts. *The Creative Capital Gains* (City of Toronto, 2011) report presents recommendations and actions to strengthen the city's creative economy. *Making Space for Culture* (City of Toronto, 2014) builds on those recommendations as they relate to the cultural infrastructure of the city. The *Toronto Music Strategy* (City of Toronto, 2016b) guides the short- and long-term growth of Toronto's music sector, while *Spotlight on Toronto* (City of Toronto, 2017d) is a strategic action plan to strengthen the film, television, and digital media industries. Finally, the *King-Spadina Cultural Spaces Retention Study* (City of Toronto, 2017e) makes recommendations to retain important cultural spaces within one of Toronto's rapidly changing areas.

The City of Toronto itself boasts over 70 museums and art galleries, including the Royal Ontario Museum and the Art Gallery of Ontario. The Greater Toronto Area has nearly 60 additional museums. Additionally, Toronto has taken an innovative approach to its heritage, establishing a de-centralized Museum of Toronto, which hosts virtual and physical exhibits online and throughout the Greater Toronto Area. In addition, Toronto City Council has voted to create a museum of Toronto across from Nathan Phillips Square, in the Old City Hall building, whose plans are forthcoming (Rider, 2018).

Similarly, in Toronto, art is not confined to galleries. Like many North American cities, the City of Toronto also has a Percent for Public Art program that works with private developers to secure public art contributions during the development review process (City of Toronto, 2010). This helps to increase the quality of Toronto's public realm.

Toronto is also host to numerous annual festivals. The Toronto International Film Festival (TIFF) is one of the largest film festivals in the world, hosted throughout the city and within the TIFF Bell Lightbox Theatre. Each year, Toronto also hosts Hot Docs, the largest documentary film festival in North America. This festival draws an audience of more than 200,000 per year (Hot Docs, n.d.).

Arts festivals also draw large crowds to Toronto. The Luminato International Arts Festival was established in 2007 and is funded by the federal government as well as the province of Ontario and City of Toronto (Luminato Festival, n.d.). Nuit Blanche Toronto attracted more than a million people in 2016 and generated approximately CAD$43 million for Toronto (Nuit Blanche Toronto, n.d.).

This is in addition to the cultural festivals for which Toronto is known. The Toronto Caribbean Festival, known locally as Caribana, has been hosted by Toronto for over 50 years and had an economic impact of CAD$338 million in 2014 (Cheung & Baksh, 2017). The Pride Toronto festival contributed an estimated CAD$352 million to Ontario's GDP in 2017 and drew over 1.3 million attendees (Pride Toronto, 2017).

The Toronto region is well known for its live theatre. Not only in terms of the City of Toronto but also the region, ranging from the Shaw Festival at Niagara on the Lake to the Shakespeare Festival in Stratford. It is estimated that there are over 168 nonprofit theatre companies as well as a number of commercial operations. Toronto is considered to be the world's third-largest center for English-language theatre, behind only New York and London (Gardner, 2009).

For sports enthusiasts, Toronto is home to eight major sports franchises, four of which are in major North American leagues: Toronto Maple Leafs (hockey), Toronto Blue Jays (baseball), the Toronto Raptors (basketball), and the Toronto FC (soccer). All of these sports enjoy a very enthusiastic and loyal fan base.

Environment/Climate Change

Toronto is a green city. It has a vast greenspace network as well as ravines and an increasingly appealing waterfront. The Greater Toronto Area itself is surrounded by a Greenbelt. The Greenbelt was established in 2005 by the provincial government to contain the Greater Golden Horseshoe area and prevent urban sprawl. The Greenbelt contains more than 2 million acres of protected lands (Friends of the Greenbelt, n.d.). It protects valuable agricultural lands and provides water filtration, flood control, climate stabilization, wildlife habitat, and recreation space (Wilson, 2008). As one of the world's largest protected greenbelts, it is part of a crucial natural infrastructure for mitigating the effects of climate change.

As of May 2009, the City of Toronto is the first city in North America to have a green roof bylaw (City of Toronto, n.d.b). This aims to allow Toronto's buildings to mitigate their contribution to the urban heat-island effect. Further environmentally friendly building policies can be found in Toronto's Green Standard, a building emissions standard mandatory as of 2010 (City of Toronto, n.d.c).

In 2016, Toronto joined the ranks of 100 Resilient Cities through a grant by the Rockefeller Centre. The Chief Resilience Office is responsible for assessing Toronto's resilience, meaning the way it can best respond to physical, social, and economic shocks and stressors that may impact the city. Toronto's Resilience Strategy is forthcoming, though the City's concern with its environment has been one of long standing. Toronto and Region Conservation Authority (TRCA) has been tasked with flood control responsibilities since 1954, following the death of 81 people due to Hurricane Hazel (TRCA, n.d.). The TRCA has authority to acquire lands for recreation and conservation purposes. 18,000 hectares have been acquired in the Greater Toronto Area, and in the aftermath of Hurricane Hazel, municipal regulations prevent construction of new buildings on floodplains (TRCA, n.d.).

At the federal level, Canada is a party to the Paris Accord. The commitments made as a country are fulfilled at a provincial level by the Province of Ontario's Climate Change Action Plan. The Climate Change Action Plan (2016) focuses on the following action areas: transportation, buildings and homes, land-use planning, industry and business, collaboration with indigenous communities, research and development, government, agriculture, forests, and lands. At the municipal level, Toronto's TransformTO Climate Action Plan sets 2050 targets for greenhouse gas emissions and notes that since 1990 the city's emissions have lowered by 24% (City of Toronto, 2016a).

Greenspace

Greenspace has a positive impact on health outcomes, and contributes to the overall livability of a city. It has been found to improve the physical health, mental health, and wellbeing of urban residents (Toronto Public Health, 2015). Toronto residents benefit from the urban forest canopy that covers nearly 30% of the city, valued at CAD$7 billion (Alexander & McDonald, 2014). Toronto has a higher tree coverage rate than New York City, which has 24% coverage (City of New York, n.d.). Toronto has set a tree cover target of 40%, and is targeting private lands to increase the canopy (City of Toronto, 2013).

In addition to a strong and growing urban canopy, the Greater Toronto Area has a strong greenspace network. Toronto ranks 27/281 OECD metropolitan areas for greenspace and contains 1,298 square meters per 1 million residents. The City of Toronto contains 1,600 parks, covering approximately 13% of Toronto's overall land (Newman, 2015). Financing or land for greenspace in Toronto is secured by parkland dedication requirements for new developments, while private greenspace is required by the green roof bylaw. Both allow the city of Toronto to combat heat island effects associated with a lack of green infrastructure in urban areas.

In addition to being a city of trees, Toronto is also a city of ravines. In fact, Toronto has one of the largest ravine networks in the world (City of Toronto, 2017b). The ravines provide parkland and hiking trails to Toronto visitors and residents and are home to important waterways such as the Humber River. Through the Ravine Strategy, Toronto seeks to increase access to these greenspaces while also protecting and managing them more effectively. The city's connection to the waterfront was the subject of a revitalization plan written by David Crombie (1992), former mayor of Toronto. Titled *Regeneration: Toronto's waterfront and the sustainable city* (1992), it advocated for increased connection to the waterfront as well as cycling and walking pathways connecting Toronto to other waterfront cities, such as Hamilton to the west. The waterfront is currently being improved by Waterfront Toronto, a multi-partner organization that shapes the development of the previously industrial shore of Lake Ontario.

Crime

Toronto is recognized as a highly safe global city. It was ranked the fourth safest city globally by the Economist Intelligence Unit (2017b). This ranking considers digital security, health security, infrastructure security, and personal security. According to Statistics Canada, the severity of crime in Toronto is on a downward trajectory as incidences of violent crime are less and less common. Further, Toronto's Crime Severity has consistently ranked below the Canadian average (Statistics Canada, 2017c).

Summary

The above themes and discussion attempt to document some of the components that make Toronto both a desirable and livable city/region. Different components or themes resonate with different people, but collectively, they make the Toronto region a very attractive place to live, work, play, and raise a family.

Responses to Toronto as a Livable City

There are several significant initiatives recently supporting Toronto's reputation as a livable city. These include the selection of Toronto as a venue for major international events and as the location for important investment by several high-profile companies. These initiatives by external organizations reflect the views of external entities that Toronto is a positive place and that they are looking to consider making significant investments in the region.

Despite the fact that Toronto failed in its bid to host the Olympics in 2008, it did succeed in bringing the Pan Am Games to the city in 2015. It is important to note that the venues for the events were not constrained to the city of Toronto but were located throughout the Toronto region. These games were an important international public relations success for Toronto. Their legacy included the construction or renovation of 27 venues, including 10 new sport facilities, which spanned all 16 municipalities in the region. Toronto followed up this success by hosting the 2017 Invictus Games.

There has also been significant progress in enhancing the development of the Toronto waterfront. As with many waterfront cities, industries focused in this area have increasingly become obsolete, leading to derelict and underutilized properties in the former port lands. To address this issue, Waterfront Toronto was created in 2001 to facilitate planning and development for the Toronto waterfront. This tri-level government initiative—federal, provincial, and local—called for each level of government to commit CAD$500 million to the project. Hence the Waterfront Toronto organization was given a 25-year mandate to transform 800 hectares (2,000 acres) of brownfield lands on the waterfront into beautiful, sustainable, mixed-use communities with dynamic public spaces (Waterfront Toronto, 2018). Their mission is to develop a leading-edge model for city-building to serve as an inspiration for global cities this century.

The approach undertaken by Waterfront Toronto has been to develop the public realm as a way of creating value for the properties it controls. These lands would then be put out for tender with a set of specifications or requirements for bidders. In this way they could maximize the values that they would receive for their properties while ensuring their mandate is met. Their international request for proposals (RFP) in regards to a partner for one of their recently available properties, Quayside, specified their mandate. Respondents should specify in their proposals how they planned to "create a globally significant community, showcasing advanced technologies, new building materials and innovative funding strategies that demonstrate pragmatic solutions toward climate-positive urban development" (Waterfront Toronto, 2018).

In 2017, Waterfront Toronto announced that they had selected Google Sidewalk as their partner in the venture, now referred to as Sidewalk Toronto. Its objective is to develop a new model for 21st-century urban living by making use of new digital technology and innovative urban design to build people-centered neighborhoods that provide affordability, sustainability, mobility, and economic opportunity.

This focus on innovative approaches to future planning in Toronto is also seen in other initiatives. The City of Toronto and the Toronto Region Board of Trade have formed a joint Smart City Working Group, which had the initial objective of gaining a comprehensive knowledge of the Smart City movement. This working group then focused on developing a position paper for the city regarding the undertaking of Smart City initiatives. As the Smart City concept has taken root on a broad international basis, Toronto is considered now to be consistent with other major cities that have embraced this concept. It has also had repercussions nationally. Partly in response to the work done by Toronto's Working Group, the federal government has become more actively involved in the Smart City movement. They have initiated a competition for the best Smart City plans initiative by both large and midsized cities. Toronto's aforementioned working group developed and submitted the bid for the city of Toronto, although the outcome of this competition is still outstanding.

Also still outstanding is the result of the international competition for Amazon's new HQ2 headquarters. When this process was launched with great fanfare to overwhelming public interest, 238 cities submitted bids. To Toronto's credit, it was selected as one of the final 20 bidding contenders. It is interesting to note that the Toronto bid did not include any direct financial incentives from government. The strength of the Toronto bid is the availability of a highly educated workforce and the financial benefits resulting from its health care system. The existence of its provincial health care system reduces the cost of employee health care benefits that would be provided for their employees.

In addition to individuals and households finding the Toronto city/region, a desirable place to live, it is clear that a number of organizations and companies have identified the city/region as an important place to locate an activity or business.

Areas Requiring Improvement

Despite these positive developments, there are several aspects of the Toronto region that require improvement to address its future as a livable city. As with all cities and urban regions, Toronto must strive to address these concerns, specifically in the areas of transit, housing affordability, and income disparity. It is also important to recognize that these issues cannot be addressed solely by local governments. Rather, they need support, and most importantly, financing, from the provincial and federal levels of government to address these issues.

In terms of transit, Toronto was once viewed as an excellent transit-based city with high ridership and good quality of service. However, as the city has grown over the last 30 years, both in terms of population and in urban expansion, investment in public transit has not kept pace. There are several reasons for this lack of investment. Prior to the creation of Metrolinx, an umbrella agency responsible for coordinating transit investments across the region had not yet been formed, making planning more difficult. The other significant factor is that there has not been a consistent stable funding program for transit from the senior levels of government. Canada, in fact, is the only G7 nation that does not have a sustainable program for funding transit investments it its urban areas. As a result of this shortfall, there has been a deficit in transit investment. A number of areas in the city and region are poorly served by public transit, including a number of the older suburbs in the city of Toronto itself, resulting in transit inequity (Hertel, Keil, & Collens, 2015).

A second area for improvement is the provision of affordable housing. This includes the entire spectrum of housing: affordable social housing, affordable rental housing, and affordable ownership housing. These are matters of longstanding concern. The federal and provincial governments curtailed their support for social housing starting in the 1990s. In 1992, the federal government terminated its funding for new social and nonprofit housing units. This was followed in 1998 by the provincial governments' *local services realignment policy*, which shifted the financial responsibility for social housing to local governments (Schwartz, 2009). Over the years, these policy shifts have led to the reduction in building new social and affordable housing units as well as the lack of funds available to repair the existing units. The long-term impact of these policies has been both the deterioration in the quality of social housing units and the lengthening of waiting lists for available units.

There has also been a shift in the market for rental units. There have been very few purpose-built rental units in recent years, as these developments compete for the same sites as condominiums. The condo market has been extremely robust and has displaced the development of units for rental purposes. This has led to condos becoming a significant component of the rental market. Especially in terms of ground associated market units, there has been significant price appreciation in recent years. This has been due partly to supply restrictions resulting from the enactment of a stringent regulatory containment plan, the lack of servicing in some areas, and the increase of exaction policies (Clayton & Amborski, 2017).

Significant recent increases in housing costs have exacerbated the lack of affordable housing over the last few years. This is a significant concern, as studies have suggested that the want of affordable housing has had impacts on both the GDP of cities and the ability to close the income disparity in urban areas (Florida, 2015; Shoag & Ganong, 2016). Housing affordability and problems in funding transit, therefore, reflect the growing income disparity between high-income and low-income neighborhoods, also a concern for Toronto's future as a livable city moving forward. When comparing the average income of census tracks over the last several census periods, the increasing polarization and disparity in these neighborhoods is clearly growing in Toronto. After the last census, the United Way extended this analysis to the broader Toronto region and found that the same pattern exists (United Way Toronto & York Region and Neighborhood Change Research Partnership, 2017).

As indicated earlier, these problems of transit funding, housing affordability, and income disparity between neighborhoods cannot be the sole purview of urban jurisdictions. These jurisdictions, other than Toronto, have very limited taxing or revenue-raising powers. Consequently, there is the need for appropriate policies and funding from the senior levels of government at the federal and provincial levels.

Access to this aid has been sporadic, as seen with the recent but not sustainable, ad hoc, funding for transit in urban areas by the federal and provincial governments. There has been more substantial progress in the question of housing affordability, as the federal Liberal government has recently established a National Housing Strategy. This reflects for the first time in many years an active interest in housing policy at a broad level. With respect to income (re)distribution, this needs to be funded from a progressive tax base. As municipalities in Ontario (excepting Toronto) only have taxing authority in relation to property tax, a regressive tax base, there is also a need for senior levels of government to address the issue in regard to both policy and funding.

Conclusion

Toronto is a livable city/region. This is clear by the growth rate, including immigration, as many people are choosing to make Toronto their home. It is also clear by the fact that many firms and organizations are choosing Toronto for their events and firms. The results are clear. As a livable city, Toronto benefits from employment, economic activity, and GDP growth.

It is important to recognize that it is the entire region, centered on Toronto, which has attracted this growth. When considering the city's appeal, it is necessary to better understand the changing government organization and structure of Toronto as a city and as a region. In the early years, the city of Toronto (or Metropolitan Toronto) was responsible for driving this growth. More recently, however, it has been the areas surrounding the city of Toronto that have played the largest role.

Toronto's reputation of livability is supported both by external analysis and by its performance on specific metrics in comparison with other cities, both in Canada and internationally. These include Toronto's educated workforce, greenspace, and low crime rate. As well, local governments have provided the basic conditions for livable communities through good governance, good planning, and in ensuring conditions are met for fiscal health. This approach is supported by legislation set out by the provincial government.

Despite this livability, the city/region, as with all governments, has issues to be addressed. In the case of Toronto, these include the need for investments in transit and affordable housing, as well as measures to address growing income inequities. As seen, addressing these issues goes beyond the scope of local government. The leadership, energy, and innovation of local government will need support from the senior levels of government in terms of finance and policy in order to move forward.

As the Toronto region is a main driver of GDP in the national economy, and given the number of initiatives and research being put forward by policymakers invested in this question, it is likely that joint efforts will be made to address these issues. This will ensure that Toronto's profile as a global and livable area will be enhanced.

Acknowledgments

The author thanks Heather Metcalfe for her assistance in preparing this chapter.

References

Alexander, C., & McDonald, C. (2014). *Urban forests: The value of trees in the city of Toronto*. TD Economics. Retrieved from www.td.com/document/PDF/economics/special/UrbanForests.pdf.

Altus Group Economic Consulting. (2018). *Government charges and fees on new homes in the greater Toronto area*. Toronto: Altus Group Economic Consulting. Retrieved from www.bildgta.ca/Assets/Bild/EducationalLibrary/BILD_Report.pdf.

Cheung, M., & Baksh, N. (2017, May 31). 50 years later, the beat goes on for the city's Caribbean festival. *CBC News.* Retrieved from www.cbc.ca/news/canada/toronto/caribana-caribbean-festival-carnival-funding-toronto-1.4136632.

City of New York. (n.d.). *About MillionTreesNYC.* Retrieved from www.milliontreesnyc.org/html/about/urban_forest_facts.shtml.

City of Toronto. (n.d.a). *Official plan review.* Retrieved from www.toronto.ca/city-government/planning-development/official-plan-guidelines/official-plan/official-plan-review/.

City of Toronto. (n.d.b). *City of Toronto green roof bylaw.* Retrieved from www.toronto.ca/city-government/planning-development/official-plan-guidelines/green-roofs/green-roof-bylaw/.

City of Toronto. (n.d.c). *Toronto green standard: Overview.* Retrieved from www.toronto.ca/city-government/planning-development/official-plan-guidelines/toronto-green-standard/toronto-green-standard-overview/.

City of Toronto. (2010). *Toronto urban design: Percent for public art program guidelines.* Retrieved from www.toronto.ca/wp-content/uploads/2017/11/9090-aoda-public-art-guidelines.pdf.

City of Toronto. (2011). *Creative capital gains: An action plan for Toronto.* Retrieved from www.toronto.ca/legdocs/mmis/2011/ed/bgrd/backgroundfile-37775.pdf.

City of Toronto. (2013). *Every tree counts: A portrait of Toronto's urban forest.* Retrieved from www.toronto.ca/wp-content/uploads/2017/12/92de-every-tree-counts-portrait-of-torontos-urban-forest.pdf.

City of Toronto. (2014). *Making space for culture: Community consultation summaries.* Retrieved from www.toronto.ca/legdocs/mmis/2014/ed/bgrd/backgroundfile-69273.pdf.

City of Toronto. (2015). *Toronto official plan.* Retrieved from www.toronto.ca/wp-content/uploads/2017/11/8fd8-cp-official-plan-chapter-1.pdf.

City of Toronto. (2016a). *TransformTO: Climate action for a healthy equitable, and prosperous Toronto—Report #1.* Retrieved from www.toronto.ca/wp-content/uploads/2017/10/8ec4-TransformTO-Climate-Action-for-a-Healthy-Equitable-and-Prosperous-Toronto-Report-1-November-2016.pdf.

City of Toronto. (2016b). *Toronto music strategy: Supporting and growing the city's music sector.* Retrieved from www.toronto.ca/legdocs/mmis/2016/ed/bgrd/backgroundfile-90615.pdf.

City of Toronto. (2017a). *Toronto action plan to confront anti-black racism.* Retrieved from www.toronto.ca/legdocs/mmis/2017/ex/bgrd/backgroundfile-109127.pdf.

City of Toronto. (2017b). *Toronto ravine strategy.* Retrieved from www.toronto.ca/wp-content/uploads/2017/10/9183-TorontoRavineStrategy.pdf.

City of Toronto. (2017c). *Vision zero: Toronto's road safety plan.* Retrieved from www.toronto.ca/wp-content/uploads/2017/11/990f-2017-Vision-Zero-Road-Safety-Plan_June1.pdf.

City of Toronto. (2017d). *Spotlight on Toronto: A strategic action plan for the film, television and digital media industry.* Retrieved from www.toronto.ca/wp-content/uploads/2017/11/972e-spotlight-on-toronto-film-strategy-2017.pdf.

City of Toronto. (2017e). *King-Spadina cultural spaces retention study: Strengthening the creative economy in Toronto's downtown core.* Retrieved from www.toronto.ca/wp-content/uploads/2018/01/8e62-King-Spadina_Cultural_Spaces_Retention_Study_2017_.pdf.

Clarke, G. E. (2009). Multiculturalism and its (usual) discontents. *Canada Watch,* Fall, 24–25. Retrieved from www.yorku.ca/robarts/projects/canada-watch/multicult/pdfs/Clarke.pdf.

Clayton, F., & Amborski, D. (2017). *Countering myths about rising ground-related housing prices in the GTA: new supply really matters.* Toronto: Ryerson University, Centre for Urban Research and Land Development.

Crombie, D. (1992). *Regeneration: Toronto's waterfront and the sustainable city: Final report.* Toronto: Royal Commission on the Future of the Toronto Waterfront.

Economist Intelligence Unit. (2017a). *The global livability report 2017: A free overview.* Retrieved from http://pages.eiu.com/rs/753-RIQ-438/images/Livability_Free_Summary_2017.pdf.

Economist Intelligence Unit. (2017b). *Safe cities index 2017.* Retrieved from https://dkf1ato8y5dsg.cloudfront.net/uploads/5/82/safe-cities-index-eng-web.pdf.

Fincher R., Iveson K., Leitner H., & Preston V. (2014). Planning in the multicultural city: Celebrating diversity or reinforcing difference? *Progress in Planning, 92,* 1–55.

Florida, R. (2015, May 18). *The urban housing crunch cost the US economy about $1.6 trillion per year.* Retrieved from http://citylab.com.

Friends of the Greenbelt Foundation. (n.d.). *About the greenbelt.* Retrieved from www.greenbelt.ca/about_the_greenbelt.

Gardner, D. (2009). *English-language theatre.* Retrieved from www.thecanadianencyclopedia.ca/en/article/english-language-theatre/.

Hertel, S., Keil, R., & Collens, M. (2015, March 9). *Switching tracks: Towards transit equity in the greater Toronto and Hamilton area.* Retrieved from https://city.apps01.yorku.ca/wp-content/uploads/2015/04/Switching-Tracks_9-March-2015.pdf.

Hodge, G., & Gordon, D. (2013). *Planning Canadian communities* (6th ed.). Toronto: Nelson Publishing.

Hot Docs. (n.d.). *Hot Docs Festival.* Retrieved from www.hotdocs.ca/p/hot-docs-festival?ep=1.

KPMG LLP. (2016). *Focus on tax: KPMG's guide to international tax competitiveness, 2016.* Retrieved from www.competitivealternatives.com/reports/compalt2016_report_tax_en.pdf.

Kymlicka, W. (2010). The rise and fall of multiculturalism? New debates on inclusion and accommodation in diverse societies. *International Social Science Journal, 61*(199), 97–112.

Levy, E. (2015). *Rapid transit in Toronto: A century of plans, projects, politics, and paralysis.* Toronto: BA Consulting Group Ltd.

Luminato Festival. (n.d.). *History.* Retrieved from https://luminatofestival.com/About.

Metrolinx. (2018). *2041 regional transportation plan for the greater Toronto and Hamilton area.* Retrieved from www.metrolinx.com.

Nakamura, Y., & Donnelly, P. (2017). Interculturalism and physical cultural diversity in the greater Toronto area. *Social Inclusion, 5*(2), 111–119.

Newman, A. (2015, May 16). Toronto's green spaces a breath of fresh air. *Toronto Star.* Retrieved from www.thestar.com.

Nuit Blanche Toronto. (n.d.). *Event history.* Retrieved from https://nbto.com/about/event-history.html.

OECD Regional Well-being. (2016, June). *Ontario OECD regional well-being.* Retrieved from www.oecdregionalwellbeing.org/CA35.html.

Office of the Premier. (2018, January 2). *Newsroom: Free prescription medications for everyone under 25.* Toronto: Province of Ontario. Retrieved from https://news.ontario.ca/opo/en/2018/01/free-prescription-medications-for-everyone-under-25.html.

Ontario Health Coalition. (2011, July 28). *Hospital overload: Backgrounder on Ontario's hospital bed shortage.* Retrieved from www.ontariohealthcoalition.ca/wp-content/uploads/backgrounder-on-hospital-bed-shortage.pdf.

Pride Toronto. (2017). *Economic impacts report 2017.* Retrieved from pridetoronto.com.

Project for Public Space. (1997). *The role of transit in creating livable metropolitan communities.* Washington, D.C.: Transportation Research Board. Retrieved from http://onlinepubs.trb.org/onlinepubs/tcrp/tcrp_rpt_22-a.pdf.

Province of Ontario. (2016). *Ontario's five year climate change action plan 2016–2020.* Retrieved from www.applications.ene.gov.on.ca/ccap/products/CCAP_ENGLISH.pdf.

Province of Ontario. (2018, February 5). *Get help with high prescription drug costs.* Retrieved from www.ontario.ca/page/get-help-high-prescription-drug-costs.

Rider, D. (2018, February 1). Old City Hall set to become home to a museum of Toronto. *Toronto Star.*

Sancton, A. (2000). Amalgamations, service realignment, and property taxes: Did the Harris Government have a plan for Ontario's municipalities? *Canadian Journal of Regional Science, 23*(1), 135–156.

Schwartz, H. (2009). Toronto ten years after amalgamation. *Canadian Journal of Regional Science, 32*(3), 483–494.

Shearmur, R. (2018). The millennial urban space economy: Dissolving workplaces and the de-localization of economic value-creation. In M. Moos, D. Pfeiffer, & T. Vinodrai (Eds.), *The millennial city: Trends, implications, and prospects for urban planning and policy* (pp. 65–80). New York: Routledge.

Shoag, D., & Ganong, P. (2016, August 4). *Why has regional income convergence declined?* Retrieved May 1, 2018, from www.brookings.edu/wp-content/uploads/2016/08/wp21_ganong-shoag_final.pdfBrookings Institution.

Srivastava, S. (2007). Troubles with anti-racist multiculturalism: The challenges of anti-racist and feminist activism. In S. Hier & B. S. Bolaria (Eds.), *Race and racism in 21st century Canada: Continuity, complexity, and change* (pp. 291–311). Peterborough: Broadview Press.

Statistics Canada. (2017a). *Labour force survey estimates (LFS), employment by census metropolitan area based on 2011 census boundaries and North American Industry Classification System (NAICS), annual (persons x 1,000).* Labour Force Survey no. 3701. Ottawa: StatsCan. Retrieved from www.statcan.gc.ca/.

Statistics Canada. (2017b). *Gross domestic product at basic prices, by census metropolitan area, 2009–2013.* Ottawa: StatsCan. Retrieved from www.statcan.gc.ca/.

Statistics Canada. (2017c). *Uniform crime reporting survey—3302.* Ottawa: StatsCan. Retrieved from www.statcan.gc.ca/.

Toronto Foundation. (2018). *Toronto's vital signs report 2017/18.* Retrieved from https://toronto-foundation.ca/wp-content/uploads/2018/01/TF-VS-web-FINAL-4MB.pdf.

Toronto Global. (2017). *Toronto region response to Amazon HQ2 RFP.* Retrieved from https://torontoglobal.ca/amazon/.

Toronto Public Health. (2015). *Green city: Why nature matters to health—An evidence review.* Retrieved from www.toronto.ca/legdocs/mmis/2015/hl/bgrd/backgroundfile-83421.pdf.

Toronto Public Health. (2016). *A healthy city for all: 2016 annual report.* Retrieved from www.toronto.ca/wp-content/uploads/2017/09/96e3-toronto-public-health-annual-report-2016.pdf.

Toronto Region Board of Trade. (2015). *Toronto as a global city: Prosperity scorecard 2015*. Toronto: Toronto Region Board of Trade. Retrieved from www.bot.com/portals/0/unsecure/advocacy/scorecard_2015.pdf.

Toronto Regional Conservation Authority. (n.d.). *History*. Retrieved from https://trca.ca/conservation/flood-risk-management/history/.

United Way Toronto & York Region and Neighborhood Change Research Partnership. (2017). *The opportunity equation in the greater Toronto area: An update on neighbourhood income inequality and polarization*. Toronto: Factor-Inwentash Faculty of Social Work, University of Toronto.

University Health Network. (2017). *2017 annual research report*. Toronto: University Health Network. Retrieved from www.uhnresearch.ca/service/annual-research-report.

Waterfront Toronto. (2018). *Quayside*. Retrieved from https://waterfrontoronto.ca/nbe/portal/waterfront/Home/waterfronthome/projects/quayside.

Wilson, S. (2008). *Ontario's wealth, Canada's future: Appreciating the value of the greenbelt's econ-services*. Vancouver: David Suzuki Foundation.

Chapter 9

VIENNA—KEEPING IT LIVABLE: HOW URBAN PLANNING INSTRUMENTS CONTRIBUTE TO A CITY'S QUALITY OF LIFE

Katharina Soepper-Quendler

Running a livable city is rewarding and challenging at the same time. This chapter discusses how urban planning contributes to the quality of life in cities using the example of Vienna, Austria.

Vienna's Status Quo

Vienna has been voted the city with the highest quality of life in the "Mercer Quality of Living Survey" eight times in a row from 2009 (Stadt Wien, 2017). Moreover, the city ranks high in tourism and provides comprehensive services for its inhabitants allowing a high quality of life in the city. Therefore, Vienna provides a variety of input for a discussion on livable cities. Reasons that make the city livable are extensive green space, such as the River Danube and its local recreation areas; moreover, affordable housing provided by the public, comprehensive social services, and much more. The following gives a short introduction into Vienna's services and facilities.

Vienna has 1.8 million inhabitants and is a dense city with a number of green spaces. Almost 50% of Vienna's area is green (Vienna City Administration, 2016). Keeping the density of new building structures high allows for maintaining the large number of parks, greeneries, rivers, etc., in Vienna. Vienna's social housing stock (including nonprofit) is around 400,000 dwellings, which are spread out all over the city (Vienna City Administration, 2016). The flats are in the possession of the city of Vienna or financial support for the construction of affordable housing is awarded by the city in accordance with a list of criteria. Providing good-quality social housing in such a number makes living affordable for people moving to and already living in Vienna. The wide distribution of social housing in each of the Viennese districts makes the city population well mixed and aids in keeping social tensions low (Vienna City Administration, 2016).

Vienna's public transport system is highly developed, very affordable (annual ticket: €365), and laid out all over the city. This provides an easy and cheap way to get around, thus reducing the necessity of using a car (Vienna City Administration, 2016). The excellent drinking water quality and its reliable water pipe system is another asset in Vienna's quality of life. It starts in a mountain area outside Vienna and transports the natural spring water right into each household (Vienna City Administration, 2016). Substantial investments are made in the technical infrastructure on a regular basis to provide reliable services for a metropolis of almost 2 million inhabitants. The waste disposal structures of the city, including wastewater purification, waste treatment, waste separation, and cogeneration, i.e., combined waste incineration and heat generation, are considered models of good practice and are followed by many other cities (Vienna City Administration, 2016). Moreover, Vienna's living quality emerges by its cultural and leisure offerings, social cohesion and personal safety, free-of-charge educational institutions, healthcare facilities as well as ecological assets (Vienna City Administration, 2014).

The aim of the city of Vienna is being and staying livable. Current challenges in the city development of Vienna are various. Global trends as well as local developments affect the city. Ongoing globalization, as well as the rapid development of new technologies, brings a new spin into how the city works and how its inhabitants use the urban fabric. On a local level, the fast growth of Vienna's population (approx. 250,000 new inhabitants during the next two decades) (Vienna City Administration, 2014) will make the city younger, more diverse, and more vibrant. All these changes bring about the current key topics for strategic urban development: growth, financing, quality of life, resources, social responsibility, and development of the Viennese metropolitan area.

Even though considerable achievements have been made, staying on top requires continuous effort: administration works together with city politics on strategies to keep Vienna livable. Therefore, various strategies and plans have been produced during recent years that aim at high quality of life, e.g., the *Smart City Wien Framework Strategy* (Vienna City Administration, 2016). This chapter focuses on another Viennese urban planning strategy, the *STEP 2025—Urban Development Plan Vienna* (STEP 2025), and illustrates what urban planning can—and has to—contribute to a livable city.

Measures from the current strategic concept are discussed below. Beforehand, the latest results of Vienna's own study on the quality of life in the city will be briefly presented. The study has provided a good empirical basis on the subject for several years and adds to the external rankings cited above.

Vienna's Own Measures and Statistics

The city of Vienna grounds its work on livability on its own periodic survey, *Quality of Life in Vienna*, which was compiled based on the study, *Basic Research on Social Science II*. In 2013, the survey was undertaken for the fourth time after 1995, 2003, and 2008. Such metrics, which are based on a solid foundation, provide a useful overview of how inhabitants experience the quality of life. The study provides numbers for all city districts and consists of 140 questions. Approximately 8,400 Viennese people aged 15 and over were interviewed by telephone starting in the autumn of 2012. This is a sample of roughly 1% of Viennese households, is representative of the area, and shows a unique monitoring project compared on an international level. Questions were asked concerning the following topics: housing, work, family, and satisfaction with public services. Viennese city planning uses the results of the study to define goals and strategies for the city's development (Stadtentwicklung Wien, 2016).

The results of the study are of particular interest because of their exact numbers and the information about each district and respective quarters. The number of respondents in all 91 districts is at least 50. This urban area typology makes it possible to work out small-scale differences between districts and quarters. Hereby, a more differentiated picture can be worked out, rather than averaging often very heterogeneous districts (Stadtentwicklung Wien, 2016, p. 7).

The study defines quality of life by 13 indicators regarding the living environment. Each indicator shows satisfaction with:

- General: (1) the neighborhood in general, (2) prestige of the neighborhood, (3) safety in the neighborhood, (4) people living in the neighborhood
- Infrastructure: (5) connection to public transport, (6) proximity to health facilities, (7) shopping facilities, (8) proximity to green spaces, (9) offers for sporting activity
- Environment: (10) air quality, (11) traffic noise
- Housing: (12) overall living quality, (13) quiet location of accommodation.

(Stadtentwicklung Wien, 2016, p. 18)

First, a few general results of the survey, which are valid for the entire city, will be presented. Afterwards, three indicators are examined in detail for clarity and later compared with the existing strategies and measures of the city of Vienna (Stadtentwicklung Wien, 2016, p. 18):

- When asked about their overall satisfaction with the residential area, 93% responded that they liked living in their residential area, and 62% liked it very much.
- 79% of respondents were satisfied or very satisfied with the people in their neighborhood. Questioned about satisfaction with the safety of the residential area, 70% agreed that they feel safe, and 72% were satisfied with the reputation of the residential area.
- The infrastructure receives a very high level of satisfaction. Between 84% and 90% of respondents were satisfied with the connection to public transport and the proximity of green spaces.

Regarding the objectives of the spatial planning concepts, which will be discussed later on, this chapter will focus on the following results (indicators) of the *Quality of Life in Vienna* survey: overall satisfaction with the neighborhood, connection to public transport, and proximity to green spaces.

Overall Satisfaction with the Neighborhood

As described above, 62% of the Viennese people are very happy to live in their own residential area. However, a closer look reveals differences between individual districts: satisfaction varies between 30% and 90% in different districts. For urban planning, these results emphasize areas with a pronounced need for improvement versus areas that have already developed successfully (Stadtentwicklung Wien, 2016, p. 20).

Connection to Public Transport

The level of satisfaction with regard to connection to public transport is already very high. For example, 80% of the residents surveyed in 75 of the 91 districts are satisfied with public transport services. However, lower satisfaction is found in a few suburban districts. (Stadtentwicklung Wien, 2016, p. 24) This reflects the advanced state of development of public transport in most areas, and indicates where further improvement should be made. In areas with already high satisfaction, it is important to keep up this high level, particularly with an increasing population in the inner districts. Further expansion and improvement in the public transport network can further increase satisfaction.

Proximity to Green Spaces

In terms of satisfaction with the proximity to green spaces within Vienna, a very differentiated picture emerges, with large differences between different districts. In summary, satisfaction with the availability of green spaces decreases in more densely built-up areas. (Stadtentwicklung Wien, 2016, p. 26) This provides a good statistical basis for further development of urban green spaces that responds to these differences and helps tailor solutions to the different situations. This will be described in more detail below using a current Viennese concept for illustration.

Vienna's Strategies and Goals

Current strategies, such as the *Smart City Wien Framework Strategy* and the *Urban Development Plan Vienna (STEP 2025)*, provide urban planning instruments for keeping the city livable while dealing with challenges like population growth, lower financial resources, and restrictions with respect to natural resource consumption, etc. This section briefly summarizes the overall goals of the *Smart City Wien Framework Strategy* and goes into more detail regarding the more distinctive measures described by the *Urban Development Plan Vienna*.

The key objective for 2050 in the *Smart City Wien Framework Strategy* is the best quality of life for all inhabitants of Vienna while minimizing the consumption of resources, which shall be realized through comprehensive innovation. The goals of resources, innovation, and quality of life are considered equally important. Vienna also emphasizes the social component while pursuing the overall goals of innovation and reduction of resource consumption by supporting technical and social innovation, which allows high quality of life for each inhabitant of the city (Vienna City Administration, 2016, p. 29). The city of Vienna is convinced that high quality of life can only be reached in a socially balanced way (Vienna City Administration, 2016, p. 30). On this note, the *Smart City Wien Framework Strategy* states an ambitious objective:

> Vienna maintains its quality of life at the current superlative level and continues to focus on social inclusion on its policy design: as a result, Vienna in 2050 is the city with the highest quality of life and life satisfaction in Europe.
>
> (Vienna City Administration, 2016, p. 36)

Looking at the quality of life goal in detail shows the focus on social inclusion, health, and environment (Vienna City Administration, 2016, p. 37). *Smart City Wien Framework Strategy* is an approach with overarching goals and precedes all strategic policies throughout Vienna.

The *Urban Development Plan Vienna* aims at a true urban spirit, and its topics range from the further development of the existing city as well as questions related to land mobilization and business location policy, to networking within the metropolitan region, the planning of open space, and the transport system. Following the overall goals and political aims, the *Urban Development Plan Vienna* lists a number of next steps and further projects. (Vienna City Administration,

2014). In the following, the three indicators of the *Vienna Quality of Life Survey* presented above are taken up again and the corresponding measures formulated in the *Urban Development Plan Vienna* are presented.

Overall Satisfaction with Neighborhood

The *Urban Development Plan Vienna* aims at high-quality urbanity for all parts of the city, i.e., the existing city as well as newly developed areas. This is pursued first of all by planning quarters contiguously instead of on a plot-to-plot basis. Moreover, the strategy follows mixed-use approaches by building urban structures that are used by different inhabitants in very different ways. Functions of the urban quarters should include compact building structures in a high-quality density which are used by a different mix of functions: living, working, leisure, shopping, etc.; this allows for low energy and land consumption. Quarters will be built to be walkable and bicycle-friendly (see below) and include necessary retail facilities as well as high-quality infrastructure. Infrastructure (green, transport, social, etc.) will be considered in the design of newly developed quarters or added where necessary in existing quarters. For example, new green infrastructure will be commensurate with the demand of the new inhabitants, while existing green spaces must be preserved and improved (see below). Ground floor zones and the public space are of particular importance for livable quarters, not only for flourishing supply facilities in the ground floors, but also for the establishment of an attractive city of short distances (Vienna City Administration, 2014, pp. 48, 49, 54).

Further strategies have already been and will further be laid out following the goal of vivid and attractive urban spaces. The city of Vienna will partner with project developers and other private partners to reach the goals—even in times of restricted public funding. For these collaborations, new regulations and laws have been established that aim for fair cost sharing ("agreements for urban development") (Vienna City Administration, 2014, p. 52). Moreover, the further development of the city can and will not be executed without the participation of its inhabitants (Vienna City Administration, 2014, p. 54). Therefore, information and participation will be intensified, following the newly established *Master Plan for Participatory Urban Development* (Magistrat der Stadt Wien, 2016). Following the Viennese tradition of affordable housing, the city continues to invest in the construction of social housing and financially supports low-income households by providing affordable and attractive options (Vienna City Administration, 2014, p. 21). This housing segment will be mixed with other housing stock to build quarters in a condensed diversity. By mixing municipal, subsidized, and free market housing, segregation shall be prevented. Instead, vibrant quarters with a good social mix shall foster further urban growth (Vienna City Administration, 2014, p. 9).

The objectives, instruments, and plans mentioned above are a useful starting point for processing the results and requirements resulting from the *Vienna Quality of Life Survey*. The needs that have become apparent in the individual districts can be addressed with the appropriate measures outlined in the *Urban Development Plan Vienna*. Particularly in areas of low satisfaction, the goal is to implement comprehensive steps to achieve a more livable neighborhood.

Connection to Public Transport

Vienna already starts from a very good modal split share: trips in Vienna are traveled by foot (28%), by bike (6%), by car (27%), and by public transport (39%). The 2025 goal is a modal split of 80–20, meaning 20% of trips made by car and 80% by foot, bike, or public transport. In order to achieve such numbers, the city of Vienna continuously improves the connection to public transport for its inhabitants, inter alia, by optimization and upgrade of public transport as well as strengthening eco-friendly modes of transport. This aims at ultimately making car use less attractive than public transport, cycling, or walking (Vienna City Administration, 2014, pp. 106, 107). Modernization and maintenance of the network as well as the vehicles takes place for each mode of public transportation. Particular impact is expected from the adaption and upgrade of the S-Bahn (urban railway) network, which will better resemble the attractive offer of the metro line in terms of shorter intervals, better equipment, and useful routes. Tram and bus routes will be accelerated by moving them onto separate lanes as well as granting them preferred treatment at traffic lights. With regard to the growing city, new lines will be established. Beside the improvements on the network in general, one focus will be the transport stops and big interchange hubs, making them more comfortable, safe, and secure as well as putting them in the right spot (Vienna City Administration, 2014, pp. 106, 107). Walking and cycling in Vienna shall become even more attractive, as these modes of transport are important on their own and they also provide access to public transport. Therefore, the walking as well as cycling network will be enhanced by including routes that are easy to find, tightly knit, and spacious. They will get preferred traffic light circuits, will be easy to ride, and include attractive surroundings and amenities (trees, areas to rest, bike garages, etc.) (Vienna City Administration, 2014, p. 108).

As the above-mentioned survey has shown, overall satisfaction with the connection to public transport is high. However, there is a need for improvement in the suburban areas, and Vienna is facing the challenge of keeping the existing network fit and attractive, while the number of residents, and thus the number of users, is increasing. This objective can be met by the above-mentioned measures of the public transport network expansion, network improvement, and also the improvement and attractiveness of walking and cycling. Special attention is given to the creation of attractive offers in non-motorized traffic in order to achieve the 80–20 goal of the modal split.

Proximity to Green Spaces

Next steps in developing the Viennese green spaces further are the upgrade of leisure zones, including new parks, as well as the further establishment of the green network in Vienna, which has to be planned, implemented, or improved (see also "Mission Statement of Green Spaces" in Vienna City Administration, 2014, p. 123). Moreover, Vienna will complement the quantitative urban space parameters established in 2005 with qualitative parameters (Vienna City Administration, 2014, p. 117). Vienna's open space network will make open spaces available to each inhabitant, which can then be reached within not more than 250 meters from home. Therefore, gaps in the network have to be closed and low-quality sections have to be improved. Planned interventions comprise the planting of trees, greening measures in the streetscape, small street-side parks (temporary or permanent), establishing places to sit down or play along the walkways, and more. These measures will also entail healthier air quality and better micro-climates in the neighborhoods (Vienna City Administration, 2014, p. 118). As part of major ongoing development projects, two large new recreation zones will be installed (Vienna City Administration, 2014, p. 119). The qualitative and quantitative urban space parameters help ensure a high-quality and quickly accessible connection to green space for each inhabitant of Vienna. Therefore, 3.5 square kilometers of green space in close proximity are mandatory per inhabitant in newly built quarters. The same number is strived for in existing quarters; however, because of the dense building environment in these quarters, this is challenging. The green space newly built in neighborhoods has to be larger than 1 hectare and fulfill some quality require-ments as being accessible by public transport or by foot, providing different zones of use, age-specific play areas for children, playgrounds, open spaces for young people, seating areas, pathways, dog zones, and nature zones. Besides the size of the green space in the neighborhood, there are higher-level regulations for necessary green space in the quarter and region as well (Vienna City Administration, 2014, p. 120; Vienna City Administration, 2015, p. 84).

The above-mentioned measures respond to the results of the *Vienna Quality of Life Survey* by striving for improvements in densely built-up areas and by building new green spaces in inner-city development areas as well as securing them in growing outer areas. In order to further increase the general satisfaction with the green spaces, the city of Vienna has formulated com-prehensive quality and quantity standards.

Vienna's Way to Stay Livable by Urban Planning

The methods, goals, and instruments described above show, using the example of the city of Vienna, how urban planning can contribute to the preservation and improvement of quality of life. On the one hand, it has been shown that the city's own data on the current living situation of the residents provides an important basis for planning work. On the other hand, the strategies serve as examples of the steps that urban planning can foresee for a city worth living in. Based on the urban planning work in Vienna, it became clear that the following points are particularly important for successfully pursuing the quality of life in a city:

1   Reliable and meaningful statistical data: As a basis for all measures, a sufficiently detailed data collection should be carried out regularly. The *Quality of Life Survey* conducted by the city of Vienna provides insights into the situation of the Viennese population and can make statements even at district level. These data provide valuable fundament for the inter-ventions of urban planning. Based on the available data, the city of Vienna was able to identify quarters that are considered worth living in (these districts can serve as models for further work) and those where improvement is needed (measures must be taken here to harmonize the quality of life in the districts). Even in areas with an overall high level of satisfaction, room for improvement can be identified and addressed (e.g., public transport). The same applies to the distribution and quality of open spaces, which are represented differently throughout Vienna and are therefore dealt with differently. In short, the data-based approach outlined in this chapter allows for efficient and effective planning.

2   Strategic documents with a holistic view and political commitment: Viennese urban planning has for decades been working with strategic documents based on a holistic

approach (Urban Development Plans 1984, 1994, 2005, 2014). The definition of over-arching objectives ensures that a uniform development can be achieved across the whole city and that resources are bundled in areas where they are most needed (e.g., development of public transport or creation of green spaces). An important factor for the implementation of the higher-level strategies is political commitment as well as the translation of the strategic goals into concrete projects (see plans for the surroundings of public transport stops or the catalogue of criteria for green space).

3   Collaborations: In times of globalization and declining public funds, it is no longer possible for the public sector alone to implement major projects and measures. Therefore, partners and new forms of cooperation are necessary in order to maintain a livable city. The city of Vienna thus sets up cooperation with private developers and has issued specific regulations and a legal framework for this purpose (see urban development contracts).

4   Large- and small-scale projects: In order to achieve the above-mentioned goals, it makes sense to start large projects and think on a large scale, while implementing measures on a small scale at the same time. The city of Vienna therefore relies on large-scale projects such as inner- and outer-city expansion by creating urban districts (urban development areas and development of entire neighborhoods), thus meeting the challenges of growth and at the same time ensuring a livable environment for its inhabitants. In addition, Vienna also implements measures on a smaller scale, for example public spaces, making cycling and walking more attractive, or further improving public transport stations.

As shown in this chapter, the city of Vienna and its urban planning instruments can contribute to a broader discussion on livable cities and illustrates how urban planning can help improve the quality of life.

References

Magistrat der Stadt Wien, MA 21 – Flächenwidmung und Stadtteilentwicklung. (2016). *Masterplan für eine partizipative Stadtentwicklung*. [online] masterplan-partizipation. Available at: https://masterplan-partizipation.wien.gv.at/site/files/2016/12/Masterplan_Partizipation.pdf [Accessed December 3, 2017].

Stadt Wien. (2017). *Lebensqualität—Wien ist und bleibt Nummer eins*. [online] Available at: www.wien.gv.at/politik/international/wettbewerb/mercerstudie.html [Accessed November 25, 2017].

Stadtentwicklung Wien, Magistratsabteilung 18—Stadtentwicklung und Stadtplanung. (2016). *Lebensqualität in 91 Wiener Bezirksteilen*. Vienna: Stadtentwicklung Wien, pp. 7, 18, 20, 24, 26.

Vienna City Administration. (2016). *Smart city Wien framework strategy* (2nd ed.). Vienna: Vienna City Administration.

Vienna City Administration, Municipal Department 18—Urban Development and Planning. (2014). *STEP 2025: Urban development plan Vienna*. Vienna: Vienna City Administration.

Vienna City Administration, Municipal Department 18—Urban Development and Planning. (2015). *Thematic concept: Green and open space*. Vienna: Vienna City Administration.

PART III

ISSUES OF POVERTY, EQUITY, AND THE ENVIRONMENT

Chapter 10

TRANSIT EXPANSION AND THE PURSUIT OF EQUITY IN DEVELOPMENT AND GROWTH IN MINNEAPOLIS-ST. PAUL, MINNESOTA
Edward G. Goetz

There are two paradoxes at the heart of politics and governance in the Twin Cities region of Minneapolis-St. Paul. First, though the region boasts a strong and thriving economy and ranks high on a number of livability measures, it simultaneously suffers from large and persistent racial disparities on those same economic and quality of life measures. Second, though the region is widely regarded as a leader in progressive and innovative policymaking, none of these policy strategies have made a dent in the racial inequities that plague the region. Racial disparities remain an important and unachieved element of livability in the Twin Cities. The rising awareness of these racial disparities since the turn of the century has put equitable growth and development at the top of the policy agenda in the region.

Equity and Livability in the Twin Cities

The Minneapolis-St. Paul region has for many years enjoyed a strong reputation for livability. Good schools, a healthy economy, and good government have produced high rankings on a range of quality of life indices covering health and fitness, educational outcomes for children, arts and culture, and levels of civic engagement (Gauto, 2012). Its relatively diversified economy allowed the region to avoid the precipitous decline of many Midwestern cities during the late-20th-century post-industrial transition. Through both national recessions and expansions since 1980, the Minneapolis-St. Paul region has boasted a vibrant economy strong in a range of industries from milling to medical products to graphic arts. It is the largest corporate center between Chicago and Denver, home to more Fortune 500 businesses per capita than any other U.S. city. The issue of livability has long been a central concern of the region's policy elite, a response in part to the competitive disadvantage that the cold, northern climate creates for the region.

The rosy picture of economic growth, social wellbeing, and high quality of life, however, has hidden another reality that reflects less well on the region. Despite the glowing economic and civic successes, the metropolitan area has a dismal record when it comes to disparities between whites and people of color. Although the region has the 13th lowest poverty rate among the 100 largest U.S. metros, it ranks 89th in the white–minority gap in poverty. The metro is also ranked 13th among the top 100 metros in median income in 2009, but it is 93rd out of 100 in the white–minority gap in median income household (Gauto, 2012). Blacks in Minneapolis are almost nine times more likely to be arrested for low-level crimes than are whites (Andersson, 2015), and only 23% of black households in the metro area own a home, compared with 73% of white households (Buchta, 2017). These disparities belie the image of a universally prosperous metropolitan area and have pushed equity to the front of the local policy agenda.

Though the metropolitan area has been long heralded as a progressive region (Nickel, 1995) that has successfully initiated innovative policies such as regional tax base sharing and regional approaches to affordable housing development—policies that most other regions are unwilling or unable to consider—it has, to this point, not made noticeable progress on the issues of racial disparities. Indeed, on some dimensions the disparities have gotten worse in recent years. The police killings of Jamar Clark in Minneapolis in 2015 and Philando Castile in a suburb bordering St. Paul in 2016 reinforced for many the problem of racial equity and justice in the metro area.

As a result, for most of the 21st century, equity in development has been a prominent goal among the region's policy elites. In this chapter I focus on how livability and equity concerns played out in recent regional development politics. The largest issue related to metro-wide development in the Twin Cities since the turn of the century has been the build-out of the regional transit system. From the completion of the area's first light rail line in 2004 policymakers and community groups have grappled with what decision-making processes should look like and how the transit system can reduce racial disparities and regional inequities.

The period of time between 2005 and 2018 has provided an unusually high number of opportunities for a regional policy conversation related to equity. Several local developments were occurring almost simultaneously that forced this regional discussion:

- The regional planning body (the Metropolitan Council) worked from 2012 to 2014 to rest its regional growth plan, setting out development objectives in transit, land use, housing, and economic development.
- Between 2015 and 2019, municipalities in the region were required to update their individual comprehensive plans, with required elements in transportation and housing, among others, that would be consistent with the Metropolitan Council's regional goals.
- The metro area has been planning and building out a regional transit system to supplement the prevailing automobile/bus system with light rail, commuter rail, and bus rapid transit.
- As a recipient of the federal Sustainable Communities Initiative (SCI) grant from HUD, the region was obligated to produce a Fair Housing and Equity Assessment in 2014, forcing local actors to articulate an equitable vision of development and address issues of racial equity.

Thus, this recent period has represented an unusually intense time of regional reflection and planning about major regional infrastructure, development, and equity. A range of public, private, and philanthropic groups came together in various bodies and in various forums; they accessed millions of dollars in federal funds and philanthropic investments, and they planned and implemented ambitious processes of community engagement to articulate transit and housing approaches, which addressed regional needs and reflected widespread concerns about participation and equity in development.

Livability, Equity, and Transit

Transit investments, especially early-21st-century light rail systems in metro areas across the nation, are frequently sold on the basis of their benefits to neighborhoods, to the cities in which they are located, and even to the region. Evidence regularly shows that these systems spur residential and commercial investments and increase property values along the line (Pan, 2013; Hess & Almeida, 2007). The phenomenon of transit-induced investment has created in many places concerns that the increased livability benefits of such investment can actually negatively impact lower-income residents by generating too much neighborhood change and spurring residential displacement, a phenomenon that has come to be called *transit-induced gentrification* (Dawkins & Moeckel, 2016).

The Twin Cities' first experience with light rail bore out these expectations. In 2004 the region's initial light rail line opened to great success. Ridership significantly exceeded estimates and studies showed that the line spurred property value increases and investment along its route and increased job accessibility for low-wage workers in the region (Goetz, Ko, Hagar, Ton, & Matson, 2009; Fan, Guthrie, & Teng, 2010).

With the first line finished and a tremendous success by virtually all measures, the Metropolitan Council looked to continue the build-out of the entire system. The next step was the construction of the Central Corridor light rail line, connecting the downtowns of St. Paul and Minneapolis. Given the spillover development benefits that were seen with the first line, officials were understandably optimistic that residents along the Central Corridor would welcome the investment that was likely to accompany completion of the line. They were wrong.

In a city (St. Paul) that was roughly 20% people of color, the Central Corridor was scheduled to run right through neighborhoods that were, on average, more than 50% people of color. The residents of this part of St. Paul had seen something like this a generation earlier. The last time, in fact, that these neighborhoods had received this much attention from transportation planners was in the 1960s, when Interstate 94 had cut a quarter-mile swath through the community, destroying the historical heart of the black community in St. Paul, displacing residents, and triggering overcrowding and decline in the areas of the neighborhood left standing. Now, the Central Corridor light rail was planned to run down the middle of University Avenue, stretching from the University of Minnesota campus in Minneapolis, east to the state capitol building, ultimately terminating in downtown St. Paul. For more than 6 miles the line would parallel Interstate 94 and, residents feared, would duplicate the devastation the neighborhood had experienced 50 years earlier.

When final plans for the line were announced in 2006, residents and advocacy groups organized in opposition around three issues. The first was the protection of the small businesses that lined University Avenue. Indeed, University Avenue was thick with locally owned, ethnically identified businesses and restaurants at the time. Preserving these businesses and thus the ethnic flavor of the corridor through the construction period and beyond was the first objective of advocates. Second, given concerns that the transit investment would drive up property values nearby, the community groups worried about the impact of the line on affordable housing and thus pursued both the preservation of existing affordable units and the building of new affordable housing along the corridor. Third, the final plans for the light rail line showed that when the line ran through the heart of the lower-income communities of color, there were to be four stations placed a mile apart from each other. This meant that residents could have walks of up to a half-mile in either direction once they reached University Avenue to use the system. This was in direct contrast to more numerous and closely placed stations at either end of the line (downtown Minneapolis and downtown St. Paul) and at the University of Minnesota. Advocates immediately identified this as discriminatory and reflective of a more general lack of equity planned by the transit planners. Up and down University Avenue signs were posted reading "Blight Rail," "Save Our Jobs," and "Save Our Businesses" (Callaghan, 2016), and community groups organized into a coalition, Stops for Us, to oppose the line.

The transit planners argued that they were responding to efficiency standards mandated by the federal funding when they had placed stations about a mile apart. Spacing the stations thusly minimized the per-rider cost as the federal government required, while simultaneously limiting the access of low-income residents to the line. Residents looked at the plans and saw a huge public investment that would cause widespread disruption in their communities and, when finished, would not even serve them well.

In the ensuing years, local and regional officials were faced with constant political pressure to look beyond basic questions of system design and the coordination of large public infrastructure investments, and focus more specifically on how the region's transit system could be built so as to achieve equity, and how development along the various transit corridors would be not only sufficiently transit-oriented, but would also meet the equity demands of community residents.

Planning and Delivering Equitable Transit-Oriented Development

Between 2006 and 2016, the movement for equity in development in the Minneapolis-St. Paul region led to an important redesign of decision-making around regional land use, transit, and affordable housing development. At the same time, it ushered in a much more participatory process that effectively incorporated the input of communities that had historically been excluded from such decision-making processes in the past. The region leaned on its historical strengths of inter-jurisdictional and cross-sectoral collaboration, designing new institutions and decision-making systems, some temporary and some designed to last.

One of the first steps taken was the 2006 creation of the Central Corridor Funders Collaborative (CCFC). CCFC was a collaboration among 14 private foundations, formed to work with the major public sector actors with an interest in the Central Corridor, including the two central cities, the counties that held each central city (Hennepin for Minneapolis and Ramsey for St. Paul), state officials, and the Metropolitan Council. CCFC was formed to help coordinate infrastructure and development investment, public and private, along the line in order to maximize equitable development outcomes.

In response to the protests and fears of organized opponents, CCFC turned its attention from the outset to the issues of affordable housing, small businesses protection, and the placement of stations along the line. The thorniest of these issues was the question of whether the line would adequately serve the low-income communities through which it was being placed. Stops for Us demanded three additional stations through the core St. Paul neighborhoods. This would place stations a half-mile apart and greatly increase the transit access of community residents. The Metropolitan Council initially opposed these demands because they would increase the cost of the line to a point where it no longer would meet federal cost-effectiveness guidelines. The Council claimed the Federal Transit Administration (FTA) rules mandated low per-rider costs could only be achieved by limiting the number of stations. With the stations, the line would forfeit its federal funding. Without the stations, community activists were adamantly opposed to the project.

Throughout 2008 and 2009 the issue remained unresolved. The federal funding that made the line possible was highly competitive and Twin Cities officials felt the strong community opposition could easily convince the federal government to divert funding to a different city to support a much less-controversial transit project. With both sides dug in, the city of St. Paul stepped forward in 2009 with $5.2 million to create one of the three stations that activists demanded. The city also pledged to create zoning restrictions to minimize gentrification and rising land values in the corridor (Orrick, 2010). Unappeased, the activists stuck to their demand for three new stations, filing a federal Civil Rights Complaint in 2009 and a lawsuit in January 2010. Referencing the damage done to the Rondo neighborhood in the 1960s when transportation planners had had their way, Nathanial Khaliq, president of the St. Paul chapter of the NAACP, simply said, "Not this time" (Orrick, 2010).

Over the course of a few months in late 2009, Stops for Us, local policymakers, and CCFC worked with the new Obama administration FTA head Peter Rogoff to find a solution. Their efforts began to focus on relaxing the cost-efficiency rules. Finally, in late January 2010, after the lawsuit and the Civil Rights Complaint had been filed, the U.S. Department of Transportation announced it would change FTA rules for rating transit projects to include, in addition to cost-effectiveness, *livability factors* such as environmental, community, and economic development benefits provided by transit. Rogoff called the Central Corridor case the poster child for the need to rethink the agency's guidelines. The policy change made the three additional stations acceptable to the federal government, preserving federal funding and keeping the entire line viable. Matching funds were quickly found and the project was completed (Babler, 2011).

Corridors of Opportunity

About the time that CCFC and Stops for Us were successfully breaking the logjam that threatened the Central Corridor, CCFC spurred additional local efforts that would ultimately lead to a new and different collaboration to manage the region's transit build-out. CCFC helped organize successful proposals to two large national initiatives, one philanthropically based, the other governmental, that in 2010 would bring more than $20 million in grants and project-based investments to the region. The first source was Living Cities, a national consortium of 22 private foundations and financial institutions. In 2010 Living Cities awarded grants in five cities, including Minneapolis-St. Paul, as part of their Integration Initiative aimed at supporting cross-sector collaboration in addressing system change in efforts to address equity. The consortium of public and private entities that received the Living Cities funds proposed to devote them to projects of the type that people around the country were beginning to call *equitable transit-oriented development* (ETOD).

Later that same year, the Metropolitan Council applied for and received a $5 million grant from the HUD Sustainable Communities Initiative (SCI). SCI was a collaboration between HUD, EPA and DOT to provide planning grants to regions to support regional planning and development efforts that would coordinate housing, urban development, and transportation investments to reduce energy consumption, environmental deterioration, and greenhouse gas emissions in major metropolitan areas (Chapple, Streltzov, Blondet, & Nape, 2017). The principles of the program emphasized transit and housing equity, coordinated local investment strategies, and growth that supports existing infrastructure investments. The recipient of the SCI grant, the Metropolitan Council, pledged to use the funds to implement their plans for building out a regional transit system.

These two large initiatives, together accounting for more than $20 million in outside investments, merged their efforts, creating a joint *policy board* for one united initiative they called Corridors of Opportunity (CoO). CoO was a remarkable body that included the regular participation of the most prominent public, private, and philanthropic leaders in the region. The mayor of Minneapolis participated regularly in meetings of the policy board, which included a representative of the St. Paul Mayor's Office, the chair of the Metropolitan Council, the commissioner of the State Housing Finance Agency, county commissioners, and leaders of local foundations and private sector business groups. All investments and planning activities for the Living Cities grant and the HUD grant were coordinated from the outset and through the entire grant periods. The policy board met monthly from January 2011 through December 2014. The initiative focused on small business assistance, affordable housing development, and land use planning for TOD along seven different transit corridors accounting for more than 100 miles of transit lines throughout the region.

Community Engagement

The success of the Stops for Us campaign in 2009 demonstrated the importance of community input for meeting equity goals in transit planning. In order to continue community involvement, the CoO initiative created a Community Engagement Team (CET). Three organizations were to constitute the CET, Nexus Community Partners, a nonprofit intermediary that supported community engagement in the region, the Alliance for Metropolitan Stability, an advocacy organization that focuses on equitable regional development, and the Minnesota Center for Neighborhood Organizing (MCNO), a capacity-building group that was part of the Center for Urban and Regional Affairs (CURA) at the University of Minnesota.

The CET quickly became a critical element of the CoO initiative. First, it was the vehicle for community participation in the regional planning initiatives in transit and housing pursued by CoO. CET used over $750,000 to make sub-grants to advocacy organizations across the region in order to support their work in transit planning in different corridors. Repa Mekha, spokesman for the CET and the executive director of Nexus Community Partners, relates:

> The Met Council, who received the HUD grant, was not set up to make small grants to a lot of different groups, but we [Nexus] were. That is what we do. We had a process and infrastructure for it. We set up a process for deciding how the funds would be distributed and we created a review committee of community people to make those decisions. There

were some who thought that even though the process had been devolved to Nexus, public officials would have some say in where the funds went. Some were not happy to find out that this was not the case. The innovation here is that the community was going to control where and to whom those funds went, not elected officials...We made those funding decisions and then reported back to the policy board. It was community folks making decisions with federal funds.

(R. Mekha, personal communication, December 15, 2017)

Three rounds of engagement grants were made (supplemented by an additional $1 million from local funders).

Second, CET was instrumental in opening up the policy board meetings to a wider range of socio-demographic representation than otherwise would have occurred. CET leaders frequently invited their community partners to attend policy board meetings to, as one CET leader put it, "let them know that people were watching." In addition, CET was able to make the policy board itself more inclusive. Early on in the process, the CET had one spot on the board, but it was nonvoting. Shortly after pointing out to the HUD officials overseeing the Twin Cities' SCI grant that he was the only person of color on the policy board and that he was in an ex-officio position, policy board leaders promoted him to a voting position and other people of color were added to the group.

Finally, the third contribution CET made to the policy board was to situate the issue of equity into the center of all conversations. As the leader of the CET, Repa Mekha, noted:

We were thinking about what would be in place when Corridors of Opportunity went away. We'd never been at those tables before [and here he is referencing the gathering of high-powered public officials and private sector leaders on the policy board]. So our strategy was to get out ahead of all of the other teams in Corridors of Opportunity. [CoO had a large number of working teams focusing on specific projects at various geographic points along the line or on various policy issues.] We got out in front. So when the policy board met during the first months, we would be able to make reports, and all eyes in the room would be on us. This made community engagement a central focus of CoO because few other projects were up and running yet. They couldn't ignore us; we were on the agenda all of the time.

(R. Mekha, personal communication, December 15, 2017)

In the summer of 2011, Community Engagement Team (CET) brought Angela Glover Blackwell, president of PolicyLink, to the Twin Cities, and the topic was the local racial disparities in the Twin Cities. As one CoO participant said, this "called the question on local disparities" and further ensured that equity was front and center in all that CoO did.

CoO disbanded when both the Living Cities and the HUD Sustainable Communities grant periods ended. Many of the actors continued to meet for an additional year afterward. CCFC ended its operations shortly after the Central Corridor line opened in June 2014.

Equitable Transit Development

The combined efforts of CCFC and the CoO initiative produced a number of significant achievements. In small business protection, CoO channeled more than $1 million in loans, grants, and technical assistance to small businesses to prepare for and survive the construction period. Though there was churn among the small businesses along the line, business starts outnumbered closures and relocations. Of the 353 businesses that received assistance from CoO, only four closed during the years of construction (Shelton, Pittman, & Steel, 2014). CCFC leveraged over $3 million in loans to 450 businesses for improvements during the construction period, and $3.9 million in Ready for Rail forgivable loans to 212 more businesses for offsetting losses due to the interruption in business caused by transit construction. The two initiatives have supported the preservation or development of over 3,500 units of affordable housing and assistance to hundreds of households to stay in their housing along the corridor. Other areas of accomplishment include a small business energy-efficiency initiative, strategies to match job skills with workforce needs in the region, and green infrastructure planning along the various transit corridors in the region.

One signal objective of CoO was *system change*, or changes in policymaking and infrastructure planning within the region. At least in the area of transit-related development, CoO seems to have had an impact on how policy is made in the region. CoO was able to shift the planning for supportive infrastructure, land use, and housing to the corridor scale, in contrast to the station-by-station, or even city-by-city policymaking that had prevailed before (Shelton et al., 2014). This allowed local governments to align transit-supportive investments across jurisdictional lines. The participation of business and philanthropic leaders also facilitated a coordination of public investment with the efforts of foundations. Most participants report increased collaborative work across sectors, jurisdictions, and issue arenas, as a result of CoO (ibid.).

The work of the CET has had lasting impacts within the region. The CET brought more voices into the process of planning and building out the regional transit system. The model of funding specific engagement efforts through mini-grants has been repeated and extended to the issue of housing policymaking. The notion of community engagement in the region was transformed by the CET. Through CoO, community groups moved from outside agitators to indispensable partners in the planning process. According to participants, the community turnout for routine meetings of the policy board, often as many as 50 observers, kept policymakers accountable throughout the process and reinforced a new and more inclusive way of planning and implementing transit and infrastructure development in the region. In sum, the process brought about a significant democratization of expertise and engagement in regional policymaking.

The region's planning body, the Metropolitan Council, was, in particular, affected by the inclusive and collaborative decision-making in CoO. The council, which was producing the regional planning framework during this time period, creating a new housing policy plan for the first time in close to 30 years, and completing a Fair Housing and Equity Assessment, adopted new forms of planning, decision-making, and engagement, and brought ideas, values, and processes from CoO into its work. Substantively, the council incorporated the five principles of CoO (equity, transparency, innovation, collaboration, and sustainability) into its regional development framework. The guiding regional documents for housing and transit in the region have been noticeably shaped by community groups typically excluded from such processes. Indeed, as one participant noted, "The Met Council lived out what we put into the Corridors of Opportunity work. The Metropolitan Council has become such a different agency through this process."

Finally, participants claim an impact on national policymaking as well: "We changed the FTA guidelines for assessing transit projects," claimed one local funder, a conclusion not contradicted by the statements of the Obama administration officials involved.

Conclusion

The Twin Cities of Minneapolis and St. Paul have a deserved reputation for good government, policy innovation, and progressive politics. These local characteristics, however, have not prevented the emergence of significant regional inequities, most notable along racial lines. As a result, the contemporary political environment within the region emphasizes questions of equity in both governance and development. These issues were prominently played out in recent efforts to plan, coordinate, and implement transit and infrastructure development within the region. These efforts were carried out through new and highly collaborative and inclusive institutions and processes. There is reason to believe that this experience will have lasting impacts in the region.

There is also reason to be more circumspect about the scope of change and its likelihood of enduring. The local efforts to orient regional development in a more equitable direction coincided with the existence of highly supportive state- and federal-level governments. In Minnesota, Democratic Governor Mark Dayton has held office since 2010. Members of the Metropolitan Council are directly appointed by the governor and thus reflect the political predilections of the governor. The council in place between 2010 and 2016 was notably more progressive than its predecessor (appointed by Republican Tim Pawlenty), and its adoption of principles of equity and inclusion could wane should the political orientation of the governor's seat change. Similarly, at the federal level, it was transit administrators in the Obama administration that shifted FTA policy to include livability indicators for assessing transit projects, and it was the Obama administration's Sustainable Communities Initiative that helped to support formation of CoO in the first place. The movement toward equity and inclusion in transit and infrastructure development in the region has benefited from a supportive state and federal political environment that will not always prevail.

The long-term impact of these events on racial and regional equity is impossible to assess at this point. Even whether development patterns in the region have changed in a fundamental way remains to be seen. The region has seen much greater investment in the core cities and a return of investment and wealth to the central cities. This has been accompanied by higher housing prices in the post-recession period and greater problems of affordability in the central cities (Jaramillo & Halbach, 2016). While the region was one of the few metro areas in the country to see an increase in average neighborhood density between 2010 and 2016 (Kaul, 2017), the transit-oriented infrastructural development pursued by the region's policymakers was a response to these trends, not their cause.

GOETZ

References

Andersson, E. (2015, May 28). *Minneapolis divided: A tale of two cities*. Retrieved from www.aclu. org/blog/racial-justice/race-and-criminal-justice/minneapolis-divided-tale-two-cities.

Babler, T. (2011, July 25). Making light rail stop for us. *Shelterforce*. Retrieved from https://shelter-force.org/2011/07/25/making_light_rail_stop_for_us/4/.

Buchta, J. (2017, August 19). Already-low homeownership rates of Twin Cities minorities fall further. *Minneapolis StarTribune*. Retrieved from www.startribune.com/already-low-homeownership-rates-of-twin-cities-minorities-fall-further-down/441087863/.

Callaghan, P. (2016, June 28). In final act, Central Corridor Funders Collaborative looks at what went right (and wrong) with Green Line development. *Minnpost*. Retrieved from www.minnpost.com/politics-policy/2016/06/final-act-central-corridor-funders-collaborative-looks-what-went-right-and-w.

Chapple, K., Streltzov, G., Blondet, M., & Nape, C. (2017). Epistemic communities or forced marriages? Evaluating collaboration among Sustainable Communities Initiative regional planning grant recipients. *Cityscape, 19*(3), 163–187.

Dawkins, C., & Moeckel, R. (2016). Transit-induced gentrification: Who will stay, and who will go? *Housing Policy Debate, 26*(4–5), 801–818.

Fan, Y., Guthrie, A., & Teng, R. (2010). *Impact of Twin Cities transitways on regional labor market accessibility: A transportation equity perspective*. Minneapolis, MN: Center for Transportation Studies, University of Minnesota. Retrieved from www.cts.umn.edu/Publications/ResearchReports/reportdetail.html?id=1940.

Gauto, V. (2012). Urban competitiveness and the Twin Cities Metropolitan Area. *CURA Reporter, 42*(2), 3–8.

Goetz, E. G., Ko, K., Hagar, A., Ton, H., & Matson, J. (2009). *The Hiawatha Line: Impacts on land use and residential housing value*. Minneapolis, MN: Transitway Impact Research Program, University of Minnesota.

Hess, D. B., & Almeida, T. M. (2007). Impact of proximity to light rail rapid transit on station-area property values in Buffalo, New York. *Urban Studies, 44*(5–6), 1041–1068.

Jaramillo, A., & Halback, C. (2016). *Sold out*. St. Paul, MN: Minnesota Housing Partnership. Retrieved from www.mhponline.org/images/Sold_Out_final_revised_small.pdf.

Kaul, G. (2017, July 13). Bucking a trend, the Twin Cities have grown more densely populated in recent years. *MinnPost*. Retrieved from www.minnpost.com/politics-policy/2017/07/bucking-trend-twin-cities-have-grown-more-densely-populated-recent-years.

Nickel, D. R. (1995). The progressive city? Urban redevelopment in Minneapolis. *Urban Affairs Review, 30*(3), 355–377.

Orrick, D. (2010, January 19). Black groups sue over Central Corridor light rail line. *St. Paul Pioneer Press*. Retrieved from www.twincities.com/2010/01/19/black-groups-sue-over-central-corridor-light-rail-line/.

Pan, Q. (2013). The impacts of an urban light rail system on residential property values: A case study of the Houston METRORail transit line. *Transportation Planning and Technology, 36*(2), 145–169.

Shelton, E., Pittman, B., & Steel, R. (2014). *Corridors of opportunity: Final evaluation report*. St. Paul, MN: Wilder Research.

Chapter 11

POST-DISASTER AMENITY POLITICS: LIVABILITY, GENTRIFICATION, AND RECOVERY IN POST-KATRINA NEW ORLEANS

Billy Fields

Introduction

One of the central challenges in the recovery planning of New Orleans following Hurricane Katrina was how to create a more livable, sustainable city. With the inundation of 80% of the city and the intense demands of housing and infrastructure rebuilding, making communities safer, stronger, and more livable seemed like a consensus mandate for planners tasked with coordinating rebuilding efforts (Fields, Wagner, & Frisch, 2015). These planning concepts formed the guiding framework for nearly all of the post-recovery plans. While terms like livability and sustainability were central planning concepts, many neighborhood residents were suspicious of efforts to improve the city in this way, with concerns of neighborhood removal, race, displacement, and equity emerging as clear issues in early recovery planning (Nelson, Ehrenfeucht, & Laska, 2007; Hirsch & Levert, 2009).

Over ten years after Hurricane Katrina, New Orleans now has a set of completed livability-based recovery projects in neighborhoods throughout the city (Reckdahl, 2014). These new community amenities, such as parks, bicycle facilities, and public spaces, were designed to improve neighborhood places and solidify recovery investment. While issues related to neighborhood abandonment have eased, issues related to gentrification, affordability, and displacement have quickly taken their place as key issues of concern (Brand, 2015) as home values have increased 54% and rental costs have gone up 50% from pre-Katrina levels (Greater New Orleans Housing Alliance [GNOHA], 2015).

This chapter provides an overview of how these tensions have been negotiated in New Orleans in the transition from disaster recovery and rebuilding to *recovered* urban planning. The chapter explores the meaning of livability through an analysis of post-Hurricane Katrina recovery planning in New Orleans. To provide more in-depth context, livability planning is then analyzed through the succession of plans impacting neighborhoods adjacent to the new Lafitte Greenway, a key livability-oriented post-Katrina recovery project.

The analysis presented here finds that most of the post-disaster recovery plans did not systematically address how new community livability amenities could alter neighborhood housing affordability even as they broadly recognized affordable housing as a key issue. From a policy perspective, livability planning in a post-disaster setting needs to be directly tied to equity and affordability issues to help address the gentrification conflict that arises as added community amenities put upward pressure on the housing market (Godschalk, 2004). This was particularly evident at the project planning level, as the Lafitte Greenway plans were virtually silent on housing affordability issues. While there is now a concerted effort along the Lafitte Greenway, and in New Orleans more generally, to address these issues, recovery planning lacked systematic, structured mechanisms for addressing the post-disaster gentrification conflict. This represents an important missed opportunity to enhance community livability for all residents.

This chapter is organized around four broad sections. First, the key tensions associated with contemporary livability planning are analyzed. These livability tensions are then linked to unique characteristics of recovery planning. To put these tensions in context, recovery plans in New Orleans associated with the Lafitte Greenway are then analyzed. Finally, key livability policy implications are discussed.

Livability: Meanings and Tensions

In the 1990s, two interrelated normative visions began to emerge about the goals of urban planning, with language related to sustainability and livability seeping into planning documents. By the early 2000s, sustainability and livability goals had become a nearly omnipresent framing device for planners who sought to structure planning goals within the relationships of economic, social, environmental, and community livability dimensions.

Godschalk (2004) provides a concise history of the rise of these planning concepts. He shows how the larger sustainability concerns related to economic, social, and environmental issues merged with the more micro-neighborhood-level concerns related to improving community quality of life. Livability, in this framing, "operates at the level of the everyday physical environment and focuses on place making" (Godschlk, 2004, p. 6). A myriad of other definitions of livability by different place-oriented coalitions focus on articulating the normative characteristics of these places. Oberlink (2008, p. 1), writing for AARP, describes livability as broadly encompassing "a range of initiatives aimed at improving community quality of life while supporting broader sustainability goals. Livability encompasses multi-dimensional issues relative to community design, land use, environmental protection and enhancement, mobility and accessibility, public health, and economic well-being."

While these definitions provide a goal-oriented framework for policy action across multiple planning spheres, the breadth of the goals often hides underlying tensions and contradictions. Godschalk (2004) connects the concepts of sustainability and livability together to highlight the key tensions that lie at the heart of these dominant planning framing devices. He begins by re-examining Campbell's (1996) planner's triangle. Campbell identifies a series of tensions that flow from implementation of the economic, social, and environmental goals of sustainability. In Campbell's orientation, sustainability planning is not so much about creating some end-state balance between potential tensions, but instead about creating community pathways to negotiate these tensions (Campbell, 2016).

Godschalk (2004, p. 6) uses this network of potential planning tensions as a base and then layers on key issues associated with livability-oriented land use design, "the three-dimensional aspects of public space, movement systems, and building design." In this way, projects within the built environment (public space, transportation, and buildings) can be linked to livability planning goals and, simultaneously, to potential tensions that result from their alteration of the economic and real estate markets, social networks, and environmental systems. This creates the Livability/Sustainability Prism of key tensions (Figure 11.1). The specific tensions added by the land-use focus of livability planning include the gentrification conflict between livability and equity values, the green cities conflict between ecology and livability values, and the growth management conflict between ecology and economic values.

Livability Gentrification Conflict in Practice: Bicycles in the City

Greenway and bicycle infrastructure projects represent a key tension in livability dialogue as these projects are often seen as a signal of neighborhood change and a "symbol of gentrification" (Stein, 2015; Badger, 2016). Overall, pedestrian and bicycle projects are not evenly distributed in cities with higher concentrations of projects in areas of greater wealth and political power (Lowe, 2016; Handy & McCann, 2010; Flanagan, Lachapelle, & El-Geneidy, 2016). As neighborhood demographics begin to change, bicycle infrastructure often follows as livability coalitions can help tip communities through the provision of public resources.

Figure 11.1 Sustainability/livability prism.

Source: Modified from Godschalk, 2004, p. 9.

While the symbolic impact of these coalitions can be powerful, the influence of livability investments on housing markets is more mixed. Studies of influence of greenways on property values have shown that the cumulative changes in property values associated with greenways result in significant increases in the tax base for community because of the linear nature of trails (Lindsey, Man, Payton, & Dickson, 2004), but the individual increase in property value associated with trails and bicycle facilities are generally estimated to be fairly modest (Parent & Vom Hofe, 2013; Krizek, 2006).

There are, however, some outliers, particularly in weak market areas, where property values have risen dramatically. Immergluck and Balan (2017) analyze the impact of proximity to the completed sections of the Atlanta Beltline greenway. They find that the Beltline greenway had a significant impact on housing appreciation, ranging from 17.9% to 26.6%. The Immergluck and Balan (2017) analysis shows both the promise of greenways as a neighborhood livability amenity and, importantly, as a potential tool for neighborhood displacement as housing cost increases. The analysis suggests that greenway planners are not simply adding livability amenities to communities, but also intervening in the housing market in ways that should require careful equity analysis of housing impacts.

The research cited above and the broader equity discussions around livability point out that livability projects are political. They build community amenities that can enhance the development potential of certain communities and put pressure on housing markets. The policy implication here is not that livability projects should be reserved for higher-income areas to avoid housing displacement, but instead that livability projects need to be directly tied to affordable housing to help offset the potential increase in housing values. This inserts equity squarely into the livability agenda and underscores both the need to distribute livability project resources across all communities and the need to recognize their importance in affordable housing debates in the livability planning process.

Conceptualizing Livability and Post-Disaster Planning

While these tensions form an underlying set of challenges, post-disaster recovery planning as a practice adds further complications. Post-disaster planning is composed of a large number of individual projects designed to help the community rebuild and simultaneously enhance resilience to future threats. These projects are selected through a highly political and technical process. Recovery planning is characterized by intense time pressure on a myriad of public and private decisions that occur within an often-conflicted political setting (Olshansky, Hopkins, & Johnson, 2012; Gotham & Greenberg, 2014). The competitive, time-compressed, and political recovery process is also immensely technical in terms of meeting the statutory requirement of federal recovery funding. For recovery projects to emerge from this process with dedicated funding, political coalitions must shepherd the nascent developments through initial planning and on through the technical federal funding parameters (Burby, 2003).

At some time point during this process, a community moves from the intensity of this recovery planning period to the long-term, usually slow-burning nature of more commonplace planning politics. For members of the community there is often no clear demarcation point between these periods, but rather the slow and simultaneously punctuated arrival of rehabilitated homes, commercial properties, and new community projects such as rehabilitated libraries, fire stations, and parks. At all phases of the process, individuals and businesses are making decisions about whether to stay and invest or cut losses and move to more stable settings (Nelson, 2014; Fields et al., 2015). In this context, creating places of choice, places where businesses and individuals choose to invest their resources and time, is a vital marker of success of recovery planning and the transition to recovered livable communities.

Livable places of choice are, however, places that are in demand. Over time, basic infrastructure, housing, and commercial corridors are stabilized and recover through the infusion of the above-mentioned government recovery resources and the hard work and investment of individuals. These new projects often alter the real estate market, increasing the cost of housing and commercial properties with the essentially new building stock. This altered market base is often augmented over time through the slower implementation of livability-oriented recovery planning projects like parks, open spaces, and bicycle and pedestrian projects that can impact housing cost.

As these projects come online, they can also begin to change the investment dynamic from one of market dysfunction, where investment dollars are sought, to a more stable or even localized strong market dynamic, where managing the intensity of development becomes more challenging. This transition from localized weak market to a stable/strong market is often accompanied by the implementation of livability projects that signal to investors that the community is ripe for transition (Fields et al., 2015).

This presents a tension. Livability-oriented recovery planning is designed to stabilize and improve local quality of life to signal market recovery and, simultaneously, to foster a more equitable community. In more economically stable communities, this issue involves ensuring that recovery resources are distributed evenly across a community. In areas that are characterized by weaker market conditions prior to the disaster like New Orleans, the goals of improved quality of life often come under more scrutiny as an improved community can quickly result in a changed community that may benefit new residents at the expense of the pre-existing population. Drawing from Godschalk's (2004) work, this can be called the *post-disaster gentrification conflict*. As we will see in New Orleans following Hurricane Katrina, the conditions necessary to generate this type of post-disaster gentrification conflict were set in motion.

Methods and Data

To examine these questions, it is useful to drill down to a set of neighborhood plans to examine what types of policies and projects have been implemented and how neighborhood demographics have changed. Sixteen plans from 2006–2014 that significantly impacted the rebuilding and livability-orientation of recovery in the Lafitte Greenway area were identified.[1]

The plans were evaluated on two levels. At the most basic level, key terms associated with livability/sustainability planning tensions (Godschalk, 2004) were identified and then searched for within the plans (Appler & Rumbach, 2016). This provides an understanding of the extent to which planners actively anticipated potential conflicts and worked to create policies to ameliorate these tensions. The geographic scope of the plan analysis includes plans impacting neighborhoods that border the greenway. The second level of analysis aims to more deeply understand the level of engagement with particular tensions that could be associated with these planning concepts. This analysis draws from more contextual plan and primary document analysis to highlight how the tensions outlined above have been negotiated in this post-disaster setting.

The Lafitte Greenway: Moving from Disaster to Recovery to Displacement?

The Lafitte Greenway is a $9 million, 2.8-mile linear trail and park that bisects New Orleans through multiple neighborhoods. This type of linear park project is increasingly used in communities around the U.S. to enhance livability and improve active transportation opportunities. The Lafitte Greenway has drawn national attention as a new type of park system that, as Nagel and Watkins (2017) argue, is "a roadmap to a more sustainable future for New Orleans, supporting public health, recreation, storm water management, neighborhood investment and job opportunities through connections to low-cost public transportation."

The Lafitte Greenway, which officially opened to the public in the fall of 2015, was explicitly planned in the aftermath of Hurricane Katrina as both a linear trail and as a recovery project designed to spur redevelopment. This type of focused, trail-oriented development (Fields, 2009) has resulted in a number of major redevelopment projects along the greenway.[2] Larger redevelopment occurring along and adjacent to the greenway corridor include a Whole Foods and nonprofit incubator at Broad Street (Bradley, 2014), the Mid-City Market at Carrolton Avenue, and a major mixed-use development planned for Bayou St. John (Sayre, 2017). In addition, adjacent development of the University and Veterans Affairs Medical Centers only blocks from the greenway has significantly altered local real estate conditions (Calder, 2015).

Overall, it is estimated by the New Orleans-based NewCity Partnership that over $5.2 billion has been invested in multiple categories of projects in the broader area surrounding the greenway since Hurricane Katrina. Among these investments was the rehabilitation of the former Lafitte Housing Development into the new Faubourg Lafitte mixed-income neighborhood development. Discussions of the future of public housing post-Katrina were particularly intense, as one-for-one unit replacement was abandoned in favor of more mixed-income redevelopment over a longer period of time. This fits with the larger pattern of what Brand (2015, p. 251) calls "free-market recovery and the larger retrenchment of social welfare policies that might have better addressed the vast inequalities in the city."

While it can be difficult to distinguish between the impact of the disaster itself and impact of recovery projects on current housing and demographic conditions of an area, it appears that these new development projects have increased pressure on housing affordability in the neighborhoods surrounding the greenway (Table 11.1). Overall, most of the neighborhoods in the study area have large percentages of the population paying 30% or more of their income for housing. Most of the neighborhoods are also at or near poverty levels associated with concentrated poverty regions. While the greenway is just one project among many that could impact housing cost, the symbolic linear project with new developments on its rim represents a visual, if not causative, link to potential gentrification.

The result of the livability investments in public space, transportation, and housing and commercial development (Godschalk, 2004) provide the raw ingredients for a potential post-disaster gentrification conflict. From a policy perspective, the question is, to what extent did recovery plans anticipate the conflicts and plan for potential consequences?

Table 11.1 Housing and Demographic Characteristics of Greenway-adjacent Neighborhoods

Neighborhood	% Pop. Change (2000–2010)	Renter 30% or More on Housing 2010–2014 (%)	Owner 30% or More on Housing 2010–2014 (%)	Race: Black Pop. 2000 (%)	Race: Black Pop. 2010 (%)	Pop. Living in Poverty 2000 (%)	Pop. Living in Poverty 2010–2014 (%)
Treme/Lafitte	−53.00	72.10	39.40	92.40	74.50	59.60	44.30
Iberville	−51.00	48.50	NA	98.00	96.40	84.20	82.80
Tulane/Gravier	−14.00	73.00	55.70	78.20	71.20	56.20	50.50
Bayou St. John	−27.00	58.00	39	67.80	49.00	32.00	26.60
MidCity	−27.00	59.70	32.40	64.30	55.00	32.10	33.00

Source: Authors; The Data Center analysis of data from U.S. Census 2000 Summary File 1 (SF1), U.S. Census 2000 Summary File 3 (SF3) and 2010–2014 American Community Survey.

Plan Analysis

Examination of the full suite of plans from 2006 to 2014 shows both the complexity of planning for recovery and the fractured nature of the response. Recovery planning in New Orleans was conducted through a series of sometimes competing public and private plans that fluctuated between focusing recovery resources to higher-ground areas and full rebuilding of the city footprint to include all impacted areas (Campanella, 2015). Each plan had a particular emphasis, orientation, and purpose, with some of the plans focused on fairly narrow issues or concerns and others focused on the broader recovery overall. It is beyond the scope of this chapter to analyze each plan in depth. Instead the goal here is to understand how the Lafitte Greenway planning processes intersected with notions of livability and sustainability and broader concerns of affordable housing, displacement, and gentrification. The analysis below highlights key issues from the series of plans to show how the issues of livability and housing affordability were sometimes addressed, but often ignored in the planning process.

Distilling over ten years of post-disaster planning work in this corridor is a complex task, as multiple streams of processes and plans overlapped. To generalize, it appears that the initial plans following the disaster recognized affordable housing as a central issue for impacted communities, but individual livability plans associated with the Lafitte Greenway were almost silent about the potential implications of the project on housing cost.

For example, the Unified New Orleans Plan (UNOP), the summary document of the multiple streams of plans undertaken in the wake of the flooding (Nelson et al., 2007), provided a strong discussion of affordable housing and its centrality to post-disaster recovery and included the Lafitte Greenway as an important recovery project. The UNOP begins by noting that "the City lost almost its entire affordable housing inventory" (Unified New Orleans Plan, 2007, p. 1.8) and faced "a crisis of affordability" (UNOP, 2007, Appendix D). Residents voiced concerns about affordable housing and gentrification, with 38% of the residents at the in-person meetings voicing the need to have policies that "preserve affordable housing and mitigate gentrification" (UNOP, 2007, Appendix C). These concerns were placed alongside the policy desire to "(r)edevelop the Lafitte corridor as an urban/mixed-use district with central greenway" (UNOP, 2007, Appendix B). There was, however, no specific discussion about the intersection of the greenway and its impact on affordable housing.

As the multiple planning processes moved forward, specific funding for the Lafitte Greenway was officially secured, and attention moved towards the more project-level work of designing and building the greenway (Fields, Thomas, & Wagner, 2017). The implementation plans, the City of New Orleans Lafitte Greenway Masterplan, and Lafitte Greenway Revitalization Plan, included a broad emphasis on sustainability and livability, but generally lacked an emphasis on affordability and displacement.

These greenway planning documents were almost silent on the impact of the greenway on housing affordability. The Lafitte Greenway Revitalization Plan mentions the broader affordable housing programs of the city but doesn't specifically target the impact of the greenway on affordable housing. The plan instead lays out a very broad "challenge" for the plan "to understand how this Greenway will spur reinvestment in the surrounding neighborhoods and make them more sustainable for the future, while reflecting each neighborhood's individual character" (Lafitte Corridor Revitalization Plan, 2013, p. 6). This broad charge is not reflected in substantive affordable housing policy proposals in the remainder of the document. Overall, the greenway-specific plans acted more as narrow project planning documents focused on planning the greenway infrastructure, but it did not actively anticipate impacts of the greenway project on housing costs. From a planning perspective, the specific greenway plans represent an important gap in equity planning for affordability.

As the immediate disaster response began to give way to longer-term revitalization, the more comprehensive Livable Claiborne Plan began to re-establish affordability as a central planning issue. The Livable Claiborne Plan was funded through the federal Partnership for Sustainable Communities, a joint project of the U.S. EPA, HUD, and DOT. This project had the explicit purpose of using a livability framework to promote "community revitalization and economic development through equity, choice and sustainability" (Heberle, McReynolds, Sizemore, & Schilling, 2017, p. 10). In crafting the plan, many residents were specifically concerned that "revitalization could result in displacement through gentrification" (Heberle et al., 2017, p. 56).

Efforts to address these concerns have led to the creation of the Housing NOLA Plan, a partnership of nonprofit and city agencies led by the Greater New Orleans Housing Alliance. The plan is designed to more fully address affordable housing issues across the city. Within the Lafitte corridor area specifically, the Faubourg Lafitte, the newly rehabilitated mixed-income housing development, plans to add 900 designated affordable housing units and 600 market rate units (Buchanan, 2015). The Faubourg Lafitte, funded in part through the HUD Choice Neighborhood program, is linked to a number of other affordable housing projects, including the Iberville redevelopment that is planned for 800 units of affordable housing and a series of projects aimed at providing affordable housing for the area's senior population. While the development of these initiatives is significant, the larger question of affordability along the corridor is still outstanding, as a number of other planned developments, such as the 382-unit MidCity development by Sydney Torres, could further alter the housing market dynamic (LaRose, 2016).

Digging Deeper: Livability Planning in Post-Disaster Setting

Two key policy implications are drawn from the review of planning processes for the Lafitte Greenway. The first is both obvious and simultaneously undervalued: livability/amenity recovery spurs redevelopment and impacts housing affordability. From the depths of the post-disaster moment, it was difficult to envision a scenario where managing success in the form of increasing housing cost would be the paramount issue. As new projects came online with the addition of the linear park-like nature of the Lafitte Greenway, housing along the corridor has become more attractive and expensive. A key lesson for livability planning is that adding neighborhood amenities like greenways impacts housing cost. Even in the most challenging of circumstances following a disaster, the greenway, in concert with the infusion of other recovery projects, raised housing costs and re-cast the narrative of many of the neighborhoods along the greenway from one of long-term decline to, at least in close proximity to the greenway, one of stronger market conditions (Buchanan, 2015; LaRose, 2016). From an equity policy perspective, planning for livability involves planning for the impacts of success.

The second policy lesson drawn from the review of the planning processes is that livability/amenity recovery does not appear to generate affordable housing without larger policy interventions. While there have been a series of public housing and broader affordable housing initiatives along the greenway (outlined above), the pace of change has put pressure on housing values. In a post-disaster setting with large shares of newly remodeled housing forming the housing base, the market alone will not produce affordable housing at a rate that maintains low-to moderate-cost housing. As noted in the introduction, home values in New Orleans have increased 50% and rental costs have increased 54% since 2005 (GNOHA, 2015). In a post-disaster setting, changes to the housing stock that make them stronger and safer will also likely make them more expensive as well. The largely "free-market recovery" approach (Brand, 2015, p. 251) utilized in New Orleans resulted in accentuating pre-existing inequalities as new, higher-quality/higher-cost housing units came online. Different types of policy interventions in the housing market are required to ensure that livability is enjoyed by all.

While often complex and time-consuming, government intervention to promote affordable housing in livability projects can have an impact. A review of government interventions and planned projects around successful greenway projects in Minneapolis and Atlanta helps to show some of the policy tools that can be used to address the cost of housing adjacent to new livability amenities (Table 11.2). Twelve broad strategies were identified that can be used to help solidify and expand affordable housing opportunities. These strategies represent the key tools in the toolbox for livability planners to address rising housing costs associated with increased community amenities.

Table 11.2 Livability-driven Affordable Housing Toolbox

Housing Affordability Tools	Location in Practice	Citation
Low Income Housing Tax Credits	Midtown Greenway Minneapolis	Ascierto (2007)
Historic Tax Credit	Midtown Greenway Minneapolis	Ascierto (2007)
Housing Revenue Bonds	Midtown Greenway Minneapolis	City of Minneapolis (2012)
Affordable Housing Trust Fund	Midtown Greenway Minneapolis	City of Minneapolis (2012)
Housing TIF District	Midtown Greenway Minneapolis	City of Minneapolis (2012), City of Minneapolis (2013), Dolezalek (2015)
Public Housing	Beltline Atlanta	Sisson (2017)
Land Trusts	Beltline Atlanta	Sisson (2017)
Affordable Housing Bonds	Beltline Atlanta	Sisson (2017)
Community Land Trusts	Proposed Beltline Atlanta	Sisson (2017)
Mandatory Inclusionary Zoning	Proposed Beltline Atlanta	Sisson (2017), Johnson et al. (2017)
Anti-Displacement Tax Fund	Proposed Beltline Atlanta	Sisson (2017), Johnson et al. (2017)
Preserve Existing Affordable Housing	Proposed Beltline Atlanta	Johnson et al. (2017)

Source: Author.

These tools do not represent an exhaustive list of all activities that could be used to improve housing affordability, but they represent a set of tools that are currently or are planned to be used adjacent to greenways around the country. This set of tools provides a starting place for livability planners to begin to envision avenues for policies to ameliorate housing cost impacts associated with greenway projects. Planners working on livability projects need to actively engage coalitions of affordable housing advocates and city agencies to work on ensuring that new livability developments do not drive displacement. Livability planning, particularly in low- to moderate-income communities, now requires attention to the impacts on affordable housing.

Conclusion

Livability planning is embedded with underlying tensions that can become significant, particularly in the wake of a disaster. The post-disaster gentrification conflict identified in New Orleans shows how livability projects can impact housing costs and potentially cause displacement of the very people the plans are designed to assist.

The review of plans for the Laffite Greenway shows a gap of attention to the impacts of livability plans on affordable housing in the impacted corridor. While the gap represents an important missed opportunity, a number of key tools are available for cities considering livability planning. While planning for affordability will not make the underlying tensions of livability planning disappear, strategic actions to enhance affordable housing outcomes can help to ensure that advantages of livable communities are enjoyed widely.

Notes

1   The plans included: the Bring Back New Orleans Plan (BNOB), Lambert Plan: Faubourg St. John, Lambert Plan: MidCity, Lambert Plan: City Park, Lambert Plan: LakeView, Lambert Plan: Tulane/Gravier, Lambert Plan: Treme/Lafitte, Unified New Orleans Plan, Friends of the Lafitte Greenway (FOLC) Greenway Masterplan, City Office of Recovery Development and Administration (ORDA) Broad/Lafitte Target Plan, New Orleans Comprehensive Plan (UNOP), New Orleans Water Plan, City Lafitte Greenway Revitalization Plan, City Lafitte Greenway Masterplan, FOC Greenway Sustainable Water Design Plan, and the Livable Claiborne Plan.

2   It should be noted that the author actively participated in planning meetings for the greenway during this period.

References

Appler, D., & Rumbach, A. (2016). Building community resilience through historic preservation. *Journal of the American Planning Association, 82*(2), 92–103.

Ascierto, J. (2007). Major Sears site serves a new use. *Affordable Housing Finance.* Retrieved from www.housingfinance.com/developments/major-sears-site-serves-a-new-use_o.

Badger, E. (2016, January 14). Why bike lanes make people mad. *Washington Post Wonkblog.*

Bradley, B. (2014, February 14). *How one determined urban planner built a job-generating lefty foodie Xanadu in New Orleans.* Retrieved from https://nextcity.org/daily/entry/whole-foods-new-orleans-refresh-jeff-schwartz-project-refresh.

Brand, A. L. (2015). The politics of defining and building equity in the twenty-first century. *Journal of Planning Education and Research, 35*(3), 249–264.

Buchanan, S. (2015, September 29). Living along the Lafitte Greenway: Is it attainable or unaffordable? *Louisiana Weekly.*

Burby, R. J. (2003). Making plans that matter: Citizen involvement and government action. *Journal of the American Planning Association, 69*(1), 33–49.

Calder, C. (2015, September 7). New university medical center, upcoming veterans affairs complex ignite New Orleans housing, commercial boom. *New Orleans Advocate.* Retrieved from www.theadvocate.com/new_orleans/news/article_51bcd173-a469-5201-bdae-cc5ffe62f568.html.

Campanella, R. (2015, May 29). The great Katrina footprint debate 10 years later. *New Orleans Times Picayune.* Retrieved from www.nola.com/katrina/index.ssf/2015/05/footprint_gentrification_katri.html.

Campbell, S. (1996). Green cities, growing cities, just cities? Urban planning and the contradictions of sustainable development. *Journal of the American Planning Association, 62*(3), 296–312.

Campbell, S. (2016). The planner's triangle revisited: Sustainability and the evolution of a planning ideal that can't stand still. *Journal of the American Planning Association, 82*(4), 388–397.

City of Minneapolis. (2013). *Greenway Heights tax increment financing plan.* Retrieved from www.minneapolismn.gov/www/groups/public/@cped/documents/webcontent/wcms1p-115222.pdf.

Data Center. (2016). *Neighborhood statistical area data profiles.* Retrieved from www.datacenterresearch.org/data-resources/neighborhood-data/.

Dolezalek, H. (2015, September 23). Greenway Heights creates room for families. *Finance and Commerce.* Retrieved from http://finance-commerce.com/2015/09/greenway-heights-creates-room-for-families/.

Fields, B. (2009). From green dots to greenways: Planning in the age of climate change in post-Katrina New Orleans. *Journal of Urban Design, 14*(3), 325–344.

Fields, B., Wagner, J., & Frisch, M. (2015). Placemaking and disaster recovery: Targeting place for recovery in post-Katrina New Orleans. *Journal of Urbanism, 8*(1), 38–56.

Fields, B., Thomas, J., & Wagner, J. A. (2017). Living with water in the era of climate change: Lessons from the Lafitte Greenway in post-Katrina New Orleans. *Journal of Planning Education and Research, 37*(3), 309–321.

Flanagan, E., Lachapelle, U., & El-Geneidy, A. (2016). Riding tandem: Does cycling infrastructure investment mirror gentrification and privilege in Portland, OR and Chicago, IL? *Research in Transportation Economics, 60,* 14–24.

Godschalk, D. R. (2004). Land use planning challenges: Coping with conflicts in visions of sustainable development and livable communities. *Journal of the American Planning Association, 70*(1), 5–13.

Gotham, K. F., & Greenberg, M. (2014). *Crisis cities: Disaster and redevelopment in New York and New Orleans.* Oxford: Oxford University Press.

Greater New Orleans Housing Alliance (GNOHA). (2015). *10 year strategy and implementation plan: For a more equitable New Orleans.* Retrieved from www.housingnola.org/main/plans.

Handy, S., & McCann, B. (2010). The regional response to federal funding for bicycle and pedestrian projects: An exploratory study. *Journal of the American Planning Association, 77*(1), 23–38.

Heberle, L. C., McReynolds, B., Sizemore, S., & Schilling, J. (2017). HUD's Sustainable Communities Initiative: An emerging model of place-based federal policy and collaborative capacity building. *Cityscape, 19*(3), 9–37.

Hirsch, A. R., & Levert, A. L. (2009). The Katrina conspiracies: The problem of trust in rebuilding an American city. *Journal of Urban History, 35*(2), 207–219.

Immergluck, D., & Balan, T. (2017). Sustainable for whom? Green urban development, environmental gentrification, and the Atlanta Beltline. *Urban Geography, 39*(4), 546–562.

Johnson, A., Diedrick, K., Scher, A., Koenig, B., Dirnbach, E., & Ball, B. (2017). *Beltlining: Gentrification, broken promises and hope on Atlanta's Southside.* Housing Justice League and Research/Action. Retrieved from http://researchaction.net/2017/10/12/beltlining/.

Krizek, K. J. (2006). Two approaches to valuing some of bicycle facilities' presumed benefits: Propose a session for the 2007 national planning conference in the city of brotherly love. *Journal of the American Planning Association, 72*(3), 309–320.

Lafitte Corridor Revitalization Plan. (2013). Retrieved from www.dropbox.com/s/2eca7w4mgf7yg 4g/Revitalization-Plan_part1_final.pdf?dl=0.

LaRose, G. (2016, July 7). Planning Commission approves Sidney Torres' 382-unit Mid-City apartment complex. *Times-Picayune.* Retrieved from http://realestate.nola.com/realestate-news/2016/06/planning_commission_approves_3.html.

Lindsey, G., Man, J., Payton, S., & Dickson, K. (2004). Property values, recreation values, and urban greenways. *Journal of Park and Recreation Administration, 22*(3), 69–90.

Lowe, K. (2016). Environmental justice and pedestrianism: Sidewalk continuity, race, and poverty in New Orleans, Louisiana. *Transportation Research Record: Journal of the Transportation Research Board, 2598,* 119–123.

Nagel, C., & Watkins, K. E. (2017, November 28). *Urban parks' emerging role as transportation infrastructure.* Retrieved from www.governing.com/commentary/col-urban-parks-emerging-role-transportation-infrastructure.html.

Nelson, M. (2014). Using land swaps to concentrate redevelopment and expand resettlement options in post-Hurricane Katrina New Orleans. *Journal of the American Planning Association, 80*(4), 426–437.

Nelson, M., Ehrenfeucht, R., & Laska, S. (2007). Planning, plans, and people: Professional expertise, local knowledge, and governmental action in post-Hurricane Katrina New Orleans. *Cityscape: A Journal of Policy Development and Research, 9*(3), 23–52.

Oberlink, M. R. (2008). *Opportunities for creating livable communities.* Washington, D.C.: AARP, Public Policy Institute.

Olshansky, R. B., Hopkins, L. D., & Johnson, L. A. (2012). Disaster and recovery: Processes compressed in time. *Natural Hazards Review, 13*(3), 173–178.

Parent, O., & Vom Hofe, R. (2013). Understanding the impact of trails on residential property values in the presence of spatial dependence. *Annals of Regional Science, 51*(2), 355–375.

Reckdahl, K. (2014, May 23). *New Orleans' dazzling post-Katrina parks boom.* Retrieved from https://nextcity.org/daily/entry/new-orleans-post-katrina-parks-boom.

Sayre, C. (2017, February 2). Lafitte Greenway spurring new real estate developments in 2017. *Times-Picayune.* Retrieved from www.nola.com/business/index.ssf/2017/02/lafitte_greenway_patio_bar_com.html.

Sisson, P. (2017, October 3). *Atlanta's Beltline, a transformative urban redevelopment, struggles with affordability*. Retrieved from www.curbed.com/2017/10/3/16411354/beltline-atlanta-affordable-housing-development-high-line.

Stein, P. (2015). Why are bike lanes such a heated symbol of gentrification? *Washington Post*. November 12. Retrieved from www.washingtonpost.com/news/local/wp/2015/11/12/why-are-bike-lanes-such-heated-symbols-of-gentrification/?noredirect=on&utm_term=.1ae899723ec2.

Unified New Orleans Plan (UNOP). (2007). Retrieved from www.nolaplans.com/plans/UNOP/UNOP_Citywide.pdf.

Chapter 12

LAS LOMAS COLONIA IN TEXAS: A LIVABLE COMMUNITY?

Cecilia Giusti

Introduction

*C*olonias (communities in Spanish) represent about 2,500 settlements that range from very small settlements to cities and house about half a million citizens, all within the U.S. These settlements are characterized by persistent poverty, minimal infrastructure, low educational attainment, and the concentration of Hispanics. Our research of more than 15 years in Texas colonias has us question if colonias are *livable* places.

This chapter analyzes colonias beyond the simplistic view of calling them *poor non-livable* places. Instead, it explores how colonia residents are creating community and livable places. Moreover, we discuss what other indicators could be used to assess livability.

While we discuss Texas colonias in general, we focus our work on Las Lomas, a colonia in Starr County, on the Texas-Mexico border. This case study of Las Lomas is relevant because of its history of engagement and civic participation as expressed in their fight for land ownership. Their struggle, against corrupt developers, led by the grassroots organization Colonias Unidas, ended up with a march to the Texas Capitol and a victory for colonia citizens. As a result, they received legal rights to their land.

In the next section a description of Texas colonias, and Las Lomas in particular, is presented. Using traditional indicators, Las Lomas is evaluated, and then a new perspective of the same colonia is discussed using alternative indicators within a livability approach. The chapter ends with a final reflection and overall conclusions.

What are Colonias?

Officially, Texas colonias are defined as "substandard housing developments, often found along the Texas-Mexico border, where residents lack basic services such as drinking water, sewage treatment, and paved roads" (Texas Attorney General, 2018). Colonias are also found in other states and away from the Mexico border counties; however, Texas has the highest number of colonias and the largest colonia population in the United States.

Research on colonias explains their existence as a result of market failures and the shortage of housing alternatives (Larson, 1995; Ward, 1999; Ward, de Souza, Giusti, Larson, & May,

2003; Giusti, Larson, Ward, de Souza, & May, 2007). These settlements have not been planned or plotted, some have emerged suddenly, and still some are out of the purview of public officials. In the majority of the cases, residents settle on land that has been acquired through transactions, though many times dubious, as will be explained later.

Figure 12.1 shows selected Texas border counties that have a concentration of colonias. There is not an exact account of the number of colonias in Texas. Different institutions have different estimates. The Texas Council on Environmental Quality (TCEQ) estimates a total of 400,000 people living in more than 2,300 colonias. The *Texas Tribune* reports about 840,000 people in Texas colonias (Esquinca & Jaramillo, 2017), while the Federal Reserve Bank of Dallas (2015) estimates about 500,000 people living in colonias. Table 12.1 shows ten counties in Texas that have a concentration of 1,836 colonias with a population of 384,761 (Office of the Texas Secretary of State, 2010). Given all these estimates, there is no official number for existing colonias. Regardless of an exact number, we estimate that there are more than 2,000 colonias with about 500,000 people living there.

By definition, colonias are poor, isolated, and *in need*. The common indicators used to characterize colonias are: income, educational attainment, poverty, and ethnicity. Table 12.2 shows

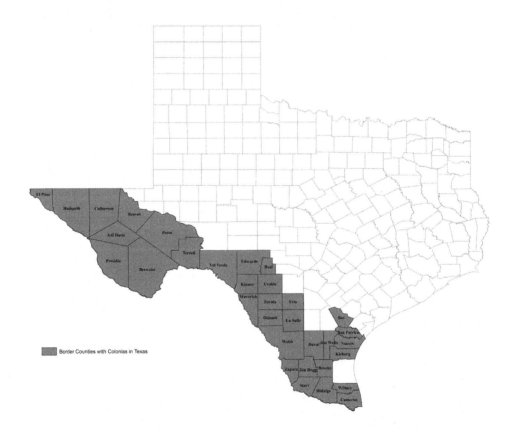

Figure 12.1 Selected Texas border counties.

Source: Attorney General of Texas.

Table 12.1 Colonias in Selected Texas Border Counties

Counties	Number of Colonias	Colonias Population
Hidalgo	934	156,132
Starr	226	34,742
El Paso	324	77,864
Cameron	178	47,606
Willacy	16	3,460
Webb	62	21,022
Zapata	41	13,807
Maverick	69	22,459
Val Verde	15	7,603
Kinney	1	66
Totals:	1,836	384,761

Source: Secretary of State (2010).

these indicators for one *typical* colonias, namely Las Lomas. Las Lomas has approximately 3,147 residents, with 90% Hispanic ethnicity. It is much higher than the 30% at the state level but lower than the 96% in Starr County. Education attainment in terms of high school or equivalent is 32%. This is very far from the 47.9% in Starr County, which is already much lower than 87% in Texas. The inequity is worse at the bachelor degree or higher level. In Las Lomas, it was less than 10% as compared with 30% in the state. Median household income in Las Lomas was about a fourth of the state. Poverty in Los Lomas is proportionally three times higher than the state of Texas. The people of Las Lomas tend to be extremely poor with limited work skills.

Table 12.2 Las Lomas Colonia, Basic Indicators

Location	2010 Census		
	Texas	Starr	Las Lomas (CDP)
Population	25,145,561	60,968	3,147
Hispanic or Latino (%)	37.6	95.7	89.6
Education (25 years and over)			
High school diploma or higher (%)	87	47.9	32
Bachelor's degree or higher (%)	30.3	9.8	9.2
Poverty			
Individuals below poverty (%)	12.7	37.6	36.3
Income			
Median household income	$55,322	$24,441	$14,107
Per capita income	$24,441	$11,659	$7,126

Source: Census Bureau (2010).

Another characteristic of colonias is their location and legal status. Most of them were established outside of the city limits in what is called extra territorial jurisdictions (ETJ). Colonias have also been involved with irregularities related to the acquisition of properties and the recording within official records.

To summarize, colonias have persistent poverty, substandard housing, minimal infrastructure, lack of public and private services, and physical isolation. Given these issues, the state and federal authorities see them as *the colonias' problem*. Furthermore, colonias are perceived as *hopeless* communities. While the colonias have poor conditions, do they have aspects of a livable community? When looking deeply into their situation, do they have hope? The next section discusses this in more detail.

Livability, Empowerment Framework

We propose to examine colonias beyond poverty. This section looks at to what extent, in the middle of this economically deprived area, and within evident physical constraints, colonias are becoming or are now-livable places. A key question is, what makes a place livable? Several authors discuss this from a variety of perspectives (Evans, 2002; Partners for Livable Communities, 2000). These authors show that the definition of a livable community varies depending on which indicators are used. We believe that non-tangible factors need to be included to assess how colonia residents feel about their communities. These factors can explain how and why colonia residents feel attachment to the places they are creating with their own efforts and how they are re-inventing their perception of what a community is. Moreover, they can describe how they are transforming seemingly uninviting spaces into welcoming places.

We have observed individual and community efforts to improve housing and basic infrastructure in colonias, and as a result of these improvements, solidarity, cooperation, and a sense of worth have been enhanced. While we still observe low education attainment and high unemployment, we also confirm that individual ingenuity, creativity, and personal drive by the residents have taken place. Additionally, colonia residents have opened up their own businesses and created their own employment. Intangible indicators such as empowerment, attachment to place, and a sense of pride are combined with tangibles, such as housing (individual) and infrastructure improvements (community). The more we observed these particular variables, the more livable colonias were.

To present these arguments, this chapter focuses on Las Lomas, a colonia with a long history of engagement and empowerment (Ward et al., 2003; Ward, de Souza, & Giusti, 2004; Giusti & Estevez, 2011). Our involvement with this colonia dates back about 15 years. Las Lomas is relevant because of the several non-tangible indicators that can be found there to help explain an expanded definition of livability. Residents have been able to improve their places in a variety of projects and policies, and as a result, stronger community ties have emerged. To accomplish such success, Las Lomas has used local and external support. Their initiatives have emerged because of their inner strength.

Las Lomas is not an isolated case of activism. There are more cases in which residents have risen to claim their rights, for example, El Cenizo in Webb County, Texas. Local residents were tired of not getting basic infrastructure and not being heard, so they took it upon themselves to become a city. This official designation allowed El Cenizo residents more access to resources and institutional support. While still a low-income community, the City of El Cenizo functions with a half-time staff (because of its limited budget). Nevertheless, the City of El Cenizo has much more autonomy in the decision-making process as a result of formally becoming a city. After early steps in city governance, El Cenizo became national news in 2001, when the city council voted to conduct its official meetings in Spanish to engage most of its only Spanish-speaking citizens. Furthermore, in 2004, they elected Mr. Raul Reyes, who was 21 years old and a part-time student, mayor. He was the youngest mayor ever elected in Texas history. Mr. Reyes is currently serving his seventh term in office. Much has been accomplished in infrastructure and in creating and supporting community improvements (Giusti, 2003).

Colonias in El Paso are another example of inner strength and courage that was shown by residents. Citizens organized and won a victory, when, in 1988, they successfully requested and got a plan from the Texas Water Development Board to build a water plant to treat 25 million gallons of water a day to serve up to 78,000 people (Donelson & Esparza, 2010). These examples are not isolated. There are many other cases where local residents, feeling strong and powerful, have organized themselves to work together in these deprived communities to make them more livable and more welcoming (Ward et al., 2003).

Las Lomas: Contract for Deed and Beyond

Las Lomas colonia is located a few miles outside of Rio Grande City, and it consists of six sub-divisions that together make it one of the oldest colonias in Starr County. Developers started selling property in this colonia in the late 1970s, but most of its growth happened in the mid-1980s. As with many other colonias, land tenure (legal rights) and physical infrastructure (water and sewage, electricity, and paved roads) were common problems. Las Lomas, as with many other colonias, was started by developers partitioning the land, as platting was almost non-existent. No plat means that there is not a map of the area, which in turn means there are no defined boundaries of each property. In addition, there is no clarity as to where streets would be located or utility easements, public access, etc. For a legally registered property or record, it is required to have the proper plat. The lack of platting resulted in many difficulties. First, there were problems amongst lot owners who could not easily resolve lot boundaries and location issues; second, problems between private owners with public land as there was not clarity from the beginning where streets were going to be. Some lots ended up with no access to public roads (Ward et al., 2003). And third, flooding was a problem, as some lots were located in the middle of a stream of water (sold during the dry season) or within a floodplain area (see Figure 12.2).

Making things even more complicated, developers did not provide proper title to residents who bought the land under a *contract for deed* instead of doing it through a mortgage deed (Larson, 1995, 2002). Contract for deed, also known as a *poor man's mortgage*, is a legal and highly flexible way to finance real estate purchases. It is used mostly when potential buyers cannot afford the down payment or when income levels of potential buyers do not qualify them for conventional financial methods (Jensen, 1996; Larson, 2002; Mettling, 1997). The caveat of contract for deed is that the actual title is not transferred until the property is paid in full.

Colonias properties were transacted away from regulated cities, and this *contract for deed* was all they had available for these very low-income families. Many of them were migrant workers who were trying to secure their investment. They would start paying for a lot in one colonia, then migrate north for a few months to work and come back to continue investing in the property.

Figure 12.2 Colonias in Texas.

Source: Author.

While it could have worked, and was the only affordable option available for colonia residents, several irregularities happened in the process, and developers quite often did not fulfill their promises. One common broken promise was on the provision of services. Residents were promised when buying land that some of the services were going to be available with time, but that did not happen. Even worse, some of the properties were resold. This happened for some families who started paying for a lot then migrated north for a few months. When they returned, they found another family on their lot (Ward et al., 2003). Without a proper contract, residents did not have a legal way to claim their rights over the contested property. This was a real problem that needed to be addressed. Las Lomas subdivisions were a typical example of some or all of these misdeeds.

After so many irregularities in several colonias, the case was taken to the Texas courts in the early 2000s. During the process, strong leaders emerged and one organization became the voice of most residents, namely Colonias Unidas.

Self-help: Colonias Unidas

Colonias Unidas is a grassroots organization located in the heart of Las Lomas. Originally it had been a local focus just dealing with water, electricity, paved roads, and the provision of basic services to colonias. Over time, it expanded its scope and became a not-for-profit organization with the goal of bettering the quality of life of all colonia residents. Colonias Unidas was a key player in the legal case against developers presented to the Texas courts in the early 2000s. The case related to the legal framework used to sell property in colonias, namely the contract for deed versus deed (Ward et al., 2003). Without the active involvement of this grassroots organization, the actual legal intervention could not have been possible. Strong leaders emerged, especially women leaders, from the community and active members of Colonias Unidas. These activists played a leadership role both in Las Lomas and in the legal representation of all colonias involved in the legal complaint.

As stated earlier, Colonias Unidas emerged from local residents. They organized as a result of the lack of response to their immediate demands. It responded to specific physical needs even before the legal complications from the contract for deed instrument for many residents was evident. While lacking services and basic infrastructure, the people had the capacity and did organize themselves. It started with leadership from within, and a network of support was established. They looked for external financial support, and they pursued strategic alliances and searched for more training on how to be better and more informed leaders. In this case, a few local leaders were trained as *community land specialists* through one of the special programs supporting low-income communities. The training came from the Minority Land Security Program of the Land Tenure Center from the University of Wisconsin at Madison in partnership with Tuskegee University. This program consisted of giving basic legal training to local leaders, who then served as resources within their communities. The explicit goal of this training was to help low-income residents retain their land, and they succeeded.

The results of community empowerment in Las Lomas are well documented (Ward et al., 2004; Giusti, 2003). After obtaining legal rights over their property, morale and self-esteem were uplifted, and a greater sense of legitimacy and a stronger sense of community were created. At the same time, it created a better relationship with local government. It needs to be reinforced that while several external actors supported colonias' claims, the strength of the community involvement made all the difference. Empowerment, a sense of belonging, and pride in local capacity are all indicators of livability in communities. While Las Lomas is a proud low-income colonia, it has demonstrated capacity to take matters into its own hands.

Through these struggles, strong networks were better developed among residents in the subdivisions of Las Lomas Colonia. Lastly, the empowerment of colonia residents involved issues far more complicated and ambitious than water and electricity. It has also showed how local capacity can be organized to formulate priorities and accomplish what they proposed.

Nuestra Casa: Our Home

After the main title and platting of Las Lomas was resolved, it was evident that residents had to face more challenges. One challenge in particular emerged as the next priority, and that was how to improve housing quality. Las Lomas residents started with what they had. Residents were already building their houses as their finances allowed them, without regulatory controls or zoning restrictions. This method was called *incremental construction*: owners improve their properties as money becomes available (Greene & Rojas, 2008). This way of building and improving housing may take several years, but residents can occupy the house while construction is still happening. This reality was acknowledged in the program run by the same not-for profit organization, Community Resources Group (CRG), that supported the legal battle for title and that ended in the receivership program. CRG continued working with Colonias Unidas in Las Lomas. The Nuestra Casa (Our Home) program was led by CRG in partnership with Colonias Unidas and was an innovative revolving funding scheme that extended micro loans for home improvements to colonia residents (Giusti & Estevez, 2011).

Colonias homeowners with proper title were eligible to take loans for home improvements. The Nuestra Casa program issued small/micro loans ($2,500 per loan) for home improvement to applicants who showed payment capacity. The money lent was to be used only for home improvements and should be paid back with interest (around 9%) in not more than three years. This interest rate was estimated as the necessary amount that allowed the fund to continue offering new loans to more residents, making the program sustainable in the longer term. If program participants paid back the loan, they were eligible for another one. The system was such that residents were able to accumulate loans and make major improvements.

The results from this loan program were positive for the residents and for the community in many aspects (Giusti & Estevez, 2011). First, Nuestra Casa proved to be a tool for the financially underserved population, like colonias residents are. Despite being low income, this program demonstrated that some people still have the capacity to go into debt and subsequently repay the loan for incremental construction. Second, it was found that Nuestra Casa delinquency rates (not paying back the loan) stayed at 3%. This means that only 3% of loan recipients missed their payments for more than three months. This tells us that the poor can be responsible financial players. Giusti and Estevez (2011) showed that program participants were so grateful for the loans they received that they were more than eager to meet their monthly payments. Third, in doing small improvements, most homeowners did some of the work by themselves. A large percentage (70%) also needed to hire some labor, which they found in the same colonia or in a nearby one. This means that the money they received from the loan circulates within the local economy. Furthermore, 47% of the loan recipients purchased lumber and related materials from colonia providers. Thus, buying materials within the colonias also has a positive impact on the local economy. Finally, though loans seem too small to make a difference in housing quality, the low starting point of the housing stock makes even these small improvements meaningful.

This alternative indicator of empowerment should be considered when discussing livability. Overall, the Neustra Casa loan program, along with grassroots organizations, proved that residents could be successful in a loan program instead of a charity program. Loan recipients, while paying back their loans, became active agents in their own future. Moreover, residents who obtained their title and were able to improve their properties were also investing in their communities. The economic impact of their investment allowed for an economic multiplier effect through labor and the local provision of construction materials.

Colonia Entrepreneurship

The last indicator discussed here is related to entrepreneurship. It is evident that colonia residents, far from being receivers or passive recipients of aid, are active economic players who are taking initiative on improving their colonias, and in doing so, are empowering themselves. Data on unemployment in Texas colonias show an estimated 50% rate, while 43% of adults are not

Figure 12.3 Businesses in colonias, entryway.

Source: Author.

even in the labor force (Federal Reserve Bank of Dallas, 2015). This reality begs the question, what other ways are available to generate income? The way this can happen is through what is called the *informal economy*. The International Labour Organization (ILO) defines the informal sector as units engaged in the production of goods and services without proper contractual agreements and with no labor laws protection (International Labour Organization, 2018).

As proposed by the Federal Reserve Bank of Dallas (2015), informality is expected in colonias given the level of income, education attainment, and employment data. Self-employment and creativity in job creation is what is expected and what is indeed found in colonias. Two more factors add to what was just presented. First, colonias are mostly separated from main urban centers and have little infrastructure or basic services; second, there are few job opportunities as there is little economic activity present. All these factors can explain why entrepreneurship is prevalent among the colonia population (Federal Reserve Bank of Dallas, 2015; Giusti & Kim, 2009).

Since the early establishment of colonias, the opening of a few new businesses spurs the opening of additional ones, such as hair salons, party supplies, arts and crafts, small food vendors, and then construction materials and services, and so on. Such businesses start supplying basic services to the growing colonia population (Giusti & Kim, 2009). With no zoning or other regulatory constraints, colonias have evolved to be multi-use areas with different housing realities that allow an *informal business* to locate within residential units.

Businesses pop up in almost all colonias, and residents benefit from such activities. As a result, there are often enough customers to make some businesses financially viable. The lack of parks or shared spaces creates opportunities to socialize at local businesses. This promotes a higher level of walking socialization (Giusti, Lee, Lord, & Wieters, 2008).

The prevalence of entrepreneurship amid a very isolated and precarious colonia reality has resulted in policies that promote local initiatives. Colonia residents, once more, show ingenuity in creating their means of income with inner strength. The residents do not expect services going to them. Instead, they are entrepreneurs working in creative ways. Serving them with several micro-lending programs has been successful through the Federal Reserve Bank of Dallas (2015). The residents in colonias are still low-income, but they are not expecting subsidies or charity. They are working to create their own sources of income through entrepreneurship.

To support these emerging businesses, colonia residents created office centers in the community. These are shared places are where several services are offered for potential and existing businesses; for example, legal advice, technical support, or financial consultancy services; regular providers include a workforce commission, micro-lending vendors and national banks, and a small business development center. The provision of services is done in these shared spaces serving local business needs in colonias.

Livability in Las Lomas: A Discussion

The Federal Reserve Bank of Dallas (FRBD) reported a somber view of colonias back in 2008, indicating that they were poor, isolated, and in need of strong investment from federal or state authorities. However, in its 2015 report, *Las Colonias in the 21 Century*, the Federal Reserve Bank of Dallas presented a very different assessment. They said that the amount of money invested in infrastructure, education, and services has allowed colonias to emerge with the potential to become communities.

The residents of the colonias have achieved a great deal through their will and sheer persistence. It was not accomplished by gifts or help. In most cases, what they received was the result of long struggles, hard work, and sometimes open protests from residents and grassroots organizations like Colonias Unidas. Second, the capacity and resilience of colonia residents have allowed them to persevere in their own communities. Third, colonia residents are defining their own priorities, like their fight for legal ownership of their property. This was especially relevant as this was the first needed step to invest in their housing improvements. It was also necessary to apply for loans. Fourth, basic infrastructure is being constructed in the colonias, making their quality of life much better. This has been very helpful. Finally, several micro-loan programs for housing and microenterprises are empowering colonia residents and improving their individual and community capacity.

When asked, after receiving a title to their home, if they were willing to move to another, *better* place, the overwhelming response was no (Ward et al., 2003). More than 80% responded that they wanted to remain in the colonia and were making accommodations for family increases within their houses. Residents found a place they could call home. Given all the indicators noted earlier, we conclude that colonias are actually becoming livable places. As colonia residents have had to fight for each of their improvements, strong community ties have emerged, as well as pride for what they have accomplished.

Colonias like Las Lomas could be characterized as a concentration of low-income, unskilled laborers with high poverty rates and little hope. However, we differ with this characterization. We have witnessed proud and committed people making their communities better. Moreover, we presented alternative indicators that define livability. In conclusion, while the colonia residents are poor and isolated, they have forged on to develop improved communities and have created a social fabric resulting in livable places.

References

Donelson, A., & Esparza, A. (Eds.). (2010). *The colonias reader: Economy, housing, and public health in U.S.-Mexico border colonias.* Tucson, AZ: University of Arizona Press.

Esquinca, M., & Jaramillo, A. (2017, August 22). Colonias on the border struggle with decades-old water issues. *Texas Tribune.* Retrieved from www.texastribune.org/2017/08/22/colonias-border-struggle-decades-old-water-issues/.

Evans, P. (Ed.). (2002). *Livable cities? Urban struggles for livelihood and sustainability.* Berkeley, CA: University of California Press.

Federal Reserve Bank of Dallas—Community Affairs Office. (2008). *Texas colonias: A thumbnail sketch of the conditions, issues, challenges and opportunities.* Retrieved from www.dallasfed.org/ca/pubs/colonias.pdf.

Federal Reserve Bank of Dallas. (2015). *Las colonias in the 21 Century: Progress along the Texas-Mexico border.* Retrieved from www.dallasfed.org/assets/documents/cd/pubs/lascolonias.pdf.

Giusti, C. (2003). Colonias along the Texas-Mexico border as an example of a pattern of city growth. In A. Petroccioli, M. Stella, & G. Strappa (Eds.), *The planned city?* (pp. 387–392). Proceedings of the ISUF (International Seminar on Urban Form) International Conference (Volume II). Bari, Italy: Uniongrafica Corcelli Editrice.

Giusti, C., & Estevez, L. (2011). Microlending for housing in the United States: A case-study in colonias in Texas. *Habitat International, 35*(2), 307–315.

Giusti, C., & Kim, S. K. (2009). Microbusinesses in colonias along the Texas-Mexico border and their contribution to sustainable economic development. *Trialog 101, 2,* 31–38.

Giusti, C., Larson, J., Ward, P., de Souza, F., & May, M. (2007). Land titling in Starr County *colonias* along the Texas-Mexico border: Planning and stability issues. *Projections, 6,* 36–55.

Giusti, C., Lee, C., Lord, D., & Wieters, M. (2008). *Transportation infrastructure and quality of life for disadvantage populations: A pilot study of El Cenizo Colonia in Texas.* College Station, TX: Texas A&M University. Retrieved from http://swutc.tamu.edu/publications/technical reports/167162-1.pdf.

Greene, M., & Rojas, E. (2008). Incremental construction: A strategy to facilitate access to housing. *Environment and Urbanization, 20*(1), 89–108.

International Labour Organization. (2018). *Informal economy.* Retrieved from www.ilo.org/global/topics/employment-promotion/informal-economy/lang-en/index.htm.

Jensen, J. (1996). *Regulation of residential contracts for deed in Texas: Senate Bill 366 and beyond* (M.A. professional report). Austin, TX: LBJ School of Public Affairs, University of Texas at Austin.

Larson, J. (1995). Free markets in the heart of Texas. *Georgetown Law Journal, 84*(2), 179–260.

Larson, J. (2002). Informality, illegality, and inequality. *Yale Law and Policy Review, 20*(1), 137–182.

Mettling, S. (1997). *The contract for deed.* Chicago, IL: Real Estate Education Company.

Office of the Texas Secretary of State. (2010). *The colonias program: Tracking the progress of state funded projects that benefit colonias.* Report presented to Senate Bill 99, 82nd Texas Legislature Regular Session.

Partners for Livable Communities. (2000). *The livable city: Revitalizing urban communities*. New York: McGraw-Hill.

Texas Attorney General. (2018). Retrieved on March 2, 2018, from www.texasattorneygeneral.gov/cpd/colonias.

Ward, P. (1999). *Colonias and public policy in Texas and Mexico: Urbanization by stealth*. Austin, TX: University of Texas Press.

Ward, P., de Souza, F., Giusti, C., Larson, J., & May, M. (2003). *Being an evaluation of the Community Resource Group (CRG) colonia lot titling program in Rio Grande City, Starr County, Texas*. Final Report. Presented to the Community Resources Group.

Ward, P., de Souza, F., & Giusti, C. (2004). Colonia land and housing market performance and the impact of lot title regularization in Texas. *Urban Studies, 41*(13), 2621–2646.

Chapter 13

LIMA: A LIVABLE CITY
Ana Sabogal Dunin Borkowski

Introduction

Currently the concept of sustainable cities implies a livable city. A livable city has to be functional and requires public spaces for good health as well as for social and cultural integration.

One characteristic of Latin American cities is that they are megacities with traffic problems and air contamination, where wealth and poverty come together. How to make this city livable is a difficult question. In this context, open spaces play an interesting scenario where all city problems can be found. In the city of Lima, like in most Latin American cities, open spaces are not always public spaces, so they don't play the role of social and cultural integrators. The division of social classes is evidenced in the spatial division and dysfunction. Slums, common to all megacities, are not planned spaces; most of them are located in degraded (Ferris, Norman, & Sempik, 2001; Francis & Chadwick, 2013) or risky areas.

In Lima the slums are situated near the river, the road, or on the slopes. In those areas family relations and organization is very important to survival, especially in new areas that are beginning to develop. Most Latin American cities have very poor peri-urban areas, where field migrants settled, and residential peri-urban areas, where the rich population live with big spaces for swimming pools and private green areas. The question is why this spatial division develops, and how this division can be used to develop a better model of a city.

The distribution of green areas and parks is not uniform and is directly related to the economic status of the people that live in the area. The poor have few parks and green areas in general, whereas, the middle class demands to be given parks and then uses them, and the higher class uses private spaces such as clubs and parks for social integration (Sabogal, Tavera, Suarez, & Pastor, 2017). The municipality data doesn't distinguish between the private and the public space, and least does it distinguish between green and cemented public spaces.

The growth of Lima is centripetal with concentric expansion. The old historical center of Lima city has been abandoned by its original inhabitants, who have been replaced by others from another social condition. The city expands from here and grows around the central historic city. In one direction we have residential areas and in the other high-poverty urban areas. Since the start of the 21st century, this city expansion has had a return phase promoted by the government, rebuilding or repairing old buildings. New pedestrian streets have been built in the city center, and the rebuilt spaces are now used as government buildings.

The livability can be determined by analyzing separate elements such as percentage of free spaces, and most others, but there is no metric to determine livability. It depends on the point of view of the citizens. It is a concept that includes sociocultural aspects that depend on the cultural groups that compose the city and the space. This chapter intends to determine the livability of the city through environmental indicators, one of them being the green areas in the city.

Livable Cities

Today a new concept for cities is the concept of *livable cities*. The question is, what determines this concept? In what way can we have a livable city? What is an ideal city? However, when we make reference to a "livable" city, aren't we just conforming and parting from the concept of an ideal city? Making a recount of the past years, before we came up with the idea of livable cities, we started thinking about sustainable cities, and if we go all the way back to the 19th century, we dreamt of a city with a lot of culture, in which fashion had to be in avant-garde, and theaters and coffee shops had to be visited by famous artists and writers. Paris, Berlin, and Warsaw were dream cities of the 19th century. Nonetheless, cities of Latin America like Lima and Petropolis also went through a period of alleged splendor that ended with the immigration bringing to evidence that this splendor was only a dream.

We are now aware that when planning a city we have to consider blue-collar workers, housekeepers, peddlers, handymen, and every person that works and lives in the city. In this sense, the concept of ideal city is actually not realistic.

A *livable city* is one where people can walk or ride a bicycle without fear. It is not possible to consider a city livable if there is no safety. Insecurity implies that inhabitants lose their freedom, which is the most important condition that a city should provide. The feeling of freedom has always been one of the main attractions of cities.

But that is also a utopia because today in all cities of the world, and more in the Latin American cities, liberty doesn't exist, and criminality is part of the city life. The problems of Lima are the same as the problems of any megacity: violence, poverty, and contamination.

Properties in Latin American cities are surrounded by high gates. It seems that people are resigned to being confined. A livable city is one that people acknowledge as their own and where they feel comfortable. People should have their favorite corners, walking routes, parks, and shops. Citizens should identify with the other people that live in their city.

Among different cities we can identify two models of organization: centralized cities with all activity concentrated downtown; and cities centered in quarters, where each quarter has its own independent dynamic, and inhabitants do not need to use transport from one part of the city to another every day. In these cities traffic problems are reduced, commuting time is minimal, and it is possible to use bicycles, reducing the air contamination. Most Latin American cities have a central distribution with a dominant downtown that congregates the ministries and political activities. In these cities the poor and rich occupy the outside of the cities. Under this model the central administration and businesses are in the city center. This has caused a fragmented city with urban *ghettos*; some of them are rich and others poor. People have excluded themselves.

While Latin American countries follow the centralized model, European cities follow the second model. Under this model people's daily activities take place in the same area they live, so a lot of time is not wasted commuting. Irracheta (2013) writes that cities in Latin America have their own character; they are characterized today by hyper-urbanization, poverty, climate change, unplanned development, cultural diversity, and migration.

Migration in Lima is not the same as migration in the cities of Europe and the United States, where migrants come from other countries. For example in Toronto, foreign migrants compose 44% of the population, whereas in Vancouver, the figure is 38% (Tomalty, 2005). These migrants are culturally very different from the non-migrant population and don't even speak the language. In Latin America, although most people that migrate to the cities come from rural areas within the same country, there is also a huge cultural difference between them and the non-migrants. Most of them do have Spanish as a common language.

The new cultural groups have exploited great business opportunities and have become an important economic force. They have grown and developed, not only in economic terms, but also in terms of education. Today more than half of the university students of Lima are part of this new generation of children of migrants whose parents don't have a university degree.

In Latin America the population is concentrated in the cities, which grow centripetally (Bähr & Mertins, 1995; Heineberg, 2017). In 2010, 79% of Latin Americans lived in cities (UNEP, 2012; Heineberg, 2017). Latin American cities expand without urban planning through land invasions by migrants from the rural areas. Areas originally planned for schools, parks, and open spaces are occupied by invasions, so the city has a lack of free space and green areas, most of which are risk areas such as river banks.

Many authors describe urban problems through the optic of urban metabolism, which we could define as the balance between the production of energy and the elimination of waste. Waste is considered anything that has to be eliminated from the environment such as carbon dioxide, heat, and others. Urban metabolism includes three aspects: society, biotic system, and abiotic system (Weiland & Richter, 2009). Urban metabolism impacts the health of the city and includes risks, vulnerability, and resilience to change. The concept of urban metabolism is influenced by the concept of human and biosphere and by the concepts of sustainable development. A sustainable city is one with an urban metabolism that incorporates a variety of environmental techniques, but also respects sociocultural aspects of its inhabitants (Hagan, 2015). The concept is simple, but the implementation is not easy because it is necessary to develop techniques that ensure the reduction of emissions and their subsequent absorption. This includes also a sustainable management of the government and the municipalities.

There is a big difference between the ecology in the city and the ecology of the city (Grimm, Grove, Pickett, & Redman, 2000; Weiland & Richter, 2009). Urban metabolism studies the ecology of the city, whereas studies of the ecology in the city deal with the urban ecosystem and include aspects like climate, topography, geology, and hydrology. The urban ecosystem is the key to designing sustainable green spaces. In this chapter we apply both concepts in Lima city: urban metabolism is the state of the environment and the state of the ecology of the city.

Lima City

Lima is an old colonial city founded by Spain in 1535. Now it includes Callao, which developed as a port city in the 16th century. Lima has old cloisters, historical buildings, and parks in ruin. The rich population abandoned the old buildings and constructed new houses. The old construction is cheaper, and the new poor population is renting the old construction. Between 20% and 30% of Lima's population live in tenement houses (Riofrio, 2003).

Now Lima is a big city of 2,672 square kilometers. The problems of Lima are similar to other megacities: violence, poverty, and environmental problems are the most important. Peru, as a result of a rapid migration from the highland to the city, has become an urban country. Lima has become a megacity, and at the moment it has about 10 million people, which represent 31% of its population (INEI, 2015; OECD/UN ECLAC, 2017) most of whom are young (OECD/UN ECLAC, 2017). The suburban space is increasing, and the city is, too. Nevertheless, the population growth rates have been declining in Latin America (Da Gama, 2008).

Each city has its own identity and its own character (Watson, 2013). Which is the identity of Lima City? What do the citizens like about it? Which characteristics are the most distinctive for the citizens? Which characteristics make the citizens proud? In a survey by the Geography faculty of the Pontifical Catholic University of Peru, the students found that the most distinctive characteristic of Lima is informality. This is also the most appreciated characteristic. They described how informality makes them feel part of the city. Through chaos each social class finds its own form of life and possibilities to reduce the abysmal social, economic, and cultural differences. The social and family relationships of the migrant are important to reach this dynamic. But they can be the cause of social injustice and marginality that replicate pre-existing social differences. Two authors study and describe the case of migration to Lima City, Golte (2001) and Doughty (1969).

In Lima, like in other Latin American cities, the slums are distributed by peri-urban areas, but there are also slums downtown. The peri-urban slums have their own dynamic. In Peru, they have their own form of waste disposal and water treatment. Furthermore, in these areas rural and city coexist. There are vegetable gardens, and there is breeding of small animals.

The informal sector in Lima, like in other Latin American cities, is very important. Shantytowns grow with illegal settlements and precarious construction (Da Gama, 2008). Most invasions are carried out in areas intended for green areas (ibid.). In this way there is a relationship between poverty and the lack of green areas. Illegal land trafficking makes pacification of the city very difficult, causing a great problem for the city. Invasions are led by land traffickers who, for a low payment, give the population a new possibility of life in the city. Many groups of poor people invade high-risk areas with bad environmental conditions. The same phenomena occurred in Mexico City, where remote and risky areas have been invaded by poor people who can live in these areas without paying taxes or for services (Irracheta, 2013). In Lima these areas are located along the river margins, in the old deteriorated houses in Lima downtown, or on the slopes of the hills surrounding the city. After some years the municipalities have supplied basic needs to these areas, such as schools and hospitals. Whenever there have been natural disasters, such as floods or earthquakes, the population has been relocated to safer areas. The invasions contribute to expansion of the city in both directions without planning, so the city will be bigger and bigger.

Economic growth of the country in the last decade has caused the shantytowns to change a lot. Between 1991 and 2003, the very low-income sector grew considerably, by 17% (Cord, Genoni, & Rodríguez-Castelán, 2015). From 2003 to 2012 the economic growth contributed to the decrease in poverty and the equity (Liebenthal & Salvemini, 2013). By 2013 the poverty rate had decreased from 54% to 24% (OECD/UN ECLAC, 2017). The population living below the poverty line fell from 52.5% to 23.9% between 2003 and 2013 (ibid.). A new middle class is emerging in the peri-urban areas. Currently many of the children of first-generation migrants have a university degree. This is changing informality in Peru. Within the informal and illegal sectors, mining and logging are the most important activities (ibid.). The unemployed rate has fallen from 10% in 2003 to 4% in 2013 (ibid.). The Gini index for Peru is 0.44 for the year 2012. Inequality in Peru is bigger than in most OECD countries, with the exception of Chile and Mexico (ibid.).

The big differences between urban and rural areas are the cause of the migration to the cities. The difference between chronic malnutrition of children under 5 years old in the city and in the rural areas is immense; in the city it is 3.5%, and in the rural areas it is 15.8% (OECD/UN ECLAC, 2017). The difference in access to water in urban areas rose to 91%. Drinking water in Lima reaches over 90% of the population, and sanitation services reach 81%, whereas in the rural areas, these services are much lower, 67% and 50% respectively (ibid.). In 2012 in rural areas, 52% of the population had water inside their homes through connections to the public network; in the urban areas this was 83% (ibid.).

Environmental Problems of Lima City

Until 2010, considering the GNP per person, Lima was the second poorest city in Latin America (Denig, 2010). In the last five years, Lima has developed and grown. As a consequence of this economic growth, in 2013 Peru was the 8th richest country out of 26 countries in Latin America (Diario Gestión, 2013). In 2011 the first metro in Lima was constructed, and in 2015 the construction of the second line began. The implementation of the bus line and the implementation of bus line routes to replace the old microbuses was an important step for the city. A huge percentage of the public transportation system remains informal (OECD/UN ECLAC, 2017). In spite of poor planning, the implementation of bicycle lanes has increased the use bicycles in Lima. All of these elements contribute to the expectation that Lima will become a livable city.

In 2014 only 15.5% of Lima citizens had a car (Lima cómo vamos, 2014), whereas in Canada in 2005, 80% of the population had a car (Tomalty, 2005). The city infrastructure is not designed to have more cars, so that will bring chaos to the city. All citizens spend a lot of time in traffic to cross the city from their houses to their workplaces, and the noise level in Lima exceeds the recommended one; the principal cause is the noise produced by motor vehicles. From 2003 to 2012 the traffic of Peru has increased as a consequence of economic growth. In 2012 in Lima there were 135 vehicles per 1,000 inhabitants (MINAM, 2014a; OECD/UN ECLAC, 2017). Monitoring of air quality in Lima is insufficient. Traffic congestion and the lack of a master plan for traffic regulation are evident. It is necessary to have adequate information and to implement a good monitoring system to measure air quality (OECD/UN ECLAC, 2017).

In Lima the poor population has decreased in the last decade, but environmental problems have increased as a consequence of population growth, particularly in the poorer sectors

(La República, 2014). But the environmental tax revenue and environmental tax for environmental uses are very low (OECD/UN ECLAC, 2017). The Economist Intelligence Unit (EIU) (Denig, 2010), with the participation of different urban experts in green cities in Latin America, constructed an Environmental Index for Latin America using the European methodology of Green Cities. The index has nine different priority parameters: energy, carbon dioxide, land use and skyscrapers, transport, garbage, water, sanitary, air quality, and environmental governability. Official databases were used to establish the values. The databases of most Latin American cities were developed using only a small sample. These databases have confirmed that the main problems in Latin American cities are traffic, waste treatment, air quality, land use, and poor planning (Denig, 2010). It is clear that neither the government nor the citizens currently believe that good planning, like that in European cities, is a possibility in Latin America. We confirm that Latin American cities are far from integrating the concept of urban metabolism in city management.

According to the environmental observatory of the Municipality of Lima, the most important environmental problem of Lima is traffic. Other big problems in Lima are water supply, water quality, and air pollution. Nevertheless, the incidence of respiratory disease and diarrhea was reduced from 21% to 6% between 2003 and 2009 (Liebenthal & Salvemini, 2013). But in Lima the percentage of children under the age of 5 that were at risk of contracting acute diarrheal disease was 13.7% in 2013 (MINAM, 2018).

In Peru the most important cause of air pollution is lead, originating from transport and industry (Liebenthal & Salvemini, 2013). In Lima, especially downtown, the PM2.5 and PM10 are the most important pollutants. These two particles are higher than the permitted 30% level of the year (MINAM, 2012). Whereas the PM emissions, nitrogen dioxide, and SO_2 emissions declined (MINAM, 2014a; OECD/UN ECLAC, 2017), pollution in Lima is alarming, with 94 microgram/m^3/day of PM particles, almost double the pollution of other cities in Latin America—except for nitrogen dioxide, which is below average (Denig, 2010). In addition, it rains very little in Lima, only 7 mm/year, but it is very foggy and humid, so this fog traps the smog. In 2013, the average of PM2.5 was 48.52, just below the limit of 50 (MINAM, 2014b). The level of air pollution depends on the part of the city you are in. In 2010 the highest concentration of PM10 was found in the south and north of Lima, with less in the east and in the city center (MINAM, 2012).

From 2003 to 2013, according to the World Resources Institute, the total greenhouse gas emissions, including land use change in Peru, reached 0.34% of global emission and only 3.5% of Latin American and Caribbean emissions; specifically in 2012, 46% of the greenhouse gas emissions in Peru were a consequence of land use change and deforestation (OECD/UN ECLAC, 2017). Total emissions in 2010 could be broken down as follows: 35.1% tropical forest degradation, 32.7% energy sector (caused mainly by transportation vehicles), 21% agriculture, 6.2% waste, and 5.1% industrial processes (ibid.). Emissions of ozone destructive substances were considerably smaller; from 2003 to 2013, the ozone destructive emission decreased 88.48% (UNEP, 2012; OECD/UN ECLAC, 2017).

Regulations to control emissions through the maximum permissible level (MPL) include CO, NO_x, SO_x, HC and PM. Regulations to control gasoline fuel vehicles have been in force since 2008, but regulations to control diesel fuel vehicles, which produce high levels of SO_x emissions, is mandatory only in some areas, such as Lima and Callao (OECD/UN ECLAC,

2017). This can be explained by the fact that the refineries at la Pampilla, Conchan (state-owned), and Talara (Repsol property) produce diesel with huge SO_x concentrations operating under a concession contract, which does not allow this to be changed (ibid.). However, since 2003 diesel does have 5% of biodiesel and gasoline 7.8% of ethanol (ibid.), reducing air pollution in recent years.

Between 2007 and 2013 PM10 concentrations decreased 29%, PM2.5 43%, SO_2 33%, and NO_2 16% for Lima and Callao (MINAM, 2015; OECD/UN ECLAC, 2017). Air pollution indicators for this period were very high, exceeding the permitted limit in the case of PM10 and PM2.5, and reaching the limit in the case of SO_2 and the NO_2 (OECD/UN ECLAC, 2017). According to the OECD, more accurate information is needed regarding the distribution and quantity of emissions. Currently, Lima does not have an adequate monitoring system that can be statistically representative (ibid.).

For Peru, the cost of urban pollution was calculated to be 0.9% of the gross domestic product and has caused over 6,000 casualties in the poor sector of the city (MINAM, 2012). The cost of the environmental degradation was estimated at about 3.9% of the country's gross domestic product in 2003 (Liebenthal & Salvemini, 2013). According to MINAM (2014b), the cost of medical care for environmental-related illnesses was estimated at US$806 million (OECD/UN ECLAC, 2017).

In Latin American cities, each person produces 465 kg/year of waste, a little bit less than the waste production in Europe, where it is 511 kg/year (Denig, 2010). In Lima and Callao, the biggest cities of Peru, the per capita waste production is 0.58 kg/day/inhabitant (OECD/UN ECLAC, 2017), which is 245.48 kg/inhabitant/year, much less than in the other cities. Informal recycling is an important part of the dynamic of Latin America cities. There are about 1,000 recycling organizations, which is more than in any other region of Latin America (Banco InterAmericano de Desarrollo, 2016). In Peru 46.2% of the waste is not adequately dealt with (OECD/UN ECLAC, 2017). There is a big difference between Lima and the countryside; in 2007 in Lima, 92.6% of the garbage was disposed of in authorized landfills, whereas in the countryside, only 26.1% was (ibid.). Currently Peru has 11 garbage deposits (ibid.), 5 of which are in Lima, the biggest being Huaycoloro, where 50% of the garbage is processed (MINAM, 2012). In 2013, a formal company collected 87.5% of the garbage in Lima, but only 41% was taken to a sanitary landfill (MINAM, 2014c). Of the solid waste 30.3% was collected and recycled by the informal sector (MINAM, 2015). Only 12% of organizations that work in recycling and garbage collection were formal (Andina, 2012). Fifty percent of the collected waste was composed of organic material and 28% of recyclable non-hazardous waste (MINAM, 2014c). One of the important issues that must be resolved and regulated is the collection and treatment of hazardous waste. There are regulations for the disposal and reduction of this type of waste. However, these regulations have not been implemented.

Waste treatment and disposal are not a resolved problem for Peru. More than half of the solid waste is not adequately disposed of; it is dumped in illegal landfills, burned, or disposed of in the ocean (OECD/UN ECLAC, 2017). In Peru in 2012, only 24.5% of the municipalities prepared reports regarding waste disposal and treatment (MINAM, 2014c). There is little information about domestic waste (OECD/UN ECLAC, 2017). There are many reasons for this, one of which is the accelerated growth of the cities. Today 81% of the population in Latin America lives in cities (Denig, 2010), whereas at the beginning of the 20th century only 10% of the population did (Berry, 1990; Francis & Chadwick, 2013). The import and use of chemicals has grown considerably, but information about it is poor (OECD/UN ECLAC, 2017).

The water consumption is distributed as follows: 85.7% for farming, 10% for human consumption, 1.5% for mining, and 1% for manufacturing (MINAM, 2014b; OECD/UN ECLAC, 2017). Access to potable water is not a problem for the majority of inhabitants in the cities of Latin America, but very few inhabitants in the countryside have access; 87% of Lima's population has access to potable water, but 38% of the water is lost (Denig, 2010) because of bad infrastructure and informal use.

The average water consumption in 17 Latin American cities is 264 liters/inhabitant/day, whereas the consumption in Europe is 288 (Denig, 2010). Consumption in Lima is only 151 liters/inhabitant/day (Denig, 2010) since the poor population has no access to it. Water treatment in Peru is inefficient; only 33% of residual water was treated in 2011 (MINAM, 2012). In the urban areas only 50% of wastewater got treatment; however, most of their effluents exceeded the MPL (OECD/UN ECLAC, 2017). Most of the water basin doesn't reach the Environmental Water Standard (ibid.). The water of Lima contains arsenic in levels above those allowed to keep inhabitants in good health.

Another problem with the cities of Latin America is related to an unstructured public policy for environmental conservation. In Peru the environmental governability is fragmented through multiple departments of state (ministerios) (Denig, 2010); as responsibilities become desegregated among different departments of state, governability becomes inefficient.

The *Ministerio del Ambiente* (Environmental Department of State) in Peru was first created in 2008 as a consequence of international pressure. This *ministerio* is considered by the liberal politics and a large number of citizens as an obstacle for investment and development. One of the political parties running for election in 2016 proposed the fusion of the Environmental Department of State and the Agriculture and Irrigation Department of State (Ministrio de Argicultura y Riego) so as to put an end to the lack of communication between two related departments and promote coherent planning. Nevertheless, this has not happened because environmental problems are always in second place behind economic problems. One characteristic of environmental management in Peru is the large number of laws with no detailed regulations and therefore no possibility for the implementation of laws. Therefore several laws are contradictory.

In 2012 a multi-sectorial commission was created and managed by the *Ministerio del Ambiente* in order to open a bridge of communication between the different departments of state (Gobierno del Perú, 2012), but it has no authority to develop any policies. Nowadays the *Ministerio del Ambiente* is responsible for the application of the Strategic Environmental Assessment, which is intended to integrate environmental policies with the roles of the other departments that currently do not coordinate properly.

Municipal management has to consider urban metabolism. In Canada, the municipalities are responsible for the adequate disposal of contaminated waste from domestic garbage, the control of emissions, the promotion of eco-markets, the reduction of domestic water uses, and transportation. They also promote the change and use of new clean technology, and in this way, reduce the footprint of the city (Tomalty, 2005). In Latin American cities, the *Ministerio del Ambiente* is responsible for all these functions, and it does not coordinate with the municipalities. Better management of the environment would be possible if both worked together.

Today Latin American countries want to be members of the Organisation for Economic Co-operation and Development (OECD); Chile is the first Latin American country to meet the conditions required for acceptance, but Peru has yet to reach international standards. One of these standards is the implementation of cycle lanes, which has been done in Lima to some extent but without reaching the required standards of quality.

Some examples of countries that have achieved urban metabolism in Latin America are: Brazil, by producing methane from waste and implementing regulations for the reduction of energy consumption in Sao Paulo, using solar energy in Belo Horizonte, making cycle lanes and green corridors in Rio de Janeiro, and reducing gas emissions in Curitiva with the implementation of the red road; Ecuador, by planting trees in Quito; Colombia, by replacing the old bus system in Bogota and implementing funicular transportation in Medellin; Argentina, by introducing articulated and hybrid buses in Buenos Aires; Chile, by expanding the subway in Santiago and building air monitoring stations; and Mexico, by developing public transport for scholars in Mexico City (Denig, 2010).

The Gwangju Declaration on Human Rights City affirms that it is essential to find financial mechanisms to ensure the city's health, such as the Clean Development Mechanism (MDL), which implements mitigation actions such as the NAMA (Appropriate Mitigation Actions). The most used MDL for the cities is the MDL for emissions. A voluntary mechanism to reduce the emissions is the POA (CDM program), which demands quantification of emissions in order to be able to make an inventory of these emissions. Emissions for each inhabitant of the city are between 11 and 8 tons per year (Kennedy et al., 2009; UNEP, 2012). Most Latin American cities don't have data regarding emissions, including emissions related to transport, electricity, waste, industry, construction, etc. However, Mexico City has worked on a program to reduce emissions, and Bogota is reorganizing public transport (Denig, 2010).

Free Spaces of Lima City

The buildings change the environment of the city. Temperature, wind, and air quality influence the social communication of its inhabitants. Francis and Chadwick (2013) suggest a classification of urban spaces, where highly developed urban spaces have 67–100% of built cover, moderately developed urban spaces have 34–66% of built cover, and sparsely developed urban spaces have 0–33% of built cover. Under this classification it is necessary to distinguish between urban and ex-urban spaces. This can be done by looking at changes in environmental indicators such as temperature, humidity, and wind, which vary between the topographical areas of Lima. The concept of public space or free space is associated with the cultural use of free space (Francis & Chadwick, 2013). The area should be able to respond to individual and collective identities and to the cultural and artistic expression of its citizens (Watson, 2013). Abbas (2013) explains that disappeared cities are those that have vanished because people could not understand what they saw. To understand a city, the characteristics of its inhabitants have to be taken into account when planning for it. In this way, the city will not be abstract but real for the citizens. But Watson (2013) explains that public spaces must be permeable in order to address transcultural participation.

Just like many cities, Lima has developed along a river, the Rimac River. Its peculiarity is its proximity to the ocean. In the 20th century Lima also expanded along the Chillon River, which has seasonal fluctuations and a high risk of flooding. However, Lima is actually located in a desert on the Pacific Ocean, so parks and green areas depend on irrigation. Considering these environmental conditions in Lima, it is not possible to think of ecosystem resilience or succession as proposed by Sukopp (1990), who affirms that an ecosystem can recover its dynamic after destruction. Furthermore, the energy and emergency theory of Odum and Barrett (2005) that postulate that ecosystems tend to recover to the energy equilibrium is not applicable either. In Lima the green areas are anthropic ecosystems.

Cities have a fragmented and artificial ecosystem, which explains the increase of animal biodiversity (Francis & Chadwick, 2013) and the decrease of plant biodiversity as a general rule (McKinney, 2008; Francis & Chadwick, 2013). Plant biodiversity is affected by the introduction of species that are not native to the area. However, in Lima the rule is broken. Although it is a desert, human intervention has caused an increase in plant biodiversity, but it is extremely expensive to maintain.

In addition, rainfall in Lima is under 100 mm/year, which is unsuitable for sustaining green areas. The green areas are not in good condition, with more than 60% of grass in need of a large amount of water. These areas could be very important for carbon absorption, reduction of the city's temperature, which can reach 30°C in summer, and carbon dioxide absorption, but irrigation and use of fertilizers can emit methane (CH_4) and nitrate (NO_2) that is very damaging to the environment (Livesley et al., 2010; Francis & Chadwick, 2013).

Traffic, security, air pollution, and lack of infrastructure are the most important factors that reduce the benefit of walking in Lima. A study done in San Isidro (El Golf, Lima) demonstrated that those who walk along sidewalks inhale more carbon monoxide than others.

In Peru, there is no legal definition for "free space" given by the municipality, and the definition of "green space" does not distinguish between public and private spaces. There are two major problems in the city: the inequity in the spatial distribution of green spaces and the lack of public green spaces, both in the poor and prosperous areas. Most green spaces are private clubs. Likewise, park statistics do not distinguish between private and public spaces, nor do they distinguish between green spaces with a high percentage of cement and green spaces that have more green areas.

There is a correlation between income and the environmental condition of the city, the density of the population, and the distribution of green public and private spaces (Francis & Chadwick, 2013). There is also a correlation between biodiversity and the city's income (Hope et al., 2003; Francis & Chadwick, 2013). Other factors that are correlated with the distribution of green spaces are the educational level and criminality (Troy, Grove, O'Neil-Dunne, Pickett, & Cadenasso, 2007; Francis & Chadwick, 2013).

Big enough green areas are needed to reduce air pollution and traffic noise. These areas also ensure a tolerable social life in the city. Lima is exposed to a large amount of pollution, and it has very few parks. This causes many health problems. Lima has only 2.9 m²/green spaces/inhabitant (Grupo GEA, 2010). Strictly speaking, this number is much lower because of the large number of cement courts in the parks. Other cities have a lot more. Hong Kong has 3 m²/inhabitant and Singapore has 7 m²/inhabitant. New York is 13% park space, whereas in the United Kingdom, 14% of the urban area is green space (Francis & Chadwick, 2013). The average of gardens in many cities can be as high as 16%, such as in Stockholm (Colding, 2007; Francis & Chadwick, 2013), or 19% in Santiago, Chile (Reyes-Paecke & Meza, 2011; Francis

& Chadwick, 2013). According to the United Nations, a city must have one park or recreational area for each half kilometer (UNEP, 2012).

In Lima, the green spaces are specially concentrated in prosperous districts, where most of the green spaces aren't public. San Isidro has 26.3 m²/inhabitant, San Borja has 12.11 m²/inhabitant, and Miraflores has 14.86 m²/inhabitant. These districts have enough green areas, but poorer districts like Villa María del Triunfo (0.34 m²/inhabitant), Breña (0.37 m²/inhabitant), and San Juan de Lurigancho (0.61 m²/inhabitant) have a very strong need for green areas (Lima cómo vamos, 2014). This distribution coincides with the incomes of the districts. To make a realistic calculation, the parks in the city should be determined in percentage/inhabitant or in percentage of city area (Austin, 2014). In Lima the calculation is made in meters per inhabitant. The average green areas should be 2 hectares for each 300 meters of residential area (Grant, 2010; Austin, 2014).

In Peru, green spaces are not a priority for politicians or the population in general. Citizens do not participate in planning and managing green areas. In other countries, such as Canada, participative monitoring is common (Tomalty, 2005). For municipalities in Peru, green spaces are a direct expense, not an income, because payments for environmental services that the green areas provide are not included in the calculation. The maintenance of green spaces in Peru does not consider ecology; pesticides and fungicides are used constantly. This does not happen in all countries; the use of pesticides and fungicides, water management, and the average of green spaces are controlled in countries like Canada (Tomalty, 2005).

Universities, municipalities, and non-governmental organizations (NGOs) are interested in urban agriculture, but the population is not interested in developing bio-gardens. On the one hand, the price of vegetables is very low, but on the other, those who have little money do not have time for bio-gardens, and the middle class is too worried about social ascent. Labor rights are minimal, so a good worker is fully committed to working beyond the eight-hour-a-day schedule. In addition, there is still prejudice against plant cultivation, which by some is considered a sign of poverty.

The use given to green spaces is associated with cultural expression. Therefore, as a consequence of cultural differences, migrant population will not give the same use to the parks as people who already inhabit the areas. One example of this in Germany involves the migrant population from Turkey. They used Tiergarten, the largest park in Berlin, as a place to grill, so this feature was introduced into the park to make it more usable for all of the people in the city. Another example, from the area of Brixton in London, involves the inhabitants of Angell Town, a large housing development, who used pathways as free spaces to mingle with one another. This was not considered in the planning, so a redesign was required so as to incorporate this aspect and make it livable for the population (Watson, 2013). In Lima football is a sport that integrates the population, so the most usable parks have a football area.

New migrants keep close relationships with relatives from rural areas; this also occurs with inhabitants that have relatives in other countries. There is a constant flow of money, in one direction, and of people and rural products, in the other. With the modernization of the city and the rupture of the traditional model, the new generation is slowly adopting the model of city farms. This contributes to a better diet in a socially diverse space and breaks the social prejudice that associates poverty with vegetable production. But there is still a long way to go in terms of having bio-gardens in schools, cafeterias, or communities, as can be found in Sweden, where having a vegetable garden is considered a sign of distinction and raises the value of a property.

Proposal

Ecological urbanism starts from the analysis of the environment and includes the identification and consideration of natural features when planning the city (Hagan, 2015), such as hydrology, geology, and ecology as well as sociocultural aspects (McHarg, 1995). In the case of Lima, the ecology of the city at the beginning was the Rimac River Valley, but as the city has grown it now includes the surrounding desert. We now identify the natural boundaries as the river, valley, desert, ocean, and water flood. This should be the design axle. In Lima we can identify the Rimac River as the line that separates the old city from the new one. Lima is surrounded by the *costanera* along the coast that connects Lima with the Pacific Ocean, the desert, and the hilly ecosystem (Lomas). The re-evaluation of the city can be planned considering all these axles. The proposal for a boulevard along the Rimac River and the construction of the *Alameda Chabuca Granda* should be mentioned. However, this design has only included a part of the river path that crosses the city.

In the last decade, Lima, as a consequence of economic growth, has changed a lot and requires a new design that should include parks and free spaces. As an example of positive action, we have the new chain of parks along the coast of Lima, the *Costa Verde*, which goes from Barranco in the south to San Miguel in the east. This park chain builds an interesting ecological corridor with a lot of activities for the citizens. At the weekend, citizens, families, and artists use it, and young people walk along it, have picnics and play sports. Another interesting development is the *Alameda de la Juventud* situated in the south of Lima in San Juan de Miraflores. This area is a narrow, long park along a main avenue that can be used to walk along. It has a water treatment area, an irrigation system, a plant production area, and an educational area where plants and trees are described. This description includes the plant's name, origin, and ecosystem. There are also areas with playgrounds and chess tabletops for board games. There is a pergola with shade for talking and social interaction.

Green area projects are intended to restore the value of downtown Lima by improving the green areas in the city center. The green spaces of old Lima used to be cloister gardens or gardens from the old colonial villages, which have now deteriorated and become too crowded. An example of a place to be restored is the garden of the first *leprosorium* of Lima in the square of Rimac behind the main square. In this place the leprous were excluded from the general population, and they had a vegetable garden to provide for themselves. Another interesting sight to visit in downtown is San Cristóbal Hill. At the top, it has an old sanctuary with a big colonial cross. This space is a fog ecosystem where flowers used to bloom in winter. Now, the ecosystem is degraded so there are no plants and least of all flowers. The municipality organizes tourist trips to the sanctuary, but these trips are not aimed at the general population. The municipality has already designed a project to increase the value of this area and reconstruct the ecosystem.

A successful reconstruction has been the old *Plaza of Santiago de Surco*, which was the old square for the slaves of the hacienda before Santiago de Surco was integrated into the city. Several festivities take place in this area, such as the design of a flower carpet at Easter, exhibitions, concerts, and dances. The local population is organized into brotherhoods, whose members are the descendants of the slaves from the hacienda, and have lived in this area for more than 100 years.

Lima's environmental management should calculate the cost of environmental degradation in order to develop realistic environmental policies. These policies would enable us to implement clean development mechanisms for several of our environmental problems. Clean development mechanisms could help us with our water shortage and maintain green areas. We would be able to use water more efficiently, and we would definitely have more water treatment plants. We could use this water to irrigate the parks, and in this way we could reduce the cost of maintenance of the green areas. Finally, we could implement green areas as ecosystem services that would enable us to reduce carbon dioxide emissions and inhibit the island effect. It is necessary to evaluate and calculate the best possibilities, including direct and indirect costs.

The development of urban forestry with community participation is essential in order to improve air quality in the walking areas of the parks. When this form of development is carried out by the city government, it is a provision of an ecosystem service and, therefore, it would entitle the city government to get some form of monetary reimbursement. Likewise, an ecological corridor is also essential to ensure the biodiversity of the city. It also becomes a green walking route surrounding and interconnecting the city, decreasing the island effect of the city, and it reduces the cost of park maintenance and decreases the use of pesticides. The plan for these corridors should include bicycle lanes to reduce carbon emissions. In Lima, green spaces like the Miraflores boardwalk ensure multiculturalism and tolerance. The citizens of Lima now use this space for many different activities, such as walking, sports, and art.

Unlike other cities, Lima has not been successful at bio-gardens. The level of humidity in Lima is 80% all year round, temperatures fluctuate between 13°C and 30°C, and rain is under 10 mm/year; therefore bio-gardens require a lot of care. Furthermore, the price of vegetables is very low, and agriculture is considered undeserving; it is an activity done by the very poor. However, in the last few years, the wealthy have begun purchasing bio-products, which have been introduced into the market as a sign of class distinction. Slowly people have begun to take care of their diets and are more careful with the market products they purchase.

It is not enough to have an adequate quantity of square meters of green space per inhabitant. It is also necessary to consider the quality of the green areas in order to establish the green areas index. This should be calculated in consideration of the density of inhabitants and the footprint of the construction. The quality of the cities depends not only on the square meter of green area per inhabitant, but also on the footprint of each construction and on the capacity of the plants to absorb carbon dioxide. In other words, it depends on the cubic meters of green space determined by the elevation of constructions and plants. Furthermore, green areas have two essential functions: cleaning the air of carbon dioxide and serving as a social space for stress reduction. To classify green areas we must distinguish between private gardens and public spaces, which have a social function. The quality of the green areas depends also on their connectivity. The ecological corridors are important to maintain the connectivity of the fauna in the city.

Finally, green area planning should consider city expansion and growth as well as the distribution of the green areas throughout the city and not only in the periphery. A healthy city has enough parks to achieve their social function. City planning must consider the present, but also the past and the future of the city development.

References

Abbas, A. (2013). Chinese cities: Design and disappearance. In L. Krause (Ed.), *Sustaining cities: Urban policies, practices, and perceptions* (pp. 111–122). New Brunswick, NJ: Rutgers University Press.

Andina. (2012, January 21). *Sólo el 12% de los recicladores trabaja de manera formal en el Perú, informan*. Retrieved from www.andina.com.pe/agencia/noticia-solo-12-recicladores-trabaja-manera-formal-el-peru-informan-396247.aspx.

Austin, G. (2014). *Green infrastructure for landscape planning: Integrating human and natural systems*. Glasgow: Rutger.

Bähr, J., & Mertins, G. (1995). *Die latinamerikanische Grossstadt. Verstadterungsprozesse und Stadtstrukturen*. Darmstadt (WBG): Ertrage der Forshung.

Banco InterAmericano de Desarrollo. (2016). *La formalización del reciclaje informal*. Retrieved from www.iadb.org/es/temas/residuos-solidos/la-formalizacion-del-reciclaje-informal,3837.html.

Berry, B. J. L. (1990). Urbanisation. In B. L. Turner III., W. C. Clark, R. W. Kates, J. F. Richards, J. T. Mathews, & W. B. Meyer (Eds.), *The earth as transformed by human action*. Cambridge: Cambridge University Press.

Colding, J. (2007). Ecological land-use complementation for building resilience in urban ecosystems. *Landscape and Urban Planning, 81*, 46–55.

Cord, L., Genoni, M. E., & Rodríguez-Castelán, C. (2015). *Prosperidad compartida y fin de la pobreza en América Latina y El Caribe*. Washington, D.C.: Grupo Banco Mundial.

Da Gama, H. (2008). *Social and environmental aspects of peri-urban growth in Latin American megacities*. New York: United Nations Expert Group Meeting on Population Distribution, Urbanization, Internal Migration and Development. Department of Economic and Social Affairs.

Denig, S. (Ed.). (2010). *Índice de ciudades verdes para América-latina. 2010*. Economist Intelligence Unit (EIU) and Siemens AG.

Diario Gestión. (2013, May 7). Peru se convirtio en octavio pais con el PBI per capita mas grande de America Latina. Retrieved from http://gestion.pe/economia/peru-convirtio-octavo-pais-pbi-per-capita-grande-america-latina-37781.

Doughty, P. (1969). La cultura del regionalismo en la vida urbana de Lima, Perú. *Revista América Indígena, 28*, 949–981.

Ferris, J., Norman, J., & Sempik, J. (2001). People, land, and sustainability: Community gardens and the social dimension of sustainable development. *Social Policy and Administration, 35*(5), 559–568.

Francis, R., & Chadwick, M. (2013). *Urban ecosystems: Understanding the human environment*. London and New York: Routledge.

Gobierno del Perú. (2012). *R.M 189–2012*. PCM.

Golte, J. (2001). *Cultura, racionalidad y migración andina*. Lima: IEP.

Grant, L. (2010). *Multifunctional urban green infrastructure*. Briefing Report. Chartered Institution of Water and Environmental Management.

Grimm, N. B., Grove, J. M., Pickett, S. T. A., & Redman, C. L. (2000). Integrated approaches to long-term studies of urban ecological systems. *Bioscience, 50*(7), 571–584.

Grupo GEA. *Reporte ambiental Lima y Callao 2010: Evaluación a 5 años del informe GEO. 2010*. Editorial: Universidad Científica del Sur.

Hagan, S. (2015). *Ecological urbanism: The nature of the city*. London and New York: Routledge.

Heineberg, H. (2017). *Stadtgeography* (5th ed.). Stuttgart: Utb.

Hope, D., Gries, C., Zhu, W., Fagen, W. F., Redman, C. L., Grimm, N. B., Nelson, A. L., Martin, C., & Kinzig, A. (2003). Socioeconomics drive urban plant diversity. *Proceedings of the National Academy of Sciences, 100*(15), 8788–8792.

INEI (National Institute of Statistics and Informatics). (2015). *Peru: Anuario de Estadisticas ambientales 2014.* Lima.

Irracheta, A. (2013). Sustainable city: Crisis and opportunity in Mexico. In L. Krause (Ed.), *Sustaining cities: Urban policies, practices, and perceptions* (pp. 13–24). London and New York: Rutgers.

Kennedy, C., Steinberger, J., Gasson, B., Hansen, Y., Hillman, T., Havranek, M., Pataki, D., Phdungslip, A., Ramaswami, A., Villalba Mendez, G. (2009). Greenhouse gas emissions from global cities. *Environmental Science and Technology, 43*(19), 7297–7302.

La República. (2014). Retrieved from www.larepublica.pe/sities/default/imagen/2014(infografía-po003.jpg).

Liebenthal, A., & Salvemini, D. (2013). *Promoting environmental sustainability in Peru: A review of the World Bank Group's experience (2003–2009) (English).* Independent Evaluation Group (IEG) Working Paper Series no. 2011/1. Washington, D.C.: World Bank.

Lima cómo vamos. (2014). *Evaluando la gestión de Lima: quinto informe de resultados sobre la calidad de vida.* Retrieved from www.limacomovamos.org/cm/wp-content/uploads/2015/01/EncuestaLimaComoVamos2014.pdf.

Livesley, J. S., Dougherty, B. J., Smith, A. J., Navaud, D., Wylie, L. J., & Arndt, S. K. (2010). Soil-atmosphere exchange of carbon dioxide, methane and nitrous oxide in urban garden systems: Impact of irrigation, fertiliser and mulch. *Urban Ecosystems, 13*(3), 273–293.

McHarg, I. (1995). *Design with nature.* New York: Wiley.

McKinney, M. L. (2008). Effects of urbanisation on species richness: A review of plants and animals. *Urban Ecosystems, 11*(2), 161–176.

MINAM. (2012). *Informe del Estado del Ambiente 2009–2011.* Lima: MIMAN.

MINAM. (2014a). Retrieved from http://sinia.minam.gob.pe/cifras-ambientales.

MINAM. (2014b). *Informe del Estado del Ambiente 2012–2013.* Lima: MINAM.

MINAM. (2014c). *Informe anual de residuos sólidos municipales y no municipales en el Perú, gestión, 2012.* Lima: MIMAN.

MINAM. (2015). Retrieved from http://sinia.minam.gob.pe/.

MINAM. (2018). Retrieved from http://sinia.minam.gob.pe/modsinia/index/php?accion=verIndicador&idElementoInformacion=1012&idformula=87.

Odum, E. P., & Barrett, G. W. (2005). *Fundamentals of ecology* (5th ed.). Belmont, CA: Thomson Brooks/Cole.

OECD/UN ECLAC. (2017). *OECD environmental performance reviews: Peru 2017.* Paris: OECD Publishing. https://doi.org/10.1787/9789264283138-en.

Reyes-Paecke, S., & Meza, L. (2011). Residential gardens of Santiago, Chile: Extent, distribution and vegetation cover. *Revista Chilena de Historia Natural, 84*, 581–592.

Riofrio, G. (2003). The case of Lima, Peru. In *The challenge of slums: Global report on human settlements 2003.* London and Sterling, VA: Earthscan.

Sabogal, A., Tavera, T., Suarez, O., & Pastor, A. (2017). *Análisis de la calidad, cantidad y distribución espacial de los parques del distrito de Santiago de Surco.* Espacio y Desarrollo. N°30. PUCP.

Sukopp, H. (1990). *Stadtökologie, das Beispiel Berlin.* Berlin: Dietrich Reimer Verlag.

Tomalty, R. (2005). *Urban environment issues.* Toronto: Canadian Environmental Grantmakers' Network.

Troy, A. R., Grove, J. M., O'Neil-Dunne, J. P. M., Pickett, S. T. A., & Cadenasso, M. L. (2007). Predicting opportunities for greening and patterns of vegetation on private urban lands. *Environmental Management, 40*(3), 394–412.

United Nation Environmental Programme (UNEP). (2012). *Cities and carbon finance: A feasibility study on an urban CDM*. United Nation Environmental Programme.

Watson, G. B. (2013). The art of place making. In L. Krause (Ed.), *Sustaining cities: Urban policies, practices, and perceptions* (pp. 76–94). London and New York: Rutgers.

Weiland, U., & Richter, M. (2009). Lines of tradition and recent approaches to urban ecology, focusing on Germany and the USA. *GAIA—Ecological Perspectives for Science and Society, 18*(1), 49–57.

Chapter 14

FIRST WE HAD TO MAKE IT LIVABLE: THE AFFORDANCES OF LIVABILITY IN SUBURBAN NEWCASTLE, NEW SOUTH WALES, AUSTRALIA

Kathleen Mee, Pauline McGuirk, Jill Sweeney, and Kristian Ruming

Introduction

Literature in geography and urban studies has long noted how *livability* has been put to use in neoliberal projects of inter-city competition to foster particular types of redevelopment, to increase the marketability of the city and win livability rankings (Jarvis, 2007), and to attract or service middle-class consumption (McCann, 2004). Perhaps for this reason, academic discussions and policy debates about fostering livability are often narrowly focused on the city center. Recent work in geography by Lewis and Murphy (2015, p. 116) has suggested that livability agendas may exceed this framing and "create spaces of (and for) politics that have not been simply erased by neoliberalism." In this chapter we explore livability by thinking about spaces beyond the inner city, such as middle ring and urban fringe suburbs, as another way to exceed the neoliberal framing of livability. And in doing so we build on the work of Kraftl (2014), who alerts us to the ways that residents "give life" to concepts such as livability and therefore to the household practices involved in making places livable.

The title of this chapter came from a resident, Lyn, whom we interviewed as part of the research we draw on in this chapter. As we set up our recording devices, we chatted about the interview ahead and how we would be discussing the changes her household had made to their home. "First," she said "we had to make it livable." During her interview she went on to discuss many of the homemaking practices we detail in this chapter as practices of livability, including structural repairs, extending the living space of the house, enhancing the garden, and making spaces to interact with family and friends. Lyn alerted us to the importance of thinking about how livability is practiced at multiple scales, including the home and the neighborhood.

In this chapter we explore the role of livability in resident experiences of two parts of Newcastle, Australia: the middle ring suburb of Charlestown, and Huntlee, a newly developing suburb on the urban fringe.

The chapter explores how livability can be understood if explored as part of the practices of assembling the suburbs in the Australian context. For residents of the suburban neighborhoods we researched, the livability of their home and suburb was based on a low-density neighborhood that provides affordable housing, an attractive physical environment, and, often, access to amenities elsewhere. We use the concept of the affordances of affordability to explore how affordable housing allowed residents to create and experience a livable home—one which was comfortable, easy to live in, and adaptable to their changing needs. Moreover, while residents pointed to the importance of being able to *access* elements of the livable city that are located elsewhere, for example employment, shopping, or cultural facilities such as restaurants and theatres, they did not necessarily want these features in their own neighborhood. For many, living in a quiet, peaceful, suburban neighborhood was crucial to their experience of the livable city. This alerts us to consider more carefully how residents practice livability in suburban areas.

Livability: A Shopping List to Make an Apple Pie or a Set of Practices of Becoming Lively?

So what does livability mean in the Australian context? Recent work by Tapsuwan, Mathot, Walker, and Barnett (2018, pp. 133–134) has provided this broad definition: livability is defined as "the degree to which a place supports quality of life, health and well-being." Such definitions are habitually associated with "shopping lists" of related characteristics of a livable neighborhood or city. According to Lowe et al. (2015), for example, it should be peaceful, safe, socially cohesive and inclusive, harmonious, attractive, high in amenity, environmentally sustainable, and with a diverse range of housing that is affordable, well linked to public transport, provides walking and cycling infrastructure, has easy access to schools, employment, public open space, shops, health, community, and social services. All these qualities contribute to people's quality of life, health, and wellbeing (Tapsuwan et al., 2018, pp. 133–134).

In exploring livability indexes that involve shopping lists such as these, Eugene McCann astutely points out that:

> the types of criteria used … in ranking cities as good places to live tend to be hard to argue with, at least when taken at face value. "Safe streets", "vibrant economy" and "high quality of education for our children" might, in the US context, be termed "motherhood and apple pie" issues. It is hard to suggest that they are not good things, but the very fact that they seem self-evidently desirable for any policy process often makes it very difficult to question the means by which these ends will be achieved.
>
> (McCann, 2004, p. 1926)

We follow McCann's understanding of livability and build on his work in two ways. First, we argue that livability is not simply a shopping list for these apple pie features that those building, regenerating, or, as Jarvis (2007) notes, marketing a city, can use to buy and sell a more livable city in neoliberal times. Rather, we see livability as a set of practices operating at a range of scales and instituted by a diversity of actors. Second, we argue that some features of this shopping list are more important to how residents practice livability than others. We agree with Tapsuwan et al. (2018, p. 124) that "it is important to know that given the vast list of sustainable, livable and resilient features of the neighbourhood and home, what it is that people really find important."

Wetzstein (2016) takes this further by arguing that debates about livable cities often ignore how important housing affordability is to livability. Considering this from the scale of the city, he argues that:

> we end up with the perverse situation that some of the cities that are proclaimed most livable on our planet are in fact those places ordinary residents increasingly can't afford to live anymore. Those people have the option to compromise their living standards, of course, and either seek housing of lesser size, lesser standard, shared with others, further away from amenities, etc, or to leave these cities altogether.
>
> (Wetzstein, 2016, p. 3)

The lack of focus on affordability as an aspect of livability has certainly been the case in the use of livability rankings for the rating of Australian suburbs, where suburbs ranked the most livable tend to be in highly resourced neighborhoods in inner city, and/or harbor-side and beach-side locations unaffordable for most Australians. For example, the recent *Sydney Morning Herald*'s Domain[1] ranking of 555 Sydney suburbs, ranked neighborhoods on levels of and access to employment, train/light rail, bus, ferry, culture, main road congestion, education, shopping, open space, tree cover, topographic variation, cafes and restaurants, crime, telecommunications, views, and beach access (Fuary-Wagner, 2016). In introducing the rankings, the article explained that:

> When we talk about Sydney property and the best suburbs to live in, the conversation invariably turns to the topic of affordability and house prices. And while it's easy to grade Sydney's "best" suburbs based on the cost of housing, there's more to the value of a suburb than just a dollar figure. Each neighbourhood has attractive qualities that draw us in and other, less appealing, attributes that we compromise on in return.
>
> (Fuary-Wagner, 2016)

Potential new residents can then use these attributes to "find their ideal suburb" on the Livable Sydney webpage (Livable Sydney, n.d.) in four potential price brackets, the lowest being less than AUS$800,000, which is above the median house price in any city besides Sydney in Australia.

The lack of inclusion of affordability in these rankings (as opposed to the sorting of suburbs after the ranking) is a problem for two reasons. First, as Lloyd, Fullagar, and Reid (2016) note, reflecting on the Australian context, "To this point, livability has been largely a process of quantifying attributes to inform and develop government policy and to market cities to internal and external audiences" (p. 351). This is problematic, therefore, when critical aspects of livability such as affordability are not adequately accounted for. Second, according to Tapsuwan et al. (2018) in their study in Canberra, affordability is the most important feature of livability for investors and owners, across income groups, age-related groups, education, and levels of adaption of green technology. So current ways of reporting on, forming policy about, or marketing livability may be missing the most important feature of livability for residents.

While affordability is critical, other aspects of neighborhoods are important too. For example, in their research in suburban Brisbane, Willing and Pojani (2017) note that a preference for suburban living remains very strong in Australia. They argue that "[w]hile planners have been seriously advocating more compact and sustainable living and relatively small portions of the population have returned to the inner city, many other sectors of the population desire to maintain the current suburban setup" (Willing & Pojani, 2017, p. 76).

They go on to note that suburban residents actively choose these areas because they value the opportunities for creating livable spaces offered by larger living spaces and gardens. Equally, life stage is important for residents, particularly creating what are seen as appropriate spaces for children based on traditional ideas of suburban areas and, importantly, their own experiences of growing up in suburbs (Willing & Pojani, 2017).

Thus, as Lloyd et al. (2016, p. 353) have suggested, theoretical constructions of livability need to be aligned with the lived experiences of residents. This requires enhanced understandings of everyday social dimensions of residents' lives, gained through qualitative interpretation of residents' experiences of new cities and communities.

We take forward this agenda, and add insights from Peter Kraftl (2014, p. 275), who explores how "livability" might "become lively… through everyday lives lived therein" and the myriad ways in which residents bring neighborhood spaces to life through their everyday practices. In the empirical sections of the chapter, then, we support previous work that argues that affordability is a key feature of livability in Australian neighborhoods. However, building on Kraftl (2014), we take this further to explore how livability impacts on the becoming-lively of suburban areas at the scale of the home, the neighborhood, and the region, through what we term the affordances of affordability. Before turning to this discussion we briefly introduce our case study suburbs.

Introducing the Case Studies: Charlestown and Huntlee

Charlestown is a 7.1 sq. km (710 hectares) middle-ring suburb in Newcastle, a New South Wales (NSW) regional city located in the Hunter region. It is situated 12 km south of the Newcastle Central Business District (CBD), in the Local Government Area of Lake Macquarie. The suburb had a population of 12,912 people living in 5,405 dwellings in 2016, with the vast majority of dwellings separate houses (77.9%), but a growing number of semi-detached/terrace (15.2%) and apartments (6.7%) constructed around its central core (Australian Bureau of Statistics, 2016). Charlestown ticks many of the boxes on the shopping list of livability. It contains one of the largest suburban shopping centers in the region, which has been an important driver of urban regeneration in the suburb (Ruming, Mee, McGuirk, & Sweeney, 2018b). Charlestown is a hub in a newly transformed bus network of the city, offering connections every 15 minutes on weekdays to central Newcastle, as well as connections to the train network, the University of Newcastle, the John Hunter Hospital (the largest hospital in the region), and other parts of suburban Newcastle. The area has surrounding bushland, as well as access to active recreational facilities including the Fernleigh track bike path.

Huntlee's 1,700-hectare site is still under construction and spans the borders of two local government areas, City of Cessnock and Singleton Council in the Lower Hunter Valley, approximately 50 km from Newcastle CBD. First proposed in 2006, Huntlee is planned to be the biggest single housing development in NSW and claims to be the first new town in the Hunter

Valley in 50 years. Residents commenced moving into the first stage of the development, Katherine's Landing, in 2016, with planned construction to take place over the next 25 years. The site will provide up to 7,500 dwellings for 20,000 people as well as spaces for commercial properties, community facilities, and conservation land. In addition to a designated town centre, Huntlee will consist of four distinct villages/land releases, areas reserved for environmental protection, walking and bike paths, schools, and shopping centers (Ruming, Mee, McGuirk, & Sweeney, 2018a). The livability of the neighborhood is crucial to Huntlee's advertising. For example the developer, LWP, claims that the first stage of Huntlee will contain:

> Two thousand homes, as individual as their owners. Housing lots of varying sizes, sporting homes of various styles, from terraces to cottages and larger country style, right through to group and retirement housing. Katherine's Landing will prove smart, thoughtful planning can deliver brilliant future lifestyle options.
>
> (LWP, 2012)

The empirical material we draw from in this chapter comes from a larger Australian Research Council Discovery Project Grant exploring regeneration in Newcastle. The project involved a range of qualitative methodologies including document analysis (of policy, planning and development documents, media reports, social media pages and posts, and webpages), a resident survey, interviews of key informants and residents, site visits, and participant observation at regeneration-related events. We interviewed key informants from government, business, and community groups about both the Charlestown and Huntlee developments as well as residents of Charlestown. Given its early stage of development, we were unable to survey or interview residents of Huntlee. As a result, our discussion below draws on the views of key informants about both Charlestown and Huntlee as expressed in interviews, the views of Charlestown residents expressed in interviews, and views of new and future Huntlee residents expressed in publicly available sources such as media reports, Facebook posts, and marketing materials.

Practices of Livability 1: The Affordances of Affordability for Homemaking

In both Charlestown and Huntlee affordability was a key factor in livability for residents. Affordability effectively acted as a gatekeeper, in that other considerations of livability that would influence the choice of a home or neighborhood would come into play if the home or neighborhood was first affordable. Once located in an affordable neighborhood, residents could engage in other practices to make their house and their neighborhood more livable. In Charlestown, 58% of survey respondents said that housing affordability attracted them to the suburb. Affordability was also frequently mentioned in Huntlee marketing material and media reports and by residents, future residents, and investors. For example:

> To buy land elsewhere was going to be quite a lot more expensive than what it was here so it was a lot more achievable for us to have, you know, the house we wanted on a decent size block of land.
>
> (Tiff, Huntlee)

"I was looking anywhere up to a two hour drive from Sydney but kept finding tiny boxes for houses where they wanted a minimum of $800K," said Gayle. "I took a tour and promptly informed Michael I would buy it! I was bowled over by the price—you can't get a two bedroom unit in Sydney for that."

(LWP, 2017, p. 1)

Similarly, affordability was a key issue for Charlestown residents:

We decided that it would be a better option to buy slightly further out from the city in a house that was about $150,000 cheaper and not have as big a mortgage.

Affordable mostly and not too far into town. I work in the city and my wife works down south, Newcastle, Lake Macquarie so yeah price and location.… I'd love to live in town, in Newcastle but it's twice the price.

(Tim, Charlestown)

Charlestown was affordable. Warners Bay[2] wasn't—even then Warners Bay wasn't. I'd got married. We wanted [laughs]—seems very old-fashioned now—but we got married and we wanted to buy a house and then have a baby. So this was the second stage of—the process was buying a house—and we could afford a house, a nice-ish house here and we could afford a house that had a big block of land, which is what we wanted.

Wetzstein (2016) argues that residents juggle affordability with other features that they value in order to enter the property market. Assessments of affordability by residents are clearly based not just on their own financial resources but also their understanding of what is available elsewhere in the property market. While some residents clearly saw Charlestown as a "compromise" location that they could afford, others actively sought out the affordability of the suburb and what this affordability would allow them to do with their homes.

The affordability of properties was, and is, important to residents' homemaking practices, which are in turn crucial to how livable they found the suburbs. In Charlestown, this involved finding an appropriate house and undertaking modifications to make it comfortable, convenient, and appropriate to the residents' needs. When Charlestown residents were asked why they undertook home renovations, the top three survey responses were to *improve the appearance* (59%), *improve living conditions* (56%), and *make home more comfortable* (44%). Residents were working with something established to make it their own, more livable space, in a variety of ways.

In contrast, some residents wanted a space that they could afford which required little in the way of maintenance or modifications for their future life because they did not have the time or the skills to perform such tasks. For example:

That's why we bought it, because we have no practical skills whatsoever, so the fact that we were looking for a house that someone had done out—so it's still an old house but it's been renovated, it has a bit of character, but it also doesn't have wiring that was done in the early 1900s.

I bought it because I was looking at low maintenance.

(Gerry, Charlestown)

Similarly, the residents of Huntlee valued buying into a space that they thought would be easy to live in with little effort. Landscaping and fencing, high-speed internet, and recycled water is built into the house and township infrastructure, and the houses were seen to be finished to a high quality. Future residents' comments conveyed a strong sense that many aspects of livable homes were being constructed by the developer around them. For example:

Having everything done for us like the landscaping at the front, you know, just different things that Huntlee have offered us is so much, is so worthwhile. You know, it saves us a lot of money, they've been really great. To think that we're all going to move in, we're all going to have our fronts landscaped, and have the whole street looking beautiful as soon as we've moved in.

(Elizabeth, Huntlee)

Elizabeth notes that the availability of these features "saves us a lot of money."

Affordability is important to livability not simply because it is about gaining access to a particular space. It is also important to enable ongoing expenditures residents felt were necessary to make a place livable over their life course. For some Charlestown residents it was crucial that the house they bought was affordable so that they could adapt it for their future needs. Kate captures this well, saying her search for a house led her to Charlestown because it was:

value for money, basically. So we're getting good-sized land, reasonable houses that we—because we're fixing it up for—yeah, for the price. So that's the main reason.

(Kate, Charlestown)

For Charlestown residents "fixing it up" often involved extending an existing structure or adapting how a space was used to accommodate a growing family more comfortably. For example, Robert from Charlestown describes how their family adapted their home over time:

a kitchen refurb,[3] bathroom refurb, couple of times, just maintenance type things where you need to do them where they get a bit old and shabby, and just general painting and external repairs. Nothing major because when we bought it, it had a [Cape Cod] on it that was probably 90% finished, and I just finished some of that off and that became our family room living area as the children grew up, because they were 4 and 2, I think—4 and 1—when we moved here so they were pretty young. It became for a long time their play area and then as it progressed, computer and TV etcetera and stereo. So the room grew with the family.

(Robert, Charlestown)

Similarly, Peter bought his house in Charlestown because he could see the possibilities of making it a livable home over time. He said:

As far as the house was concerned we, at that stage, had just one 18-month-old. So there was—it was a larger place than what we had. Just a comfortable three-bedroom suburban home with decent living areas and with the size of the block we could see the opportunities to garden or expansion as and when the family might expand.

(Peter, Charlestown)

For some residents, the changes that they wanted to make to their home took time as they grappled with the initial financial demands of servicing a mortgage. These residents increased the livability of their homes slowly, as this quote from Christine reveals:

Well the house is an old house that was more or less completely re-gutted and then insulated and rewired and stuff like that, but the heritage style was kept. Then it was extended with more living areas and it had a garden in it that wasn't particularly native. So it took me a long time to make changes because [I had] the mortgage first.

(Christine, Charlestown)

It is critical to note here that affordability is crucial to allowing modifications that make homes more livable. Often the affordability of housing is considered only in terms of the gatekeeper role we discussed earlier in the chapter, as something that allows people to gain access to a particular neighborhood and maintain that access if they can afford their mortgage repayments. In our research, we found that affordability was also critical to the modification and maintenance of housing, and the capacity to transform homes into comfortable, convenient, and appropriate dwellings for their residents.

For the residents of Charlestown, these transformed spaces were important for the home-making practices that they enabled. A family room was important as a space for socializing within the family and with guests. Kristen sums this up nicely, arguing that these spaces are important for:

Lifestyle. Yeah the boys would be growing up, they'd be wanting to have friends over and we wanted somewhere to have people.

(Kristen, Charlestown)

The affordances of affordability allowed the transformation of properties into livable homes in other ways too. Many residents in both Charlestown and Huntlee mentioned the importance of their front and back yards. In the Charlestown interviews, residents stressed the importance of gardens as places for children to play, spaces for pets, spaces to nurture plants and attract native species such as birds, and spaces to grow fruit, vegetables, and herbs for the household. As Paul said:

Yep, we put in a little frog pond down the back. We've got lots of trees in the back yard…we've got a lot of trees in there that we'd like to keep. It can be a nuisance but they're good to have because we get birds and possums and all that sort of stuff.

(Paul, Charlestown)

Yards provide shade, play spaces, socializing spaces, spaces to dry clothes, nurture gardens, and grow vegetables. They are part of what made suburban living livable for Charlestown residents.

The affordances of affordability were important for other household practices too. These included modifications to improve the environmental performance of the building, such as increasing the shading of the building through trees or blinds, installing insulation, solar hot water systems, or solar electricity generation systems. All of these practices made dwellings more comfortable and convenient to live in, and so are part of suburban livability.

In this section we have focused on the importance of affordability for livability of housing in the suburbs. Affordability is important in allowing people to gain access to the places they want to live (the gatekeeper role of affordability) and for allowing people sufficient resources to support their home-making practices through constructing spaces that make the home comfortable and convenient for growing families, for entertaining guests, for accessing appealing outdoor spaces, and for modifying the house to be more environmentally efficient, through the additions of heating and cooling technologies, for example.

As we have shown, in all these ways residents actively make their suburban homes livable. While, for the residents we interviewed, there were some trade-offs between the housing they could afford and their reduced access to other aspects of livability they may prize in more expensive parts of the city, residents remained actively involved in making their home livable. They sought out the features of suburban homes (such as greater floor space and the outdoor spaces of yards and gardens) in order to do so. Such stories give us greater understanding of both the continued preferences of many Australian households for suburban living (Willing & Pojani, 2017) and the active role of residents in the becoming-lively of the suburbs.

In the next two sections, we briefly turn our attention to the features of livability that were important at the neighborhood and regional scales.

Practices of Livability 2: Accessing the Livable City in the Neighborhood

Shifting from the scale of home to the scale of the neighborhood, what features of the shopping list of livability did residents of Charlestown and prospective residents of Huntlee indicate were most important? Two sets of features were most important: access to facilities in the suburb and the natural environment.

As a middle ring suburb with a large regional center, Charlestown had many facilities the residents could access locally that made the suburb livable for them, including shopping, medical, education, transport, and community facilities. The examples from Peter and Graeme below are indicative of the comments of many interviewees about the most appealing features of Charlestown:

> I've got shopping and I've got all the services I want around here. Lake Macquarie Hospital out there's excellent. So you've got the services around here; so if you live close to those services, you've got the bushland gully so you've got even nature around you.
>
> (Peter, Charlestown)

> We had two teenage kids at the time and this area was close to the school, close to the unit, close to sport, shops, close to the beach. It just seemed to be a bit central and it was a nice leafy sort of area.
>
> (Graeme, Charlestown)

In the case of Huntlee, buying into a place with a plan to build local facilities for residents was important, as Tiff and Elizabeth suggest below:

> Well, you know you're going to have the amenities; you're going to have, like [a major supermarket] is coming, so there'll be shops and parks and there's going to be childcare, schools, you know, medical center, everything that you'll need. You know you don't have to travel to the next town to get those things. You know it's all going to be here and you'll have access to everything you'll need as your family grows.
>
> (Tiff, Huntlee)

> It's going to be our own little town. You know, it's going to have everything there that we want.
>
> (Elizabeth, Huntlee)

The natural environment was also important to residents in both suburbs as a feature that enhanced livability. Residents of Huntlee mentioned the retention or future construction of an appealing natural environment was important. For example:

> When we looked at the plans we could see that they'd retained a lot of natural habitat-type area. So it wasn't like we were going to be plonked out in the middle and there was nothing around the development. There's bushland, there's going to be parks.
>
> (Jenifer, Huntlee)

Residents of Charlestown also talked about aspects of the natural environment, including: trees and green spaces, quiet, sea breezes, wildlife, parks, gardens, recreation, lifestyle, ocean views, space for children to play, and distance from other people and noise and bustle. Their discussion on these topics frequently tapped into a sense of the neighborhood being pleasant, relaxed, connected to/embedded in the natural world, enjoyable, easy, and livable. For example:

> As I say it was nice to be able to look over the back fence and just see eucalypts as far as you could. Which is why we're very happy we've got the screening plants. But effectively people could come here and almost imagine that we still don't have neighbors.
>
> (Paul, Charlestown)

> I mean there's some parts over on the west side are nice but this side over here it gets all the benefit of the cooler breezes. It's got a lot of trees so you'd get a bit of cooler temperatures through here. But when the winds come through the breeze is—especially in the summer—you get the southerly breezes, you get the north easterlies and it's beautiful. You get the westerlies but that doesn't last very long. Particularly here we're right on top of the ridge and we just get those breezes, it's beautiful. You know it's a really nice—a really particularly good area here and this is just a great outlook you know. The bird life and you get the possums come up here … You know just beautiful, really nice.
>
> (Graeme, Charlestown)

I used to be in the habit of sleeping with my bedroom window wide open. There's a little creek down there. You can hear the frogs at night and the crickets and stuff like that.

(Nigel, Charlestown)

The sense of the natural environment is not simply derived from being located in this particular neighborhood. Rather residents are actively involved, in a myriad of ways, in the *becoming-lively* of the natural environment of the suburb at a neighborhood scale (Kraftl, 2014; Jones, 2016, 2017). Though still at an early stage of development, in Huntlee the developer LWP encouraged the participation of residents and future residents in planting the local threatened plant species North Rothbury Persoonia throughout the development (Ruming et al., 2018a).

In Charlestown, the resident-led Greater Charlestown Sustainable Neighbourhood group has produced an action plan that includes as its top priority:

1   Protect and care for the natural environment
    a   Develop a prioritised list of local conservation and regeneration activities
    b   Run local clean up events, organise lagoon and creek clean ups
    c   Advocate to protect and enhance existing local green spaces and to improve public access to local bushland (for example, develop educational and artistic walkways through bushland)
    d   Support existing local Landcare groups and develop new groups when necessary
    e   Inform and encourage residents to follow responsible pet care principles
(Greater Charlestown Sustainable Neighbourhood Action Plan, 2014)

A number of our interviewees mentioned the importance of these sorts of activities to the livability of their suburb. Patrick, for instance, discusses the involvement of residents of his street in practices that nurture the natural environment and therefore the livability of Charlestown:

The trees are put in but they're all so close to the development because no one supervised it. I kept them alive by watering them because no one watered them. I kept them alive but they're blueberry ash. They're going to grow 4 meters and they're too close to the development now so they'll probably have to take them out.... Then we're getting privet and lantana out. My next-door neighbor's planted those trees in there, which have grown up. We've now got... a Landcare group tied in with the council's Landcare group and Phil's the coordinator next door. What we've had is they're zoning it and they've given us the mulch and we've had other Landcare volunteers through them cleaning out more lantana down there.... I like working with people. That's why I like this Landcare group. We asked other people who work with us. Like the young bloke next door gives a hand and I was talking to Phil about this and so he's asking a few people. So it's to get some people in and some activity and it's neighbors talking to each other and that sort of thing.

(Patrick, Charlestown)

The natural environment is not experienced as simply a characteristic on a list of desirable features for a livable neighborhood. Residents in our case studies were active in nurturing the natural environment in their own yards as well as at the neighborhood scale.

The natural environment is not only implicated in livability via the space, privacy enjoyment, and nurturing of nature, it is also connected to the heating and cooling, and thus comfort, of the home. Recent research from Amati et al. (2017) shows a significant difference between average temperatures in wealthy, leafy suburbs in Sydney's north, and average temperatures in lower-income suburbs in Sydney's west and south, with poorer suburbs being up to 10 degrees hotter (Lutton, 2017). This suggests another facet of the affordances of affordability in terms of experiences of livability. The greater affordability of the suburbs allows residents to buy into neighborhoods that have more livable natural environments. Being able to afford to purchase into these suburbs, with greater access to locally based facilities than suburbs that are predominantly dormitory suburbs, allows, or will allow, residents access to these suburbs as livable. Affordability could therefore be understood more broadly, as part of an assemblage of livability that intertwines residents with the non-human, human, material, economic, and social elements of their environment.

Practices of Livability 3: Accessing the Livable City Elsewhere and the Benefits of Being *Far Enough Away*

Not all the features residents wanted to access were available in their suburbs. Therefore accessing these features was a crucial aspect of livability. In Charlestown, this included easy access to places of work and proximity to the inner city and beaches:

> [I]f you look at Charlestown it's a really interesting position, because if I want to go to the beach where I am takes me eight minutes. It doesn't matter what the time of day is or the traffic, eight minutes to the beach. If I want to go down to the lake I can go to Warners Bay or Belmont in about 10 minutes. If I want to go into town, as long as it's not peak hour, it takes me 12 minutes. If I want to go to the university, all the bus routes that go through here go to the university.
>
> (Peter, Charlestown)

Comments from future residents of the much more distant Huntlee show that residents are not making simple choices about accessing livable spaces available in a city core like Newcastle. They felt that there were livable spaces spread throughout the region that they may wish to access, and their Huntlee location put them closer to some of these, as opposed to outer suburban locations that may be closer to Newcastle:

> We looked at other places, for other subdivisions and they were sort of in between Newcastle and here, whereas here we're close to something just down the road; you can just pop down and go wine tasting or go to dinner, whereas if you bought in between Newcastle and here you've got to drive either way.
>
> (Lincoln, Huntlee)

Usually, these kinds of points would be seen as residents trading off the affordability of their suburban location with the access to aspects of livability provided better by locations elsewhere. As Dodson and Sipe (2008) and Li, Dodson, and Sipe (2017) remind us, such trade-offs are only possible for households with the financial resources to afford higher transport costs. This is particularly the case for Huntlee, where public transport access is very limited (Ruming et al., 2018a), and the distances travelled to access resources in other neighborhoods are much greater. The implication is that if transportation costs were to rise steeply, the affordances of housing affordability may be much more limited in the future.

However, in our work with Charlestown residents, a more complex picture emerged than simply having the financial resources to afford the transport to access facilities elsewhere in the city. Some residents liked being further away from neighborhoods that tick more boxes on the shopping list of livability. While such neighborhoods might have more facilities, they were considered less livable in other ways, principally due to traffic congestion and noise:

> I love Charlestown, I think it's great because it's far enough away—we can still access the shopping centers and stuff if we have to but where we are is far away enough to still see green and it's quiet.

> (Christine, Charlestown)

The valuing of peace and quiet reflects Willing and Pojani's (2017) findings on what Australians value about suburban living (Saulwick, 2018), which shows that access to aspects of the natural environment is the thing most valued by residents across Sydney. These findings are also consistent with broader discussions in Australia about how urban change—including population growth, increasing densification and congestion, and decreasing access to green spaces—is associated with perceptions of decreasing livability, despite the increase in other features such as walkability and access to inner urban centers (Alcorn, 2018; Benson, 2018; Collins, 2018; Miller & Schneiders, 2017; Sloan, 2017; Ticher, 2018; Visentin, 2018). It reflects residents' understanding that living in a neighborhood that ticks all the boxes of the livability shopping list may not allow for living well. Such findings accord with the calls from Lloyd et al. (2016) for more qualitative studies of residents' perceptions of livability. We would add that such research needs to consider how livability is experienced by residents at multiple, interconnected scales.

Conclusion: Livability and the Suburbs in Australia

Our chapter makes three key contributions to broadening the understanding of livability. First we argue that livability is not simply given by a shopping list set of neighborhood attributes. Rather, residents are actively involved in the becoming-lively of their houses and neighborhoods through their home-making practices, their interactions with the neighbors and the natural environment, and their movements in the city. Second, livability is not simply experienced at the scale of a particular neighborhood or city. Practices of livability operate at multiple interconnected scales. Here we have explored the interconnections between the home, neighborhood, and city or regional scales. Future research could turn its attention to other ways that livability is practiced at multiple interconnected scales. Third, we argue that some features of livability are more important than others. Like Tapsuwan et al. (2018), we found that housing affordability was a particularly important aspect of livability for residents. However, our research showed the importance of the affordances of affordability. Access to affordable housing was critical at all the scales we explored, allowing residents to participate in home-making practices, particularly those related to comfort and convenience (Shove, 2003), as these features were part of how homes became livable for residents.

Notions of comfort and convenience were also critical to help us unpack how access to resources at the neighborhood and regional scale were linked to livability. Furthermore, affordability enabled residents to participate actively in their neighborhoods and to access resources elsewhere in the city. While Charlestown and Huntlee are not markedly affluent neighborhoods, neither are they neighborhoods where most residents we interviewed were struggling to meet their housing costs. Future research could consider the ways in which a lack of affordable housing or the unaffordability of housing impacts affordances of affordability and therefore on the livability of our cities at a range of scales.

Notes

1   Domain is the real estate arm of Fairfax newspapers. Like many of those groups involved in livability rankings, such as the Property Council of Australia, which sponsors a set of livability rankings of Australian cities, it has a vested interest in real estate sales and providing enhanced information about neighborhoods and cities through real estate transactions.
2   Warners Bay is a suburb to the south west of Charlestown, located on the shore of Lake Macquarie.
3   The term "refurb" is Australian slang for refurbishment or renovation.

References

Alcorn, G. (2018, April 9). The struggle for Melbourne: Has the world's "most livable" city lost its way? *Guardian*. Retrieved from www.theguardian.com/cities/2018/apr/09/the-struggle-for-melbourne-has-the-worlds-most-livable-city-lost-its-way.

Amati, M., Boruff, B., Caccetta, P., Devereux, D., Kaspar, J., Phelan, K., & Saunders, A. (2017). *Where should all the trees go? Investigating the impact of tree canopy cover on socioeconomic status and wellbeing in LGAs*. Sydney: Horticulture Innovation Australia Limited. Retrieved from www.urbanaffairs.com.au/downloads/2017-9-28-2.pdf.

Australian Bureau of Statistics. (2016). *2016 Census QuickStats*. Retrieved from http://quickstats.censusdata.abs.gov.au/census_services/getproduct/census/2016/quickstat/SSC10885.

Benson, S. (2018, February 22). Plan now or quality of city life will decline, says Infrastructure Australia. *The Australian*. Retrieved from www.theaustralian.com.au/national-affairs/plan-now-or-quality-of-city-life-will-decline-says-infrastructure-australia/news-story/cd780088976dbd5b087535efdf67cfb9.

Collins, A. (2018, April 9). NSW government invests in more green, open space in Sydney to improve quality of life. *Australian Broadcasting Corporation News*. Retrieved from www.abc.net.au/news/2018-04-09/government-introducing-more-green-spaces-for-sydney/9633678.

Dodson, J., & Sipe, N. (2008). Shocking the suburbs: Urban location, homeownership and oil vulnerability in the Australian city. *Housing Studies, 23*(3), 377–401.

Fuary-Wagner, I. (2016, July 30). *What makes a suburb livable? The 16 factors that make or break a neighbourhood*. Retrieved from www.domain.com.au/news/what-makes-a-suburb-livable-the-16-factors-that-make-or-break-a-neighbourhood-20160730-gqhdkw-281398/.

Greater Charlestown Sustainable Neighbourhood Action Plan. (2014). Retrieved from www. sustainableneighbourhoods.org.au/uploads/6/7/0/6/6706950/greater_charlestown_sustainable_ neighbourhood_action_plan.pdf.

Jarvis, H. (2007). Home truths about care-less competitiveness. *International Journal of Urban and Regional Research, 31*(1), 207–214.

Jones, R. (2016). Making Moorhen. In K. Archer & K. Bezdecny (Eds.), *Handbook of cities and the environment* (pp. 385–408). Northampton: Edward Elgar Publishing.

Jones, R. (2017). Really shit work? Bodily becoming and the capacity to care for the urban forest. *Social and Cultural Geography.* doi: 10.1080/14649365.2017.1384046.

Kraftl, P. (2014). Livability and urban architectures: Mol(ecul)ar biopower and the "becoming lively" of sustainable communities. *Environment and Planning D: Society and Space, 32*(2), 274–292.

Lewis, N., & Murphy, L. (2015). Anchor organisations in Auckland: Rolling constructively with neoliberalism? *Local Economy, 30*(1), 98–118.

Li, T., Dodson, J., & Sipe, N. (2017). Examining household relocation pressures from rising transport and housing costs: An Australian case study. *Transport Policy, 65*, 106–113.

Livable Sydney. (n.d.). Retrieved from www.domain.com.au/news/livable-sydney/.

Lloyd, K., Fullagar, S., & Reid, S. (2016). Where is the "social" in constructions of "livability"? Exploring community, social interaction and social cohesion in changing urban environments. *Urban Policy and Research, 34*(4), 343–355.

Lowe, M., Whitzman, C., Badland, H., Davern, M., Aye, L., Hes, D., Butterworth, I., & Giles-Corti, B. (2015). Planning healthy, livable and sustainable cities: How can indicators inform policy? *Urban Policy and Research, 33*(2), 131–144.

Lutton, E. (2017, September 27). *Why our poorer suburbs could be up to 10 degrees hotter than their wealthier neighbours.* Retrieved from www.domain.com.au/news/why-our-poorer-suburbs-could-be-up-to-10-degrees-hotter-than-their-wealthier-neighbours-20170927-gypj82/.

LWP. (2012, October 17). *Huntlee: Your new town in the heart of the Hunter* [video file]. Retrieved from www.youtube.com/watch?v=wVwomzOmhL8.

LWP. (2017). *Huntlee Pulse*, Summer, Issue 10.

McCann, E. J. (2004). "Best places": Interurban competition, quality of life and popular media discourse. *Urban Studies, 41*(10), 1909–1929.

Miller, R., & Schneiders, B. (2017, July 1). *4 million, 5 million, 8 million: How big is too big for livable Melbourne?* Retrieved from www.theage.com.au/national/victoria/4-million-5-million-8-million-how-big-is-too-big-for-livable-melbourne-20170630-gx1uo9.html.

Ruming, K., Mee, K., McGuirk, P., & Sweeney, J. (2018a). On the fringe of regeneration: What role for greenfield development and innovative urban futures? In K. Ruming (Ed.), *Urban regeneration in Australia: Policies, processes and projects of contemporary urban change.* Oxford and New York: Routledge.

Ruming, K., Mee, K., McGuirk, P., & Sweeney, J. (2018b). Shopping centre-led regeneration: Middle ring town centres and suburban regeneration. In K. Ruming (Ed.), *Urban regeneration in Australia: Policies, processes and projects of contemporary urban change.* Oxford and New York: Routledge.

Saulwick, J. (2018, January 4). Bushland for some, bars for others: What matters to Sydney communities. *Sydney Morning Herald.* Retrieved from www.smh.com.au/national/nsw/bushland-for-some-bars-for-others-what-matters-to-sydney-communities-20180104-h0dc90.html.

Shove, E. (2003). *Comfort, cleanliness and convenience: The social organization of normality.* Oxford and New York: Berg.

Sloan, J. (2017, August 8). We're squeezing the life out of our cities. *The Australian.* Retrieved from www.theaustralian.com.au/opinion/columnists/judith-sloan/were-squeezing-the-life-out-of-our-cities/news-story/c9ef0c2c59ec79a12ec983247e2eba20.

Tapsuwan, S., Mathot, C., Walker, I., & Barnett, G. (2018). Preferences for sustainable, livable and resilient neighbourhoods and homes: A case of Canberra, Australia. *Sustainable Cities and Society, 37,* 133–145.

Ticher, M. (2018, January 3). The crane mutiny: How Sydney's apartment boom spun out of control. *Guardian.* Retrieved from www.theguardian.com/australia-news/2018/jan/04/the-crane-mutiny-how-sydneys-apartment-boom-spun-out-of-control.

Visentin, L. (2018, April 1). The Sydney suburbs facing a major shortfall in sports grounds. *Sydney Morning Herald.* Retrieved from www.smh.com.au/national/nsw/the-sydney-suburbs-facing-a-major-shortfall-in-sports-grounds-20180328-p4z6mh.html.

Wetzstein, S. (2016, May 5). *Intervention: Reclaiming the livable city as normative reference point: Against totalising aspirational political discourses.* Retrieved from https://antipodefoundation.org/2016/05/05/reclaiming-the-livable-city/.

Willing, R., & Pojani, D. (2017). Is the suburban dream still alive in Australia? Evidence from Brisbane. *Australian Planner, 54*(2), 67–79.

INDEX